John Baron Moyle

The contract of sale in the civil law

With references to the laws of England, Scotland and France

John Baron Moyle

The contract of sale in the civil law
With references to the laws of England, Scotland and France

ISBN/EAN: 9783743345546

Manufactured in Europe, USA, Canada, Australia, Japa

Cover: Foto ©ninafisch / pixelio.de

Manufactured and distributed by brebook publishing software (www.brebook.com)

John Baron Moyle

The contract of sale in the civil law

Clarendon Press Series

THE CONTRACT OF SALE

IN THE

CIVIL LAW

WITH

*REFERENCES TO THE LAWS OF ENGLAND
SCOTLAND AND FRANCE*

BY

J. B. MOYLE, D.C.L.

OF LINCOLN'S INN, BARRISTER-AT-LAW
AND FELLOW AND TUTOR OF NEW COLLEGE, OXFORD

Oxford
AT THE CLARENDON PRESS
1892

PREFACE

THIS little book, in a sense, is an experiment. So far as any attempt has hitherto been made to provide English readers with a full knowledge of the Roman law relating to some small and compact subject, it has taken the form of commentary upon the text of some Title in the Digest. Mr. Roby's work on Usufruct, and Dr. Grueber's on the lex Aquilia, are the best-known examples of this method of treatment, though in his 'systematic exposition' the latter has thrown his preceding commentary into a form nearly approaching that which I have here adopted. To the generality of English lawyers, however, such an exposition of a foreign system, interesting and instructive though it may be, is distasteful in its method, nor does it lend itself to comparison with English principles, or enable a reader to find with ease the passages which bear upon the case which he is considering, or on which he has to advise.

The law of Sale, as laid down in the Corpus Iuris, appears admirably suited for a different mode of treatment. It is expounded with extraordinary fullness, being the subject of some twenty Titles in the Code and Digest: it admits of being easily treated in continuous and connected form, with perhaps less of technicality than would be presented by any other branch of law: and finally its interest to an English lawyer is probably greater than that of any other similar topic, if only for the reason given by

His Honour Judge Chalmers, that 'there is hardly a judgment of importance on the law of Sale in which reference is not made to it.' At the same time, for the convenience of those who from choice or necessity may desire to study the original, I have printed at the end of the book the two Titles in the Digest (xviii. 1 and xix. 1) which bear most directly on the subject, and which are usually prescribed, in connection with it, in examinations, and I have prepared a kind of Index which shows the references in the body of the work to most of the other Titles in the Corpus Iuris which relate to this contract.

No attempt has been made to trace the historical evolution of the law of Sale. What was its actual origin, as a consensual contract, in the Roman system is a question of very great interest, which has been investigated by some of the most learned and penetrating of the historical jurists on the Continent, and which has engaged others, both there and in England, in speculations which have hitherto led to no very satisfactory results. Until some sure ground has been reached it would be foolish to discuss such a matter in a book which it is intended and hoped will be of real use to lawyers in this country, and accordingly I have in the main contented myself with setting forth the principles of the contract, as they are to be found in the Code, Digest and Institutes, although I have not refrained from historical disquisition where the actual origin of a rule is known beyond all question.

It would be improper for me to close these few words of preface without acknowledging the great obligation which I am under, in relation to this book, to His Honour Judge Chalmers. It will be apparent to every reader how easy the task of comparing the Civil Law with the English has been made by my possession of his invaluable work on the Sale of Goods. But I owe him still more for the courtesy and readiness with which he has constantly spared his scant moments of leisure to advise me upon points of contact and contrast between the English and the Roman law, and to suggest topics upon which a comparison, at first sight by no means obvious, becomes on examination of prime importance in illustrating the fundamental principles of the two systems. It is hardly too much to say that nearly everything which can give the book any value in the eye of an English lawyer is due to him.

J. B. M.

OXFORD, *April*, 1892.

CONTENTS

CHAPTER I.

NATURE OF SALE, AND ITS RELATION TO OTHER COGNATE
   CONTRACTS 1–8

   Definition of sale (1). The contract is consensual (1) and synallagmatic (2). Fundamental points of difference between the English and the Civil Law (3). Relation of Sale to Exchange (3) and to Hiring and Letting (6).

CHAPTER II.

WHO CAN BUY AND SELL 9–15

   Persons entirely unable to contract (9). Special restrictions: tutors and curators (9): public officials (10). Effect of contract of sale entered into by pupillus without auctoritas (11): is he bound? (13).

CHAPTER III.

WHAT CAN AND CANNOT BE BOUGHT AND SOLD   16–27

   The general principle (16). Sale of servitudes (17): of res alienae (17): of res extra commercium (19): of freemen (20): of res furtivae (20): of things whose alienation is forbidden by law (20): of things which have ceased to exist (21). Purchase of res sua (22). Sale of free services (24). Restrictions on right of sale imposed by testament (24) or by contract (25). Note A: sale of res alienae in French and English law (26).

CHAPTER IV.

CERTAIN SPECIAL SUBJECTS OF SALE 28–38

   Emptio generis (28). Sale of article to be made or procured by the vendor: is it really sale? (29). Emptio spei (30). Purchase

CHAPTER X.

The effects of the Contract. (c) The Purchaser's
  Duties 142–155

Payment of the purchase-money: the purchaser must make it the property of the vendor (142). By whom and to whom payment may be made (143). Passing of property in the goods, even when delivered, usually conditional on payment (144). Interest due on unpaid purchase-money (146). Purchaser's duty to accept delivery, and to reimburse the vendor his charges (147). Consequences of the purchaser's mora (148). The Civil Law on the subject of vendor's lien (149) and stoppage in transitu (151).

CHAPTER XI.

Conditional Sales 156–177

Conditions in general distinguished into suspensive and resolutive (156). Conditions distinguished from terms in the contract (157). Conditions affirmative and negative (159). Conditions attached for the benefit of the vendor: (i) Addictio in diem: what is a 'better offer'? (160). Effects of addictio when the condition is suspensive (163) and resolutive (164). When is the condition satisfied? (165). Sales by auction (167). (ii) Lex commissoria (169): the condition here always resolutive: when it is satisfied (170). Effect of a sale subject to a lex commissoria (171). Conditions attached for the benefit of the purchaser (173): (i) Emptio ad gustum (174): (ii) pactum displicentiae (175). Common terms in sales: reservation by vendor of right of preemption (176): pactum de retrovendendo (176) and de retroemendo (177).

CHAPTER XII.

Modes of Discharge 178–220

Contraria voluntas, or mutual waiver before performance by either party (179). Partial discharge by subsequent variation of terms (180). Rescission by the vendor for inadequacy of price (laesio enormis, 180): difficulties of the texts on the subject (182). When the price is deemed to be inadequate (183). The courses open to the vendor (183). Effects of successful action for rescission (184). Cases in which the vendor may not rescind (186): other doubtful cases (187). The purchaser's right of rescission on account of undisclosed defects (188). Historical sketch of the vendor's liability for non-disclosure: the old Civil Law (189): the practice of exacting a covenant as to quality (192):

the Ædilician Edict (192). Extension of its rules to all sales by juristic construction (194). What defects render the contract liable to rescission? (195). Distinction between slaves (196) and animals (197). The defect must exist at the date of the contract, and be unknown to the purchaser (197). Purchase by agents with knowledge (198). Defect in accessions: in one of several things purchased together (199): in part of an universitas (200). Vendor's duty to disclose defects of these kinds (200). The purchaser's remedies: (1) by exceptio, (2) by actio redhibitoria (201). Effects of this action: what must be done by the purchaser (202) and by the vendor (203). Covenants sometimes demandable by either party (206). Points in which the parties are differently treated under the actio redhibitoria (207). The period of limitation (209). (3) By actio quanti minoris or aestimatoria (210): its period of limitation and effects (211). Reaction of these Ædilician remedies on those of the Civil Law (212). Cases in which they are inapplicable (214). Note A: Implied warranty of quality in Scotch and English law (216).

DIG. XVIII. 1.

DE CONTRAHENDA EMPTIONE . . . 221

DIG. XIX. 1.

DE ACTIONIBUS EMPTI VENDITI 239

REFERENCES TO OTHER TITLES IN THE DIGEST AND CODE   261

INDEX 266

LIST OF PRINCIPAL WORKS REFERRED TO

ARNDTS, *Lehrbuch der Pandekten*, 9th ed. 1877.
BECHMANN, *Der Kauf nach gemeinem Recht*, 1876.
BELL'S *Principles of the Law of Scotland*, 9th ed. 1889.
BENJAMIN, *On Sale*, 4th ed. 1888.
CHALMERS, *Sale of Goods*, 1890.
DEMANTE, *Cours analytique de Code Civil*, vol. vii.
GLÜCK, *Ausführliche Erläuterung der Pandekten*, 1867.
IHERING, *Geist des römischen Rechts*, 4th ed. 1878.
MOMMSEN, *Beiträge zum Obligationenrecht*, 1853.
MUIRHEAD, *Historical Introduction to the Private Law of Rome*. 1886.
POTHIER, *Traité du Contrat de Vente*, 1772.
SAVIGNY, *Obligationenrecht*, 1851.
——— *System des heutigen römischen Rechts*, 1840.
TREITSCHKE, *Der Kaufcontract in besonderer Beziehung auf den Waarenhandel*, 2nd ed. 1866.
VANGEROW, *Lehrbuch der Pandekten*, 7th ed. 1876.
VERING, *Geschichte und Pandekten des römischen und heutigen gemeinen Privatrechts*, 5th ed. 1887.
WÄCHTER, *Pandekten*, 1880.
WINDSCHEID, *Lehrbuch des Pandektenrechts*, 4th ed. 1875.

THE CONTRACT OF SALE IN THE CIVIL LAW.

CHAPTER I.

NATURE OF SALE, AND ITS RELATION TO OTHER COGNATE CONTRACTS.

Definition of Sale. The Contract is consensual and 'synallagmatic,' entailing obligations on both parties. Fundamental points of difference between the English and the Civil Law on the subject. Relation of Sale to Exchange: to Hiring and Letting.

THE Contract of Sale (Emptio Venditio), or more shortly, Sale, is the contract by which two parties promise one another respectively, the one to transfer a thing, the other to pay a determinate price for that thing[1]. What precisely is meant by the words transfer, thing, price, will be more fully considered hereafter. *Definition of Sale.*

The contract belongs to the class known to the Roman lawyers as consensual[2]. With possibly one slight exception, *The contract is consensual,*

---

[1] Le Contrat de Vente est un Contrat par lequel l'un des contractans, qui est le vendeur, s'oblige envers l'autre *de lui faire avoir librement à titre de propriétaire* une chose, pour le prix d'une certaine somme d'argent que l'autre contractant, qui est l'acheteur, s'oblige réciproquement de lui payer: Pothier, Contrat de Vente, 1. La vente est une convention par laquelle l'un s'oblige à livrer une chose, et l'autre à la payer: Code Civil, Art. 1582. See a similar definition in Bell's Principles of the Law of Scotland, § 85

[2] Code Civil, Art. 1583.

it is binding on both parties so soon as they are agreed, definitely and without conditions, upon the thing to be bought and sold, and on the price to be paid. How that agreement is expressed is immaterial. It may be done by word of mouth, by messenger, by correspondence, or by conduct: no form is necessary[1], nor is part performance ever or in any degree an essential condition of the obligation, as was the case with the contracts which the civilians term Real[2].

and synallagmatic. The contract is further synallagmatic: that is to say, it must be for the benefit of both parties, and each must be bound[3]. It is possible that the obligation of one or other of them may be 'naturalis' only, so that he cannot be sued for breach, while he has the right of enforcing it against the other: but if either of them is not bound at all, then neither is the other[4].

From this it is clear, that promises to sell (the other party not being bound to buy), or promises to buy (the other party not being bound to sell), or promises made between A and B respectively to buy of and sell to one another, if required, though they seem to play a somewhat prominent part in the laws of those European countries which are founded on the Civil Law[5], are not enforceable

---

[1] Est autem emptio iuris gentium, et ideo consensu peragitur: Dig. 18. 1. 1. 2.   [2] Dig. 44. 7. 52. 1.

[3] Ce contrat est *synallagmatique*, c'est à dire qu'il contient un engagement réciproque de chacun des contractans, l'un envers l'autre, ainsi qu'il resulte de la définition que nous en avons donnée. C'est un contrat *commutatif*, dans lequel l'intention de chacun des contractans est de recevoir autant qu'il donne : Pothier, 2.

[4] Bona fides non patitur ut, cum emptor alicuius legis beneficio pecuniam rei venditae debere desiisset antequam res ei tradatur, venditor tradere compellatur, et re sua careret ; Dig. 19. 1. 50. For a very complete examination of certain cases in which it is alleged by some writers that the contract is unilateral only, or at any rate 'imperfectly bilateral,' see Bechmann, Kauf, §§ 161–186.

[5] See Code Civil, Art. 1589, 1590; Demante, Cours analytique de Code Civil, pp. 16–31 : Pothier, 476–495 : Bechmann, Kauf, §§ 190–195.

in the Roman system; they are merely *pacta nuda*, and cannot be sued upon.

Two respects in which the Roman differs from the English law upon the subject may be mentioned at once. Firstly, the law relating to the sale of land is in no way different from that relating to the sale of goods; and secondly, the contract itself never transfers property in the thing sold. In England, as is well known, and as will be more fully shown hereafter, a contract for the sale of specific or ascertained goods usually *ipso facto* transfers property therein to the buyer: but the Romans distinguish the sale clearly from the alienation [1], and it will be seen that in their law the contract never operates as a conveyance, though it may in some measure alter the legal relation of the purchaser to the thing which he has purchased. <small>Fundamental points of difference between the English and the Civil Law.</small>

Even those whose study of the Civil Law has not passed beyond its elements will remember the reference in the Institutes of Gaius [2] and of Justinian [3] to a controversy as to whether Exchange was not a species of sale, and was not governed by the rules peculiar to that contract [4]. The jurist Paulus tells us [5] that sale in fact originated in and was a species of exchange. There was a time when money had not been introduced, and when the distinction between the price and the thing sold (merx) was unknown. Men gave what they had to spare for something else of which they stood in need. The inconvenience of this led in time to the invention of Money—pieces of metal stamped with their exchange value by the authority of the State, which impression (rather than their actual cost) represented the measure of their usefulness in commercial transactions [6]. <small>Relation of Sale to Exchange.</small>

---

[1] 'Alienatum' non proprie dicitur, quod adhuc in dominio venditoris manet: 'venditum' tamen recte dicetur: Dig. 50. 16. 67.

[2] iii. 141. [3] iii. 23. 2.

[4] Pothier, 619. [5] Dig. 18. 1. 1. pr.

[6] Eaque materia forma publica percussa usum dominiumque non tam ex substantia praebet quam ex quantitate: Dig. loc. cit. So too

Thus purchase and sale took rank as an independent contract: merx is one thing, pretium is another, and Vendor is distinct from Purchaser: and although the controversy alluded to between the Sabinians and Proculians continued for many generations, it was finally set at rest in A.D. 294 by a rescript of the Emperors Diocletian and Maximian[1]. By this enactment it was settled that an agreement to exchange one thing for another, instead of for a money price, was not binding on either party until there had been performance on one side accepted by the other: permutatio henceforth definitely belonged to the class of agreements termed by civilians innominate 'real' contracts[2], enforceable by the party who had performed his side of the bargain, but not till then, by an actio praescriptis verbis[3]. In a single case an exception to this rule appears to have been allowed. Gaius[4] adverts to an opinion of Caelius Sabinus, that if one man has a thing for sale (venalis) and another takes it, giving another thing 'pretii nomine,' the transaction is sale, not exchange: and this doctrine is reproduced in a rescript of the Emperor Gordian[5]. The question which was at issue was of no small practical importance, for it is

Papinian says, 'in pecunia [quis) non corpora cogitat sed quantitatem': Dig. 46. 3. 94. 1.

[1] Cod. 4. 64. 7.   [2] Dig. 19. 4. 1. 2.

[3] Pothier says (621), 'parmi nous la convention d'échange, dès avant qu'elle ait reçu aucune exécution, et aussitôt que le consentement des parties est intervenu, produit, de part et d'autre, une obligation civile, et elle est un contrat consensuel, de même que le contrat de vente.' So by the Code Civil (Art. 1703) exchange is declared a consensual contract, and with certain exceptions (1704-1706) is regulated by the rules governing sale (1707).

[4] iii. 141.

[5] Si cum patruus tuus venalem possessionem habeat, pater tuus pretii nomine—licet non taxata quantitate—aliam possessionem dedit, idque quod comparavit evictum est, ad exemplum ex empto actionis non immerito id quod tua interest, si in patris iura successisti, consequi desideras: Cod. 4. 64. 1.

not difficult to imagine one who had negotiated an advantageous exchange, of which the other party had repented and refused to accept execution, striving to convince a court that the agreement, being a variety of sale, was consensual in principle, and therefore binding on both parties from the moment it was concluded. One at any rate of the fundamental doctrines of sale was extended to exchange, viz. the liability of each party for undisclosed defects in the article which he had exchanged for the other [1]. On the other hand, there is a material difference of rule in three particulars. We shall see that a purchaser could not rescind a contract of sale because the vendor had in fact no right to sell the article which was the subject-matter of the contract: but it is essential to exchange that each party should vest in the other the property in the article which he conveyed [2]. Secondly, in sale the purchased property as a rule is at the risk of the purchaser from the instant that the contract is concluded: if it perishes without fault in the vendor, he must pay the purchase money, and if he has paid it already he cannot recover it back: whereas, on an exchange, if *A* has given *B* what he promised, and what *B* was to give perishes without his fault before conveyance to *A*, the latter can recover back what he has conveyed himself [3]. Thirdly, in exchange the property passes on delivery, and before counterperformance by the other party [4]: in sale, as we shall see, it passed only if in addition to delivery the price were paid or credit were given.

---

[1] Sed si quis permutaverit, dicendum est utrumque emptoris et venditoris loco haberi et utrumque posse ex hoc edicto experiri: Dig. 21. 1. 19. 5: aliter, The Code Civil, Art. 1706.

[2] Dig. 19. 4. 1. 3: 12. 4. 16: Code Civil, Art. 1704: Pothier, 621.

[3] Dig. 12. 4. 16. The Contract having become consensual in the French law of Pothier's time, the rule is laid down in the contrary form by him, 625, and it is the same in the modern law: Code Civil, Art. 1707.

[4] Cum precibus tuis expresseris placitum inter te et alium permutationis intercessisse eumque fundum a te datum vendidisse, contra

and to Hiring and Letting. Another contract, between which and sale the Roman lawyers were at one time unable to precisely define the limits, is Hire, in two of its three forms, viz. locatio conductio rei, and locatio conductio operis faciendi. Hire is consensual, and consequently cannot be distinguished, like exchange, from sale by reference to the moment at which the obligation is generated. Locatio conductio rei is the letting another have, for a pecuniary consideration, the use and fruition of a thing which one has in one's de facto possession. What differentiates it from sale is the letter's intention not to part permanently with his own interest. In most instances of letting, whether of land or of chattels, this is so obvious that no question as to the true nature of the transaction can arise: but there was one case in which there was a long controversy, namely, that of ager vectigalis. If land was let in perpetuity, subject to an annual rent, there were some who inclined to the view that the contract was sale, though Gaius[1] says that according to the better opinion it was hire. The Emperor Zeno eventually ruled[2] that it should be governed by special rules of its own, though in principle it was judged to be a case of letting and hiring. The determining consideration was perhaps less the periodical accruing of the money payment than the fact, that the lessor had the right of avoiding the transaction as regards the future if the rent were in arrear, and in certain other events. We shall see that sometimes a sale was concluded on somewhat similar terms[3]: but where a sale was thus avoided the avoidance related back to the moment of conclusion, which was not the case with the contract now under consideration.

Locatio conductio operis faciendi is where one man

emptorem quidem te nullam habere actionem perspicis, cum ab eo susceperit dominium, cui te tradidisse titulo permutationis non negasti, Cod. 4. 64. 4. pr.

[1] iii. 145. [2] Cod. 4. 66. 1.
[3] See Index, s.v. lex commissoria.

employs another at a fixed remuneration to make him some definite object, such as a carriage or a piece of furniture, out of materials belonging to, or to be procured by, the employer. If they belonged to or were to be procured by the employé, Cassius held that the transaction must be broken up into two distinct contracts; a purchase of the materials, and a hiring of the skill and labour. No one appears to have thought that it was hire pure and simple, but Gaius says[1] that the prevalent opinion was (at least where the materials belonged at the time to the employé) that it was merely a sale, and this was finally accepted as the law[2]. The true criterion is supplied by Javolenus, who says that it is sale if property passes[3]. This however

[1] iii. 147.

[2] Inst. iii. 24. 4: Dig. 19. 2. 2. 1. Demante, Cours analytique de Code Civil, commenting on Art. 1788, observes that (though the case is treated under the contract of louage), 'lorsque l'entrepreneur fournit la matière, il y a proprement vente de la chose, qu'il s'oblige à faire, par conséquent vente d'une chose future, vente nécessairement conditionnelle.'

[3] Si ex fundo meo tegulas tibi factas ut darem convenit, emptionem puto esse, non conductionem: toties enim conductio rei alicuius est, quoties materia in qua aliquid praestatur in eodem statu eiusdem manet: quoties vero et immutatur et alienatur, emptio magis quam locatio intellegi debet: Dig. 18. 1. 65. Precisely the same question has arisen in English law, in consequence of § 17 of the Statute of Frauds, and it was finally settled, in the same way as at Rome, by *Lee* v. *Griffin* (30 L. J. Q. B. 252), which was an action brought by a dentist to recover £21 for two sets of artificial teeth made for a deceased lady, of whom the defendant was executor. Crompton J. said, 'When the contract is such that a chattel is ultimately to be delivered by the plaintiff to the defendant, when it has been sent, then the cause of action is goods sold and delivered.... I do not agree with the proposition, that wherever skill is to be exercised in carrying out the contract, that fact makes it a contract for work and labour, and not for the sale of a chattel:' and Hill J., 'When the subject matter of the contract is a chattel to be afterwards delivered, then the cause of action is goods sold and delivered, and the seller cannot sue for work and labour.' See the cases reviewed in Benjamin on Sale, pp. 96–110. He points out that in America the rule in *Lee* v. *Griffin* is not generally approved.

requires one qualification. Property may pass in consequence of the relation of principal and accessory having been established between something delivered by lessor to lessee, and something originally belonging to the latter: and where the thing delivered under the letting is principal, its owner becomes owner also of the accessory by the title of accession, not by a delivery in performance of a sale. Thus if a land owner gives a building lease, the house built under the lease is his, and yet the contract is locatio conductio only[1].

[1] Nec posse ullam locationem esse, ubi corpus ipsum non datur ab eo cui id fieret: aliter atque si aream darem ubi insulam aedificares. quoniam tunc a me substantia proficiscitur: Dig. 18. 1. 20. So too if one hires a builder to build one a house, it is locatio conductio only: quam insulam aedificandam loco, ut sua impensa conductor omnia faciat, proprietatem quidem eorum ad me transfert, et tamen locatio est: locat enim artifex operam suam, id est faciendi necessitatem: Dig. 19. 2. 22. 2. So too, in English law, the consideration to be paid to the builder is not for a transfer of chattels, but for work and labour done and materials furnished in adding something to the land: *Cotterell* v. *Apsley*, 6 Taunt. 322: *Tripp* v. *Armitage*, 4 M. & W. 687: *Clark* v. *Bulmer*, 11 M. & W. 243.

CHAPTER II.

WHO CAN BUY AND SELL.

Persons entirely unable to contract. Special restrictions: tutors and curators: public officials. Effects of Contract of Sale entered into by a pupillus without auctoritas: is he bound or not?

THE rules governing the capacity to enter a contract of sale are in substance merely part of the general law relating to contractual capacity, and for that reason do not here require any prolonged discussion. Some persons cannot either buy or sell, because they cannot make any sort of contract whatsoever. Others are, for special reasons, disabled by law from buying certain kinds of property. Lastly, though certain persons can enter into the contract either as vendors or purchasers, it does not, owing to the status of the contracting party, produce all its usual legal consequences.

Those who cannot contract at all are infants, that is to say, children under the age of seven years[1]; spendthrifts judicially interdicted from the management of their own affairs[2]; and idiots and lunatics[3], except in lucid intervals[4]. *Persons entirely unable to contract.*

The following special restrictions on the capacity to purchase are mentioned in the authorities:—

(1) Tutors and Curators may not buy on their own account property belonging to those placed under their charge[5], because, as Ulpian remarks[6], one cannot be both *Special restrictions: tutors and curators:*

---

[1] Inst. iii. 19. 10.   [2] Dig. 45. 1. 6.
[3] Dig. 50. 17. 5.   [4] Cod. 4. 38. 2.
[5] Dig. 18. 1. 34. 7: Pothier, 13: Code Civil, Art. 1596.
[6] Dig. 26. 8. 5. 2.

vendor and purchaser at the same time: in origin no doubt the prohibition rests on the principle 'tutor in rem suam auctor fieri non potest'[1]. But such a purchase will be good if authorised by a co-guardian[2], or if made at a public auction[3] or a sale lawfully authorised by a creditor of the ward[4], or if ratified by the ward himself on attaining his majority[5]. These rules were extended generally to agents managing the affairs of other people[6], unless the transaction was expressly authorised or subsequently ratified by the principal.

Public officials.

(2) Public officials may not buy, either personally or through an agent, property which they have to sell in the exercise of their public functions: and by an enactment of Severus and Antoninus those who infringe this rule will not only forfeit the property itself, but are mulcted as well in a penalty of four times its value[7].

(3) Persons serving in a Roman province, whether in a civil or in a military capacity, may not purchase land situate therein, except estates belonging to their own family, and sold by the Treasury[8].

The cases in which, owing to the peculiar status of one

---

[1] Inst. i. 21. 3.
[2] Dig. 26. 8. 5. 2.   [3] Cod. 4. 38. 5.
[4] Dig. 26. 8. 5. 5. Cette nullité n'est établie que pour empêcher les fraudes par lesquelles un tuteur, pour son propre intérêt, pourroit ou acheter à vil prix, ou se rendre acheteur de choses qu'il n'est pas de l'intérêt de son mineur de vendre : l'effet de la loi cesse, lorsqu'il il n'y a aucun lieu de soupçonner ces fraudes. C'est sur ce principe qu'il est décidé qu'un tuteur est reçu à enchérir et à acheter les biens saisis par les Créanciers de son mineur : Pothier, 13.
[5] Dig. 26. 8. 5. 2.   [6] Dig. 18. 1. 34. 7.
[7] Dig. 18. 1. 46 : cf. Code Civil, Art. 1596, 1597.
[8] Dig. 18. 1. 62. pr. : cf. Cicero in Verr. iv. 5. The Code Civil, Art. 1595, declares void, except in three cases, all purchases and sales entered into between husband and wife. Such sales were not contrary to the civil law, unless entered into at an undervalue merely to evade the rule which prohibited gifts between persons married to one another: Dig. 18. 1. 38: Pothier, 39.

or other of the parties, the contract does not produce its full effects, are those of slaves, persons in paternal power, and pupilli acting without the authority of their guardians. Into the first two it is not proposed to enter, for the capacity of slaves and other persons in power to bind either themselves or those to whom they are subject is the same in sale as in other contracts generating bilateral obligation, and no special light is thrown on the matter by the authorities dealing with the particular contract with which we are concerned[1]. As to the precise effect of a contract of sale entered into by a pupillus without his guardian's authorisation there is more to say, and that for two reasons: firstly, because there is a considerable amount of textual authority on the problem in the Titles of the Corpus Iuris dealing with our contract, and secondly, because, according to the construction which some writers put upon those passages, they present us with an example of a sale binding one of the parties only, and therefore conflicting with the principle,

Effects of contract of sale entered into by pupillus without auctoritas.

---

[1] In Dig. 18. 1. 2. pr. it is said, 'inter patrem et filium contrahi emptio non potest, sed de rebus castrensibus potest.' It is well known that in dealing with his castrense peculium a filius familias was deemed sui iuris, and upon a contract relating to it entered into between himself and his paterfamilias each party could sue and be sued precisely as if there had been no relation of potestas between them. It can, however, hardly be held that the passage excludes the creation of a natural obligation between father and son by a contract of sale relating to peculium adventitium. It was of course written before this kind of peculium had any existence. That a natural obligation could be generated by contract between father and son is shown by Dig. 12. 6. 38 : 46. 1. 56. 1 : ib. 71. pr., and by the application of the doctrine of deductio de peculio (Savigny, Oblig. i. pp. 48, 49): and there seems to be no reason why a purchase by a son (having peculium adventitium) from the father should not be good, or a purchase by the father of some thing forming part of that peculium. Under the republic, no doubt, when the only kind of peculium known was that subsequently termed profectitium, a contract of emptio venditio entered into between filius and paterfamilias must have been void, for it could have had no effect whatever.

which has been laid down in the preceding chapter, that the contract always gives rise to bilateral obligation.

The authorities upon the point can in fact hardly be made consistent with one another. The first conclusion which they suggest is that, though the other party is bound, the pupillus, whether vendor or purchaser, is laid under no obligation of any sort or kind by such unauthorised contract. Thus, in his Institutes [1] Justinian says

> Unde in his causis ex quibus obligationes mutuae nascuntur, ut in emptionibus, venditionibus, locationibus, conductionibus, mandatis, depositis, si tutoris auctoritas non interveniat, ipsi quidem, qui cum his contrahunt, obligantur: at invicem pupilli non obligantur:

and this is confirmed by Ulpian, who qualifies Justinian's language by observing that the pupillus emptor is suable so far as he has been enriched or benefited by the other party's performance of the contract:

> pupillus vendendo sine tutoris auctoritate non obligatur, sed nec in emendo nisi in quantum locupletior factus est[2]:

and elsewhere[3] he uses language even more explicit of a pupil vendor, which if literally construed would certainly dispose finally of the theory that the obligation produced by the contract is of necessity bilateral, or what Pothier calls synallagmatic. Similar expressions are found in one passage of Paulus:

> si pupilli persona intervenit, qui ante sine tutoris auctoritate, deinde tutore auctore emit, quamvis venditor jam ei obligatus fuit, tamen quia pupillus non tenebatur, renovata venditio efficit ut invicem obligati sint[4].

---

[1] Inst. 1. 21. pr.   [2] Dig. 26. 8. 5. 1.

[3] Si quis a pupillo sine tutoris auctoritate emerit, ex uno latere constat contractus, nam qui emit obligatus est pupillo, pupillum sibi non obligat: Dig. 19. 1. 13. 29.

[4] Dig. 18. 5. 7. 1. It may perhaps be suggested that Ulpian, who is the author of most of these statements that the pupillus was not

What however, it may be asked, is the meaning of the words obligatur, obligatus, tenebatur, in these passages? We are certainly not bound to interpret them as meaning that the pupillus was laid under no obligation whatever, for they are quite reconcileable with the view that, though not suable except 'in quantum locupletior factus est,' he was bound by his promise naturaliter, and that that natural obligation might have all or any of the effects incident to naturalis obligatio in general[1]. In support of this it may be said that (1) a pupillus who borrowed money without the guardian's authority, although not suable, was nevertheless under a natural obligation to repay it[2]: (2) a pupillus who made a promise in the form of stipulation was bound by it naturaliter, for such a promise could be guaranteed by a surety[3]: (3) such natural obligation could be released[4], and could form the subject of a novation[5]. It may be replied that these arguments are drawn from the field of unilateral obligations. There is however one clear instance of a pupillus being bound naturaliter by a transaction of quasi-contractual character, and giving rise to obligations binding on both parties. If a pupillus acted without his guardian's authority as a negotiorum gestor, and sued for his out-of-pocket expenses, he could be met by a set-off of the sum due from him in respect of the business to the person on whose behalf he had acted[6]: and nothing

Is he bound?

bound in any sense, was habitually lax in his use of words denoting obligation, or used 'obligatus' to mean 'suable.' No one probably will dispute the proposition that a pupillus to whom a thing was lent (commodata) was bound naturaliter by the ordinary duties which arose from that contract: and yet in Dig. 13. 6. 1. 2 Ulpian himself uses language which, if strictly construed, would entirely negative the possibility of such an obligation.

[1] Savigny, Obl. i. pp. 44–51.   [2] Dig. 46. 3. 95. 4.
[3] Dig. 45. 1. 127.   [4] Dig. 46. 3. 95. 4.   [5] Dig. 39. 5. 19. 4.
[6] Pupillus sane si negotia gesserit, post rescriptum Divi Pii etiam conveniri potest in id quod factus est locupletior: agendo autem compensationem eius quod gessit patitur: Dig. 3. 5. 3. 4.

could be set off which was not owed, at any rate naturaliter. (4) If a thing were sold at a fixed price subject to the condition subsequent that no better offer were made within a certain time (in diem addictio[1]) a better offer made by a pupillus without his guardian's authorisation, and accepted by the vendor, was sufficient to defeat the first sale:

> Sed et si pupillus postea sine tutoris auctoritate pluris emerit consentiente venditore, abibitur a priore emptione[2].

Now no second offer could have this effect, unless it were more advantageous to the vendor than the original sale:

> quidquid enim ad utilitatem venditoris pertinet, pro meliore conditione haberi debet[3]:

and how, under these circumstances, is it conceivable that the pupillus should be under no obligation whatever to the vendor?

These considerations recommend the conclusion[4] that in contracts of sale such as we have been examining the other party, if under no disability, is always bound; but that, although he can sue the pupillus so far as his own performance has enriched him, his other rights engendered by the contract are enforceable only in the indirect methods by which natural obligation is enforceable in general.

It may be convenient to briefly summarize three other theories upon the subject advanced by eminent authorities. (1) The contract is primarily void as regards both parties: but its invalidity is remediable by the pupillus' ratifying it, either alone when his disability has terminated, or before with his guardian's sanction. Such ratification must be acquiesced in by the other party, who himself has no similar privilege: it relates back to the moment at which the contract was

---

[1] See Index, s. v.   [2] Dig. 18. 2. 14. 3.   [3] Dig. 18. 2. 5.
[4] Held by Bechmann, Kauf, ii. §§ 169-172: Vangerow, Pandekten, i. § 279: cf. Ihering, Geist des römischen Rechts, iii. p. 192.

concluded, and the contract must be regarded as though it had bound both parties in every respect from the outset[1].

(2) The contract in part is void, for the pupillus acquires rights, but incurs no liabilities under it: he can enforce it against the other party, but it cannot be in any way enforced against him[2].

(3) The contract in part is void, for the pupillus is not bound, while the other party is: but the former cannot enforce it against the latter unless he is ready to perform his own side of the bargain[3].

[1] Wächter, Pandekten, i. § 84, Beilage ii A. For a slightly modified view see Savigny, System, iii. p. 40.
[2] Arndts, Pandekten, § 234.
[3] Windscheid, Lehrbuch, § 321, note 22.

CHAPTER III.

WHAT CAN AND CANNOT BE BOUGHT AND SOLD.

The general principle. Sale of Servitudes: of res alienae: of res extra commercium: free men: res furtivae. Things whose alienation is forbidden by law, or which have ceased to exist. Purchase of res sua. Sale of free services. Restrictions imposed on right of sale by Testament or Contract. Note A. Sale of res alienae in French and English Law.

The general principle.

THE general principle is stated thus by Paulus:

> omnium rerum quamquis habere vel possidere vel persequi potest venditio recte fit: quas vero natura vel gentium ius vel mores civitatis commercio exuerunt, earum nulla venditio est [1].

Putting aside then for the moment those things which from their nature [2] cannot, or which the law says shall not, be the subject matter of a contract of sale, we find that the contract may validly relate to tangible or corporeal things, whether moveable or immoveable [3]; to things in-

---

[1] Dig. 18. 1. 34. 1. Tout ce qui est dans le commerce peut être vendu, lorsque des lois particulières n'en ont pas prohibé l'aliénation: Code Civil, Art. 1598.

[2] Paulus was perhaps referring to 'res naturali iure omnium communes' (Inst. ii. 1. 1: Dig. 1. 8. 2. pr.), such as air, the sea, running water. But water may under given conditions be bought and sold, and it seems reasonable to say that there is nothing which in itself cannot be bought and sold except where it is to be freely had by all in such quantities that it can possess no exchange value: Si alimenta fuerint legata, dici potest etiam aquam legato inesse, si in ea regione fuerint legata, ubi venumdari aqua solet . . . . . . in ea regione Africae vel forte Aegypti . . . . . ubi aqua venalis est: Dig. 34. 1. 1: ib. 14. 3.

[3] 'Mercis' appellatio ad res mobiles tantum pertinet: Dig. 50. 16. 66.

corporeal, such as (1) servitudes or other iura in re aliena, and the release of property from such burdens; and (2) rights of action, and debts due to the vendor from some third person: to the mere right of possession: and to aggregates or 'universities' of things, corporeal and incorporeal. Whether these things belong to the vendor or not, and whether they are actually in existence or not at the time when the contract is made, is as a rule immaterial. As to two of these subjects of sale some explanation may conveniently be given at once: others are reserved for a detailed examination in the next chapter.,

Servitudes can be sold only by the owner of property, who agrees for a consideration to create them in favour of the purchaser: that is to say, a man may agree to sell a right of way over his land, or a usufruct over his slaves, and for breach of such an agreement he is suable by actio ex empto. But although a sale of land will ordinarily carry with it the praedial servitudes thereto appurtenant, a man to whom a personal servitude belongs cannot sell it (except by way of release to the owner of the servient property), nor can an existing praedial servitude be sold without the land to which it belongs, because they are by law intransferable apart from it[1]. But the usufructuary may sell the enjoyment of his usufruct[2], and iura in re aliena which are not servitudes, such as emphyteusis and superficies, being transferable, admit of sale[3]. Sale of servitudes:

A contract of sale is in no way invalid because the thing sold does not belong to the vendor, or because he has no right to sell it: of res alienae,

rem alienam distrahere quem posse nulla dubitatio est,

---

[1] But if the owner of a praedial servitude mortgages it to an adjoining proprietor, the latter may apparently, in the event of non-payment, sell it to another adjoining proprietor: Dig. 20. 1. 12.

[2] Dig. 18. 6. 8. 2: 7. 1. 12. 2: ib. 38.

[3] Dig. 18. 1. 32.

nam emptio est et venditio: sed res emptori auferri potest[1].

As will be seen more fully hereafter, the vendor's obligation is not necessarily to vest property in the purchaser: he is bound only to give him undisturbed possession, and to indemnify him for all loss which he may sustain through having to give up the thing which he has bought to its rightful owner. If one sells a thing which does not belong to one, but with the owner's consent (as in all sales effected by agents), the owner obviously is estopped from disputing the purchaser's title: and if the vendor has a mortgage or similar security given him over the property by the owner himself, and sells on non-payment of the debt at the time agreed upon, he is taken to sell as the owner's agent[2]. If however the vendor has in fact no rights over the property, and no authority to dispose of it, the owner can always recover it from the purchaser by actio in rem, unless (1) the latter has in the meanwhile acquired a valid title to it by usucapion[3], or (2) the former has become the vendor's heir[4], or (3) has ratified the vendor's action[5]. As between the vendor and the purchaser of property of which the former has no right to dispose, the validity of the contract depends upon the state of their knowledge. (1) If both are aware of the facts, but nevertheless are acting in good faith (as where an agent has received authority to sell from a person who is not owner, but whom both believe to be such) the contract is binding on each, whereas it is void if they are *in mala fide*[6]. (2) If neither of them knows the facts, it would seem that both are

---

[1] Dig. 18. 1. 28.   [2] Inst. ii. 8. 1: cf. ii. 1. 41.
[3] Cod. 4. 52. 1.   [4] Cod. 4. 51. 5.
[5] In this case he can compel the vendor by actio negotiorum gestorum or by condictio sine causa to surrender to him the purchase money, or to assign to him his rights against the purchaser: Cod. 2. 18. 19: 3. 32. 3: 4. 51.
[6] Dig. 18. 1. 34. 3.

bound[1] by the ordinary duties arising from the contract[2]. (3) Knowledge on the part of only one of the parties that the property is not the vendor's is material only when he is acting in bad faith. (*a*) Where it is the vendor, he is bound, if he has received the purchase money, to deliver the property, and the purchaser is not only entitled to compensation on eviction, but may sue ex empto even before the rightful owner evicts him[3]. If he has not received the purchase-money, he is debarred from demanding it unless he will give security against eviction[4]. (*b*) Where it is the purchaser who knows that the vendor has no right to dispose of the goods, he cannot be compelled to pay the price until the property has been delivered[5], but the vendor cannot be compelled to deliver it, or to indemnify the purchaser in the event of eviction[6].

The following classes of things cannot be the subject of a contract of sale, except where the purchaser, without fault on his part, is in error as to their real nature[7].

(1) Things which are extra commercium, such as res sacrae or religiosae[8] and res publicae[9]. *of res extra commercium.*

---

[1] See Dig. 18. 1. 70.
[2] E.g. Dig. 19. 1. 11. 7 and 8.
[3] Dig. 19. 1. 30. 1.
[4] Dig. 18. 6. 19. 1.
[5] Dig. 18. 1. 34. 3.
[6] See note A at the end of this chapter on the modern law of France and England as to the effect of sales by non-owners of what they purport to sell.
[7] See Chap. VI, inf.
[8] Inst. iii. 23. 5 : Dig. 18. 1. 4 : ib. 73. pr.
[9] Dig. 18. 1. 22 : ib. 62. 1 : Pothier, 10. Only those things which were publico usui destinatae were governed by this rule : things of which the State reserved to itself the use and disposal, such as slaves or military stores, could be bought and sold just like any other res aliena: Celsus filius ait ... te emere non posse ... sacra et religiosa loca, aut quorum commercium non sit, ut publica, quae non in pecunia populi, sed in publico usu habentur, ut est Campus Martius : Dig. 18. 1. 6. pr. Public offices were incapable of sale, Cod. 9. 27. 6. In French law too they are deemed extra commercium, and 'il faut placer dans cette catégorie la convention par laquelle le function-

of free-men,

(2) Free men[1]. The only trace left in the law of Justinian of the paterfamilias' privilege of selling those in his power is the right given by an enactment of Constantine[2] to parents in extreme poverty thus to dispose of children immediately upon birth. The effect was to make them slaves, but any one might redeem and make them free again.

Res furtivae,

(3) Property which has been stolen cannot validly be bought and sold, if the parties are aware of the circumstances. The rules here are the same as those which have been already stated in connection with the sale of property known not to belong to the vendor by the parties or either of them[3].

things whose alienation is forbidden by law,

(4) Things whose alienation is expressly prohibited by law[4]. Of these it will be sufficient to give examples. The husband was prohibited by a lex Julia from parting with land which came to him as a dowry with his wife[5]. The father might not alienate the peculium adventitium of the child in power[6]. Res litigiosae, i.e. property the title to which is in dispute in a pending action, could not be the subject of conveyance and therefore not of sale[7]. Purchases of the material of which standing houses were built, and which the owner proposed to take down for speculative

naire stipule un certain prix pour donner sa démission:' but by a law of 1816 certain public officers have received the right of nominating their successors to the Government, and this may be done for a consideration. Contracts for the sale of offices are void by the English Common law, as contrary to public policy (*Garforth* v. *Fearon*, 1 Hy. Bl. 237, and other cases cited by Benjamin, pp. 501–504), and it is the same with the sale of a pension, unless it was granted exclusively as a reward for past services: *Wells* v. *Foster*, 8 M. & W. 149.

[1] Dig. 18. 1. 4–6 pr.: ib. 34. 2: ib. 70.   [2] Cod. 4. 43. 2.
[3] P. 18 supr.
[4] Nullum enim pactum, nullam conventionem, nullum contractum inter eos videri volumus subsecutum, qui contrahunt lege contrahere prohibente: Cod. 1. 14. 5. pr.
[5] Inst. ii. 8. pr.: Dig. 23. 5. 4.   [6] Cod. 6. 60. 1. 1.
[7] Dig. 44. 6. 1 & 2: Cod. 8. 36. 2.

purposes, were forbidden and penalised by law[1]. Gaius inclined to the view, which Justinian seems to have adopted by incorporating the opinion in the Digest[2], that a sale of poison was void if it were of such a kind as could not be of any beneficent use even in combination with other substances.

(5) If the thing which it has been agreed to buy and sell has, unknown to both parties, ceased to exist at the time at which the contract is made, the contract is void[3]. The vendor must return the purchase money, if he has been paid[4]: and if he alone knew that the property no longer existed he is further liable to compensate the purchaser in damages for any loss which he may sustain through non-performance, whereas if the purchaser alone knew it, he is bound to pay the purchase money, and has no rights himself against the vendor[5]. If both were aware that the property no longer existed, the contract is void[6]. Where

things which have ceased to exist.

---

[1] Dig. 18. 1. 52 : 39. 2. 48 : Cod. 8. 10. 2 : Pothier, 12.

[2] Dig. 18. 1. 35. 2 : Pothier, 11. 'The thing sold may be such as in its nature cannot form the subject of a valid contract of sale, as an obscene book or an indecent picture, which are deemed by the common law to be evil and noxious things. The article sold may be in its nature an innocent and proper subject of commercial dealings, as a drug, but may be knowingly sold for the purpose, prohibited by law, of adulterating food or drink. . . . . In all these cases the law permits neither party to maintain an action on such a sale:' Benjamin, p. 491.

[3] Dig. 18. 1. 15. pr.: Pothier, 4. The rule is sometimes put upon the ground of mistake, but it may equally rest on the ground that one of the essential conditions of the contract has failed : nec emptio nec venditio sine re quae veneat potest intellegi : Dig. 18. 1. 8. pr. In English law 'when there is a contract for the sale of specific goods, and the goods unknown to the seller have ceased to exist at the time of the contract, the contract is void (*Couturier* v. *Hastie*, 5 H. of L. Cases, 673 : *Strickland* v. *Turner*, 7 Ex. 208). As there can be no sale without a thing transferred to the purchaser in consideration of the price received, it follows that if at the time of the contract the thing has ceased to exist, the sale is void :' Benjamin, p. 81.

[4] Dig. 18. 1. 57. pr.   [5] Dig. ib. 57. 2.   [6] Dig. ib. 57. 3.

the thing has ceased to exist only in part, the contract is void, and the purchaser can recover any purchase money which he has paid, only where less than half of it is left, or where the portion wanting is the portion for which mainly the purchaser can show that he bought it [1]. Otherwise the contract stands, the purchase money being proportionately abated [2]. On the same principle a sale of the inheritance of a living third person, or of a person who does not and never has existed, is void [3], though Justinian [4] legalised sales of the inheritance of a living person to which the vendor hoped to succeed, provided that person assented, though he was not thereby bound to leave it to the vendor at all [5].

Purchase of res sua.

(6) An agreement to purchase a thing which already belongs to the purchaser is void [6], irrespective of his know-

---

[1] Dig. 18. 1. 57. pr.

[2] Dig. loc. cit. Pothier, 4. Si au moment de la vente la chose vendue était périe en totalité, la vente serait nulle. Si une partie seulement de la chose est périe, il est au choix de l'acquéreur d'abandonner la vente, ou de demander la partie conservée, en faisant déterminer le prix par la ventilation : Code Civil, Art. 1601. There seems to be no such rule in English law: *Barr* v. *Gibson*, 3 M. & W. 390. 'The only question is, whether the article has been so far destroyed as no longer to answer to the description of it given by the contract:' Chalmers, Sale of Goods, p. 11.

[3] Dig. 18. 4. 1. Cum hereditatem aliquis vendidit, debet esse hereditas, ut sit emptio. Nec enim alea emitur, ut in venatione et similibus, sed res: quae si non est, non contrahitur emptio, et ideo pretium condicetur: Dig. ib. 7.

[4] Cod. 2. 3. 30.

[5] On ne peut vendre la succession d'une personne vivante, même de son consentement : Code Civil, Art. 1600. In English law the sale of a man's possible interest as the devisee of a living owner, on the terms that he shall return the purchase money if he does not become the devisee, is perfectly good : *Cook* v. *Field*, 15 Q. B. 460 : and see Pollock on Contract, 4th Ed., p. 302.

[6] Suae rei emptio non valet: Dig. 18. 1. 16. pr. : Cod. 4. 38. 4, ib. 10. La raison est que le Contrat de Vente consiste dans l'obligation que contracte le vendeur de faire avoir la chose à l'acheteur : et par conséquent il consiste à rendre l'acheteur créancier de la chose qui lui est

ledge of the facts : such knowledge however affects his right to recover the purchase money, if paid, for he is not allowed to do this if he was aware that the property which he was buying was already his own [1]. Hence if what he is buying belongs to him in part ownership, the sale is good only in respect of the part which does not belong to him, and he can be compelled to pay for that part only [2]. But if one man is entitled to the possession of property belonging to another, the latter can validly agree to purchase that possession [3]. So too a man may knowingly purchase a thing which will belong to him on the fulfilment of a suspensive condition or condition precedent, because the condition may fail, and he wishes to become its owner in all events [4], though if he is not aware of his conditional rights, and the condition is satisfied, it avoids the sale, and he can recover the purchase money which he has paid [5] : and similarly although an absolute and unconditional purchase of what already belongs to one is void, one can buy it under the condition and to meet the contingency of its ceasing to be one's property [6].

vendue : or, il est évident que cela ne peut avoir lieu par rapport à une chose qui appartiendroit déjà à l'acheteur : car personne ne peut être créancier de sa propre chose : l'acheteur ne peut pas demander qu'on lui fasse *avoir* une chose qui est déjà à lui : Pothier, 8.

[1] Dig. 18. 1. 16. pr.   [2] Dig. 18. 1. 18. pr.

[3] Rei suae emptio tunc valet, cum ab initio id agatur, ut possessionem emat, quam forte venditor habuit, et in possessionis iudicio potior esset, Dig. 18. 1. 34. 4. It is possible that for *et* we ought to read *ut* with Haloander, for otherwise there is no construction, and for *esset*, *sit* or *fiat*, to bring it into line with agatur and emat. The sense would then be 'if the object of the contract is to buy a possession vested in the vendor, which has actually enabled or is such as to enable him to succeed in an interdict retinendae possessionis ' : see Treitschke, Kauf-contract, § 11 : Glück, Pandekten, 16. p. 40.

[4] Dig. 18. 1. 61.   [5] Dig. 19. 1. 29.

[6] Par exemple, si je suis propriétaire d'une maison comprise dans une substitution dont je suis grevé envers vous : quoiqu'avant l'ouverture de la substitution je sois propriétaire de cette maison, je puis l'acheter

24 WHAT CAN AND CANNOT BE BOUGHT AND SOLD.

Sale of free services.

(7) It would seem that a man cannot sell his services, skill, or labour: for even if he should agree to render them for a money consideration for the whole of his lifetime, the contract cannot be anything except one of hiring and letting. There is also some question whether money can be bought and sold. As to coins, which are not, or which have ceased to be, legal tender in a country, but which are sought after for their rarity or beauty, little or no doubt can be felt: but in respect of the ordinary currency it is difficult to say that any such transaction can be more than an exchange:

> alioquin non posse rem expediri, quae videatur res venisse, et quae pretii nomine data esse: nam utramque videri et venisse et pretii nomine datam esse rationem non pati [1].

The question however is one upon which, apart from such passages as this, there is no Roman authority [2].

Restrictions on right of sale imposed by Testament,

Restrictions imposed on the power of selling property au cas et sous la condition qu'il y auroit par la suite ouverture à la substitution. Mais si j'ai acheté purement et simplement ma propre chose, le contrat est nul, et ne deviendra pas valable, quoiqu'elle cesse par la suite de m'appartenir : Pothier, 9. Similarly Blackstone says (Comm. ii. 450), 'if a man buys his own goods in a fair or market, the contract of sale shall not bind him so as that he shall render the price, unless the property had been previously altered by a previous sale': and in accordance with this in *Bingham* v. *Bingham* (1 Ves. Sr. 126), where a purchaser was dealing with his own property, not knowing it to be his, the contract was held void as being legally impossible and because the supposed subject matter of the transaction totally failed. But in *Scotson* v. *Pegg* (30 L. J. Ex. at p. 226) Wilde, B. said that a man might validly buy his own goods from another in whose possession they were, and who was entitled to retain such possession : and what may be called 'quasi exceptions' to the rule are of daily occurrence, as where a farmer buys in his goods when sold under a distraint for tithe rent charge, and in sales by sheriff's generally.

[1] The Proculian argument in Inst. iii. 23. 2.

[2] See Bechmann, Kauf, ii. § 154, and the references in Windscheid, Lehrbuch, § 385, note 3.

by the directions or stipulations of private persons do not, as a rule, prevent it from being sold, or affect the validity of a contract for the sale of it.

I. If a testator charges an heir or other person taking a benefit under his will not to sell property thereby bequeathed to him, and the charge is imposed for the advantage of some specific and determinate person [1], the property can be sold so as to vest an absolute title in the purchaser only with the assent of such person or persons [2]. If sold without such assent, the contract, as such, is good between vendor and purchaser: as regards the person for whose benefit the trust was created it is governed by the ordinary rules relating to sales of res alienae [3]. If a family settlement of land be made by a will, and the owner for the time being becomes insolvent, the purchaser of the estate will hold it only *pur autre vie* [4]: a voluntary sale by the owner for the time being merely causes the land to shift immediately to the person next entitled in remainder [5].

II. A contract entered into by the owner of property, or by Contract. and purporting to bind him not to sell it, as a rule is void:

> nemo paciscendo efficere potest . . . ne vicino invito praedium alienet [6]:

The reason being that, speaking generally, the promisee has no interest in the performance of the promise [7]. But there can be no doubt that the desired effect may be attained by the owner promising a penal sum by stipulation if he should in fact sell [8]: and there are two exceptions, one narrow and the other wide, to the general principle. (*a*) If

---

[1] Dig. 30. 114. 14 : 32. 38. 4.   [2] Dig. 30. 120. 1.
[3] Cod. 6. 43. 3. 2 and 3 : Pothier, 15 : see p. 18 supr.
[4] Dig. 31. 69. 1.   [5] Dig. 31. 69. 3 : ib. 77. 27.
[6] Dig. 2. 14. 61.
[7] Inventae sunt enim huiusmodi obligationes ad hoc, ut unusquisque sibi adquirat quod sua interest: Inst. iii. 19. 19.
[8] Arg. Dig 11. 7. 11.

the mortgagor or hypothecary debtor agreed with his creditor not to sell the property mortgaged or charged, a sale in contravention of the agreement was void [1]: the anomaly is usually explained by the fact that the creditor has rights *in rem*, and some civilians would extend the exception to all cases in which the promisee is invested with similar rights over the property to which the contract relates [2]. (*b*) The vendor of property might bind the purchaser by a pactum de non alienando, adiectum to the contract of sale [3]: but the effect of such a term in the contract was not to avoid a sale made in violation of it, but merely to entitle the original vendor to sue ex vendito for such damages as he could shew he had sustained [4].

[1] Dig. 20. 5. 7. 2.   [2] E.g. Glück, Pandekten, 16. p. 56.
[3] Dig. 19. 1. 21. 5 : 18. 1. 75 : 2. 14. 48 : and compare Cod. 4. 54. 9. with Dig. 2. 14. 61.
[4] Dig. 18. 1. 75 : 19. 1. 21. 5 : cf. Dig. 45. 1. 135. 3 : Cod. 4. 6. 3.

Note A.

Sale of res alienae in French and English Law.

The French law of the eighteenth century as to sales of res alienae is stated in accordance with the civil law by Pothier, 7 : le Contrat de Vente ne consiste pas dans la translation de la propriété de la chose vendue : il suffit, pour qu'il soit valable, que le vendeur se soit valablement obligé de faire avoir à l'acheteur la chose vendue : et l'obligation qu'il en a contractée ne laisse pas d'être valable, quoiqu'il ne soit pas en son pouvoir de la remplir, par le refus que fait le propriétaire de la chose, de consentir à la vente : il suffit que ce que le vendeur a promis ait été quelque chose de possible en soi, quoiqu'il ne fût pas en son pouvoir : il doit s'imputer de s'être témérairement obligé. By the Code Civil the law of France was altered : la vente de la chose d'autrui est nulle : elle peut donner lieu à des dommages-intérêts lorsque l'acheteur a ignoré que la chose fût à autrui : Art. 1599. The change seems to have been due to the assumption that the purchaser intends to bind himself only on the condition of becoming owner. The article of the Code is interpreted by Demante (by reference to Art. 1184) to mean that such a sale is not void, but merely voidable at the option of the purchaser. That article provides that in synallagmatic contracts either party can demand rescission on failure by the other to perform what he has undertaken : and as according to the principles of French law the vendor is bound to transfer property in the goods sold (Fréméry, Etudes du Droit Commercial, p. 5, cited by Benjamin, p. 383), the purchaser on discovering that he had no right to sell can avoid the transaction even before the true owner has taken any steps to recover the goods from him. But the provision of the Code has no application to purchases of things in genere to be procured by the vendor, nor apparently to a contract to deliver a thing in exchange for money and to guarantee the possession, with an express stipulation that one does not engage to give a good title as owner: Demante, Cours analytique de Code Civil, p. 51.

The law of Scotland appears to be in accordance with that of Rome: 'possession of moveables presumes property: and in the rapid intercourse of trade the buyer of goods is not allowed to stop the bargain on pretence of want of title, or on mere doubts as to the possibility of a challenge:' Bell, Principles of the Law of Scotland, i. p. 114.

In English Law, Benjamin (pp. 6, 7) states that 'in general no man can sell goods and *convey a valid title to them* unless he be the owner, or lawfully represent the owner: nemo dat qui non habet' (*Peer* v. *Humphrey*, 2 A. & E. 495), but a man may make a valid *agreement to sell* a thing not yet his. A good title, however, will be acquired through a sale of goods which do not belong to the vendor, if sold in màrket overt and the purchaser is acting in good faith, though the vendor remains liable to the rightful owner (*Delaney* v. *Wallis*, 14 L. R. Ir. 31): and other exceptions to the rule are found in sales of negotiable instruments (24 & 25 Vic. c. 96. s. 100): sales by pawnees (but is not the reason of this that given by Gaius, Inst. ii. 64: sed hoc forsitan ideo videatur fieri, quod voluntate debitoris intellegitur pignus alienari?): by public officers, such as sheriffs selling the goods of defendants in execution: by agents entrusted with the possession of goods for the purpose of sale: and by masters of ships in cases of absolute necessity (*the Gratitudine*, 3 Rob. Adm. 259). The question whether in English law the vendor is to be taken by implication to warrant his title will be examined in connection with a later chapter.

CHAPTER IV.

CERTAIN SPECIAL SUBJECTS OF SALE.

Emptio generis. Sale of article to be made or procured by the vendor: doubts as to its true legal character. Emptio spei. Purchase of an inheritance. Purchase of a debt, or of a right of action, whether availing in rem or in personam: rules relating to assignment.

Emptio generis.

WHEN what is bought is not a specifically determined article, such as this particular estate Blackacre, or this particular horse, book, watch, or what not, but a quantity of goods of a certain description, determined by number, weight or measure (such as 100 quarters of red British wheat, 100 dozens of Château Lafitte claret, vintage 1883, 1colb. potatoes of the crop actually gathered from a particular field), or even a single thing not specifically determined, but by description merely (as an order for 'one of your patent rapid filters') the transaction is called emptio generis. As a rule the goods belong to the class of things known as 'fungible,' but this is not necessary: and (according to the generally received opinion) it is immaterial whether the vendor already has such goods in his possession, or has to manufacture or procure them. Where the goods bought have to be selected from a larger quantity (as for instance where one orders a dozen shovels from an ironmonger's stock, or agrees to buy fifty out of a larger number of lambs born in the past season) the selection in cases of doubt rests with the vendor, who may, if the genus comprises different qualities, send the worst if he pleases[1]. As

[1] Dig. 18. 1. 60, cf. ib. 25. 1: 45. 1. 99. pr.: 17. 1. 52: 12. 6. 32. 3.

will be seen hereafter, this species of sale is an exception from the rule that the goods purchased are at the purchaser's risk from the moment of the conclusion of the contract [1].

It has been already pointed out that an agreement by *A* to make an article for *B* out of his own (*B*'s) materials [2], is a sale, nor is there any doubt that an agreement to sell a certain thing or number of things out of a larger quantity actually belonging to the vendor is a good sale as well. It has however been questioned whether an agreement to procure and deliver a certain quantity of goods of a particular kind, or to make an article of a given kind out of materials to be procured by one from some one else, can be deemed a sale on the principles of the Civil Law. It is urged [3] that no contract of this kind can be considered to be performed at all, unless both (1) property is vested in the other party, so that one fundamental principle of the Civil Law—that embodied in the rules relating to eviction—has no application to the case, and (2) the article made or

Sale of article to be made or procured by the vendor:

Is it really Sale?

According to English law, if there is an executory contract of sale, or an agreement to sell goods to be selected and appropriated to the buyer, the rule on the subject of selection is 'that when, from the nature of an agreement, an election is to be made, the party who is by the agreement to do the first act, which, from its nature, cannot be done till the election is determined, has authority to make the choice, in order that he may be able to do that first act, and when once he has done that act, the election has been irrevocably determined, but till then he may change his mind' (Benjamin, p. 319). 'Thus if *A* sells a thousand bricks out of a stack to *B*, who is to send his cart and fetch them away, *B* is to do the first act, and cannot do it till the election is determined : he may choose first one part of the stack and then another, and repeatedly change his mind ... until he has put them in his cart to be fetched away. But if the vendor is to despatch the goods, or do anything to them that cannot be done till the goods are appropriated, he has the right to choose what the goods shall be :' Benjamin, loc. cit. : cf. Blackburn on Sale, p. 128: *Heyward's Case*, 2 Coke, 36 : *Aldridge v. Johnson*, 7 E. & B., 885, 901.

[1] Dig. 18. 1. 35. 7.
[2] Ex auro *suo* : Gaius, iii. 147 : Inst. iii. 23. 4.
[3] E. g. by Bechmann, Kauf, ii A. p. 332.

procured possesses the marks and attributes bargained for, so that a second fundamental principle—that of implied warranty of quality—is also excluded: and further that the application of the doctrine of periculum to the cases raises difficulties towards the solution of which the authorities give little or no assistance. This opinion seems to be gaining ground among modern writers on the Civil Law [1], and it cannot be disputed that the texts contain no single case in which transactions of these kinds are clearly described as sales [2].

Emptio spei.

When what is bought is a thing which does not as yet exist, and which may never exist at all, or the quantity or value of which is so indeterminate that it may, as we say, come to nothing, the transaction is called emptio spei. If the intention of the parties is that the purchase money shall be paid in any case, whether the hoped for equivalent comes to anything or not, it is commonly termed, for the sake of distinction, emptio spei simplicis: if it is that it shall not be paid unless something at any rate is forthcoming, or shall only be paid in proportion to what the purchaser actually gets, it is termed emptio rei speratae. The first is presumed to be intended in such cases as where one agrees to buy the fish that shall be caught in such or such a net or nets, the game that shall be killed in such or such a battue,

---

[1] 'Es mehren sich in neuer und neuester Zeit die Stimmen, welche den grundsätzlichen Gegensatz zwischen beiden Gebieten betonen und zugleich mehr oder weniger entschieden anerkennen, dass das Lieferungsgeschäft jedenfalls in den Quellen des römischen Rechts nicht als Kauf vorkommt:' Bechmann, op. cit. p. 331, note 4. On the other hand, it is said in Holtzendorff, Rechtslexicon, ii. p. 664, 'the defenders of the view that a "Lieferungsvertrag" is a contract of sale affirm that just as a thing to be made by one [out of one's own materials?] may be the subject of a sale, so can a thing which one has to procure. There is no doubt that this view is correct.' But on German or on Roman principles?

[2] The nearest are Dig. 18. 1. 20 : 18. 6. 15. 1. Of course there is no doubt that they are sales both in Scotch (Bell, §§ 90, 147) and in English law : *Hibblewhite* v. *McMorris*, 5 M. & W. 462, Benjamin, p. 311.

the minerals that shall be extracted from such or such a mine to be opened:

> aliquando tamen et sine re venditio intellegitur, veluti cum quasi alea emitur. Quod fit, cum captum piscium vel avium vel missilium emitur: emptio enim contrahitur etiam si nihil inciderit, quia spei emptio est[1].

The second, which is in fact the purchase of a future thing conditionally on its coming into existence, is presumed to be intended when one buys a thing which may reasonably be expected to come into existence in the ordinary course of nature: e.g. the offspring of a slave woman now actually with child, the lambs to be born in the following spring on a particular sheep run, or next season's yield from a certain farm, garden or vineyard. In such a case the quality of the produce has no effect upon the amount of the purchase money, which, as it cannot be increased because the quality is better, similarly cannot be diminished because it is worse in fact than was expected. The presumption, however, in favour of either construction can be rebutted by evidence of a contrary intention. For instance, if one were to agree to buy for a fixed sum the whole of next year's vintage on a particular vineyard, this

---

[1] Dig. 18. 1. 8. 1: cf. Dig. 19. 1. 11. 18: ib. 12. The case is criticised by Benjamin, p. 87. The Scotch law is the same: Bell, § 91 (2). Cette espèce donna lieu à cette fameuse contestation, rapportée par Plutarque dans la vie de Solon. Des Milésiens se trouvant dans l'Isle de Cos, avoient acheté de quelques pêcheurs leur coup de filet: ces pêcheurs pêchèrent un trépié d'or: les acheteurs le prétendirent. On doit décider qu'ils étoient mal fondés: les vendeurs et les acheteurs n'avoient entendu vendre ou acheter que le poisson qui seroit pris: le trépié d'or auquel aucune des parties contractantes n'avoit pensé, ne faisoit donc pas partie du marché: et c'est une bonne fortune dont les pêcheurs seuls doivent profiter. Cette décision est plus juste que celle de l'Oracle, qui, consulté sur cette contestation, adjugea le trépié au plus sage des mortels; afin qu'aucune des parties n'osant s'attribuer cette qualité, le trépié d'or demeurât aux Prêtres: Pothier, 6.

would be an emptio spei [1]; but if the agreement were for ten casks of the wine which so and so should make next year from his vineyard, it would be an emptio rei speratae, and if only five casks were made, or none at all, the purchaser would have to pay only for five or none: while conversely the vendor would not be liable to deliver more than was made in fact, though he might have agreed to sell more [2].

Purchase of an inheritance.

The purchase and sale of an inheritance, that is to say, of the whole estate of a deceased person, or of some aliquot share of such estate as one is entitled to as coheir, is a peculiar transaction requiring some brief explanation. An inheritance may be sold either before or after it is 'delata' to the heir, in other words, either before or after the time has arrived at which he may accept it. If, for instance, one is a substitute under a will, and sells before the event occurs upon which one's right to accept is to accrue, or if one is instituted subject to a suspensive condition, and sells before the condition is satisfied, the sale is an

---

[1] Arg. Dig. 18. 1. 78. 3.

[2] Dig. 18. 1. 39. 1. For the different ways of interpreting this passage see Glück, Pandekten, 4. p. 189, sqq.: Vangerow, Pandekten, § 632, note i. 1.

'In relation to things *not yet in existence*, or not yet belonging to the vendor, the law considers them as divided into two classes, one of which may be *sold*, while the other can only be the subject of *an agreement to* sell, of an executory contract. Things not yet existing which may be sold, are those which are said to have a *potential existence*, that is, things which are the natural product or expected increase of something already belonging to the vendor. A man may sell the crop of hay to be grown on his field, the wool to be clipped from his sheep at a future time, the milk that his cows will yield in the coming month, and the sale is valid. But he can only make a *valid agreement to sell, not an actual sale*, where the subject of the contract is something to be afterwards acquired, as the wool of any sheep, or the milk of any cows that he may buy within the year, or any goods to which he may obtain title within the next six months:' Benjamin, pp. 82 and 83: *Grantham* v. *Hawley*, Hob. 132: *Wood* and *Foster's* case, 1 Leon. 42: *Robinson* v. *Macdonnel*, 5 M. & S. 228: *Reed* v. *Blades*, 5 Taunt, 212, 222.

emptio spei [1], and is governed by the rules. recently stated, by which such transactions are regulated. A sale after the inheritance is 'delata,' but before it has been actually accepted, lays the heir under an obligation to the purchaser to accept, and the position then becomes similar to a sale after acceptance.

Where that is the case, it is important to distinguish between the effects of the contract, as between the vendor and the purchaser, and as between either of them and third parties who are in any way concerned with the inheritance.

In the first place, the vendor is bound to the purchaser by an implied warranty of his title as heir: if it turns out to be invalid, the latter can recover his purchase money [2], and such further damages as he has sustained [3]: if it is incomplete, or of a different kind from that represented, he is equally liable in damages [4]. Unless however he has given an inventory [5] of the inheritance, or made representations as to its value [6], he is under no liability if it prove less valuable than was supposed [7]. The sale does not make the purchaser heir in lieu of the vendor [8]; but the latter is bound to put him in possession of all property which was

---

[1] Dig. 18. 4. 10. 11 & 13: Pothier, 527, 528.
[2] Dig. 18. 4. 7.   [3] Dig. 18. 4. 8 & 9.
[4] E. g. si quasi heres vendideris hereditatem, cum tibi ex Sco. Trebelliano restituta esset hereditas, quanti emptoris intersit teneberis: Dig. 18. 4. 16.
[5] Dig. 18. 4. 14. 1 & 15.   [6] Dig. 18. 4. 15.
[7] Celui qui vend une hérédité sans en spécifier en détail les objets, n'est tenu de garantir que sa qualité d héritier: Code Civil, Art. 1696: Demante, Cours analytique de Code Civil, vii. p. 202.
[8] Gaius, ii. 251: Inst. ii. 23. 3. Lorsqu'on vend une hérédité, ce n'est pas le titre et la qualité d'héritier qu'on vend: ce titre et cette qualité sont attachés à la personne de l'héritier, et ne peuvent s'en séparer, d'où il suit qu'ils ne peuvent se vendre: car comme personne ne peut s'obliger à l'impossible, je ne puis m'obliger envers un autre à lui faire avoir une chose, qui par sa nature ne peut subsister dans une autre personne que dans la mienne: Pothier, 529.

comprised in the inheritance at the time when the contract was made, including fruits and accessions which have accrued since the decease of the person to whom he has succeeded:

> in hereditate vendita utrum ea quantitas spectatur, quae fuit mortis tempore, an ea, quae fuit cum aditur hereditas, an ea quae fuit, cum hereditas venumdatur, videndum erit. Et verius est hoc esse servandum, quod actum est: plerumque autem hoc agi videtur, ut quod ex hereditate pervenit in id tempus, quo venditio fit, id videatur venisse [1].

Consequently (apart from debts or legacies which he may have paid) if the vendor has alienated anything belonging to the inheritance before the sale, he must allow a proportionate abatement of the purchase money [2], for the words quoted do not mean that he is not answerable for what he has parted with, but that he is answerable for accessions accruing between the time of the death and the time of the sale [3]. He must also permit the purchaser to bring all actions which are necessary for the recovery of such portions of the inheritance as he has not yet reduced into possession [4]. On the other hand, if after selling the inheritance itself, but before conveyance to the purchaser, he sold anything which it comprised to a third party, he was deemed the negotiorum gestor of the first purchaser [5]: and consequently if such thing perished without his fault before conveyance to the third party, so that the latter had no alternative but to pay what he had agreed to give for it,

---

[1] Dig. 18. 4. 2. 1 : Pothier, 530, 534: Code Civil, Art. 1697.

[2] Si (le vendeur) avait déjà vendu quelques effets de la succession, il est tenu de les rembourser à l'acquéreur : Code Civil, Art. 1697.

[3] Haec est sententia legis, in venditionem hereditatis venire non ea tantum, quae fuerunt mortis vel aditionis tempore : sed etiam ea, quae post mortem aut post aditionem accesserunt : Cujacius.

[4] Dig. 18. 4. 2. 4-10 : ib. 3 : ib. 25.

[5] Dig. 18. 4. 21 : Cod. 4. 39. 6 : Pothier, 531.

he received and held the money for the use of the purchaser of the inheritance[1]. The sale of the inheritance is deemed to be an assignment from the heir to the purchaser of all the choses in action of the deceased, and the purchaser can sue upon them, including even those which may have been due to the deceased from the heir himself, or from other persons to whom also he may have succeeded[2]: but in a case of joint inheritance the purchaser of an heir's portion has no right to the portions of co-heirs accruing to his vendor after the sale to him by the latter of his own share in the succession[3].

In addition to paying the purchase money, the purchaser of an inheritance is under an obligation to the vendor to pay the outstanding debts of the deceased, including those due to the vendor himself[4], and to regrant to the latter any servitudes over property of the deceased which might have been extinguished by the confusio resulting from the succession. On the same principle, if the vendor, while still having an unsettled claim against the purchaser of the inheritance, became heir to the latter, and sold his estate in turn, he could sue the second purchaser on the original claim[5]. The purchaser is further under an obligation to the vendor to pay legacies and trusts, including those due to the vendor himself as heir to a legatee or other beneficiary under the will[6]. Finally, he must reimburse him all costs which he has incurred in connection with the inheritance[7], such as funeral expenses, taxes on land[8], payment of debts[9], or debts for which he remains liable[10].

---

[1] Pothier, 532. [2] Dig. 18. 4. 20. pr.: Pothier, 537.
[3] Arg. Dig. 18. 4. 2. 1: cf. Dig. 50. 17. 34. The point is very fully discussed by Pothier, 545.
[4] Dig. 18. 4. 2. 18: Pothier, 542. [5] Dig. 18. 4. 2. 15.
[6] Dig. 18. 4. 24. [7] Pothier, 540.
[8] Dig. 18. 4. 2. 16. [9] Dig. 18. 4. 2. 11.
[10] Dig. 18. 4. 2. 10.

When we turn to consider the effects of a contract for the sale of an inheritance from the point of view of third parties who may be debtors or creditors of the estate, it is obvious that, so far as they are concerned, the contract not having made the purchaser heir instead of the vendor, it is *res inter alios acta*[1]. Hence the vendor—at any rate until notice—retains against the debtors of the estate all rights of action which he might have exercised in his own behalf, had he not sold the inheritance, though whatever he recovers by enforcing them he can be compelled to surrender to the purchaser. Similarly, as no one can be required to accept performance of an obligation from any one except the party bound[2], the creditors, legatees, and other persons who could have sued the heir before the sale are not debarred from suing him still, and if they do so, he can only resort to his remedy over against the purchaser:

> quamvis heres institutus hereditatem vendiderit, tamen legata et fideicommissa ab eo peti possunt, et quod eo nomine datum fuerit, venditor ab emptore vel fideiussoribus eius petere poterit[3]:

and even though the purchaser has expressly promised the vendor to pay them, he can, if he pleases, refuse to let them sue him, for with them he has made no contract at all[4]; except where the Treasury is the vendor, for in that case the purchaser alone can be sued[5]. But every action that can be brought by the heir can be brought (alternatively) by the purchaser under the assignment implied in the sale[6]

Purchase of a debt, or of a right of action, whether in rem or in personam. The last peculiar subject of sale upon which a few observations are necessary is a debt or a right of action. Whether the action was *in rem* (for the recovery of property) or *in personam* (for the enforcement of an obligation) was immaterial[7]: if it were *in personam*, the

---

[1] Pothier, 529. [2] Arg. Cod. 2. 3. 2. [3] Cod. 6. 37. 2. [4] Cod. 4. 39. 2.
[5] Cod. 4. 39. 1. [6] Dig. 5. 3. 54. pr.: Cod. 4. 39. 5. [7] Cod. 4. 39. 9.

obligation might be absolute, conditional, or subject to a time limitation[1], and its source, whether contract or private delict, was, speaking generally, a matter of indifference[2], but the obligation must not be based on purely personal grounds, as in such cases as an actio injuriarum or a querela inofficiosi testamenti. A sale of the documentary evidence of a debt is deemed to be a sale of the debt and of the action for its recovery[3].

The effect of the sale of a right of action is that it operates as an assignment, entitling the assignee to sue either by direct action in the name of the assignor, or in his own name by actio utilis: but the law relating to the form and effects of assignment does not belong to a treatise on the law of sale, except so far as such assignment for a money consideration is subject to the ordinary principles of that contract. The only points to which it seems at all necessary to call attention are the following. The sale of a right of action carries with it all securities[4], whether in the nature of mortgage or charge[5] or of suretyship[6]. The implied warranty by which the vendor is bound extends to the existence of the right of action, but not to the certainty of its being effectively enforced: *Rules relating to assignment.*

> si nomen sit distractum, Celsus libro ix Digestorum scribit, locupletem esse debitorem non debere praestare: debitorem autem esse, praestare, nisi aliud convenit, et quidem sine exceptione quoque[7].

[1] Dig. 18. 4. 17. [2] Dig. 50. 16. 11 & 12. pr.
[3] Eum qui chirographum legat, debitum legare, non solum tabulas, argumento est venditio: nam cum chirographa veneunt, nomen venisse videtur: Dig. 30. 44. 5; qui chirographum legat, non tantum de tabulis cogitat, sed etiam de actionibus quarum probatio tabulis continetur: appellatione enim chirographi uti nos pro ipsis actionibus palam est, cum, venditis chirographis, intellegimus nomen venisse: Dig. 32. 59.
[4] La vente ou cession d'une créance comprend les accessoires de la créance, tels que caution, privilège et hypothèque: Code Civil, Art. 1692.
[5] Dig. 18. 4. 6.   [6] Dig. 18. 4. 23. pr.   [7] Dig. 18. 4. 4 & 5.

Qui nomen quale fuit vendidit, duntaxat ut sit, non ut exigi etiam aliquid possit, et dolum praestare cogitur [1].

That is to say, if the right assigned does not belong to the vendor at all, the ordinary principles apply which regulate the sale of a res aliena [2], and the fact that the action can be met by a peremptory exception puts it on a par with an action which does not exist at all [3]: but in the absence of fraud or express warranty, the vendor is not liable if the person chargeable proves unable to satisfy any judgment which may be recovered. The sale of a debt or right of action is also governed by the ordinary principles as to periculum and commodum rei [4], which will be fully set forth in a later chapter.

---

[1] Dig. 21. 2. 74. 3. Celui qui vend une créance ou autre droit incorporel doit en garantir l'existence au temps du transport, quoiqu'il soit fait sans garantie. Il ne répond de la solvabilité du débiteur que lorsqu'il s'y est engagé: Code Civil, Arts. 1693, 1694: cf. Demante, Cours analytique de Code Civil, pp. 194-199: Pothier, 559-572.

[2] Dig. 18. 4. 8: Code Civil, Art. 1691.

[3] Dig. 50. 17. 112.

[4] Actiones autem eas non solum arbitrio, sed etiam periculo tuo tibi praestare debebo, ut omne lucrum ac dispendium te sequatur, Dig. 19. 1. 31. pr.

CHAPTER V.

HOW THE CONTRACT IS CONCLUDED.

Necessity of complete agreement between the parties. No forms (such as writing) required for the validity of the contract. Justinian's enactment in Inst. iii. 23. pr. as to writing: it relates to negotiations, not to a sale definitely agreed upon. Contracts made by correspondence, and through agents. Arra or earnest.

It is not necessary to say much of the mode in which the contract of sale was concluded, for the law left the parties to make it as they pleased. All that it required was that they should be agreed upon the thing to be bought and the price to be paid, and that each should be aware of that agreement [1]. In fact, however, they must be agreed not only on the essential points of the bargain (merx and pretium), but on all its subsidiary or ancillary terms as well, in this sense, that if the negotiations have dealt with such terms, and any of them are still unsettled, or have been reserved for further consideration, the

Necessity of complete agreement between the parties.

---

[1] Trois choses sont nécessaires pour le Contrat de Vente: une chose qui en soit l'objet, un prix convenu, et le consentement des contractans: Pothier, 3; (la vente) est parfaite entre les parties .... dès qu'on est convenu de la chose et du prix, quoique la chose n'ait pas encore livrée ni le prix payé: Code Civil, Art. 1583. 'Written evidence of the consent is required in Scotland to complete the contract of sale of land, of copyright, of ships, and of goods bonded for duties in the warehouse of the importer. But the sale of goods and merchandise in general is effectually proved by evidence *prout de iure*; parole, written, or confession. When the bargain is made by the principals without writing, the evidence of two witnesses, or one corroborated by circumstances, is necessary: or the letters of the parties, holograph, or signed by them, are good proof': Bell, § 89.

presumption is that they did not intend as yet to be bound at all:

> in venditionibus et emptionibus consensum debere intercedere palam est: ceterum sive in ipsa emptione dissentiant, sive in pretio, sive in quo alio, emptio imperfecta est [1].

Similarly, if the intention was that the perfection of the contract should depend on the fulfilment of a suspensive condition, there is no obligation until it is fulfilled:

> si id quod venierit appareat quid quale quantum sit, sit et pretium, et pure venit, perfecta est emptio: quod si sub conditione res venierit, si quidem defecerit conditio, nulla est emptio [2].

No forms required for the validity of the contract. It is certain that until the time of Justinian no form, written or otherwise, was prescribed as the necessary condition of either the validity or the enforceability of the contract, whether its subject matter might be moveable or immoveable, corporeal or incorporeal, valuable or worthless. But according to what may perhaps be considered the accepted interpretation of an enactment of that Emperor [3], if the parties agreed, as part of their contract, that it

---

[1] Dig. 18. 1. 9. pr. Le contrat de vente peut se faire entre présents, verbalement et sans écrit: il faut néanmoins bien prendre garde, si ce que les parties ont dit exprime une vente ou un simple pourparler de vente, qui n'oblige point, et laisse la liberté de changer de volonté: Pothier, 33.

[2] Dig. 18. 6. 8. pr.

[3] Sed haec quidem de emptionibus et venditionibus quae sine scriptura consistunt obtinere oportet, nam nihil a nobis in huiusmodi venditionibus innovatum est. In iis autem quae scriptura conficiuntur, non aliter perfectam esse venditionem et emptionem constituimus, nisi et instrumenta emptionis fuerint conscripta, vel manu propria contrahentium, vel ab alio quidem scripta, a contrahentibus autem subscripta, et si per tabelliones fiant, nisi et completiones acceperint, et fuerint a partibus absoluta: donec enim aliquid ex his deest, et poenitentiae locus est, et potest emptor vel venditor sine poena recedere ab emptione: Inst. iii. 23. pr.

should be reduced into writing, it was to bind neither until the condition had been fulfilled, and the writing had been signed by both. It is generally held that it was necessary for them to agree that its validity should depend on its expression in a written form[1], and where that was the case either vendor or purchaser might go back from the agreement until it had been signed by both, but if it was the purchaser, he forfeited anything which he might have given by way of earnest: if it was the vendor, he had to give it back, and its value in money as well[2]. Where the parties did nothing more than agree that a contract in fact made between them by word of mouth should be put into a written form, the writing was merely evidentiary[3].

But although this interpretation of the passage in the Institutes, which assumes the existence of a complete agreement between the parties, is the most simple and

Justinian's enactment in Inst. iii. 23 pr. as to writing: it relates to negotiations,

---

[1] The Code Civil enacts that the sale 'peut être faite par acte authentique ou sous seing privé;' and Demante (Cours analytique de Code Civil. p. 4) says, 'il est certain que, dans ce cas, la perfection de la vente dépend de celle de l'acte, et, par conséquent, de l'emploi de la forme particulière, soit authentique, soit privée, à laquelle la volonté des parties aurait, de fait, assujetti cet acte.... La vente en pareil cas n'est pas parfaite, le consentement n'est pas donné, les parties peuvent se dédire, en un mot rien n'est fait. Il n'y a pas même un contrat conditionnel: ceci est important à remarquer, car si la rédaction de l'écrit était considérée comme une condition suspensive de la vente, lorsqu'elle serait réalisée elle aurait un effect rétroactif.' It is interesting to find an English case very much in point. In *The Governor, Guardians, &c., of the Poor of Kingston-upon-Hull* v. *Petch* (10 Ex. 610, 24 L. J. Ex. 23) the plaintiffs advertised for tenders to supply meat, stating 'all contractors will have to sign a written contract after acceptance of tender.' The defendant tendered, and received notice of the acceptance of his tender, and then wrote that he declined the contract. It was held that, by the terms of the proposal, the contract was not complete till the terms were put in writing, and signed by the parties, and that the defendant had the right to retract.

[2] Cod. 4. 21. 17.

[3] See Dig. 22. 4. 4: Treitschke, Kaufcontract, p. 19, note.

obvious, it fails in leaving Justinian's enactment isolated, apparently motiveless, and unconnected with anything, so far as we know, which had preceded it in the history of the law. A comparison with the terms of his constitution in the Code[1], which beyond doubt relates to the same point as the text of the smaller work, strongly suggests that he had not in his mind a complete contract to buy and sell, but preliminary negotiations undertaken with a view to such a contract. As early as the time of Diocletian and Maximian we read of 'pacta arralia' in relation to sales[2], and we hear of them also in connection with other contracts. A pactum arrale is the giving of something by way of earnest by one person to another, between whom there have been pourparlers with a view to some contract, coupled with an agreement that if the contract shall actually be concluded, or shall fail to be concluded only by reason of the fault of the receiver, it shall be returned, either simply or with its value in addition. That such agreements often related to very important transactions is shown by the passage in the Code, which proves that they themselves were sometimes executed in writing[3]: for it can hardly be doubted that the passage contemplates not an actual sale, but negotiations preceding a sale which may subsequently be made ('emptio facienda')[4], and the

[1] Illud etiam adicientes, ut et in posterum, si quae arrae super facienda emptione cuiuscunque rei datae sunt sive in scriptis sive sine scriptis, licet non sit specialiter adiectum, quid super isdem arris non procedente contractu fieri oporteat, tamen et qui vendere pollicitus est venditionem recusans in duplum eas reddere cogatur, et qui emere pactus est, ab emptione recedens datis a se arris cadat, repetitione earum deneganda: Cod. 4. 21. 17. 2.

[2] Cod. 4. 49. 3: A.D. 290.

[3] The words 'sive in scriptis sive sine scriptis' clearly belong to 'arrae datae sunt,' not to 'super facienda emptione.'

[4] The later expressions in the enactment, which seem to imply an actual agreement—vendere recusans—ab emptione recedens—are used loosely, just as we speak of backing out of a bargain to which we have not yet actually committed ourselves.

only difficulty in reconciling the passage of the Institutes with this hypothesis is the occurrence in it of the expression venditio *celebrata*, which must be taken to mean 'celebranda[1].' According to this view, the arra spoken of is not given as evidence that a contract has been concluded (of which we shall speak later in this chapter): it is the so-called 'arra contractu imperfecto data,' and the case contemplated is where there are negotiations pending for a sale: the intending purchaser gives earnest, and it is agreed that the contract, if it comes off, shall be reduced to writing and signed by the parties. Justinian then gave no *new* right to either party of withdrawing from a *contract*, for in the case supposed there is merely a refusal to complete a bargain which so far has not advanced beyond the stage of pourparlers. All that was new in his enactment was that if arra had been given by the would-be purchaser in the course of such pourparlers, and he backed out of them, he should forfeit it, while, if it was the intending vendor, he should have to return it and its value besides, whether there had been an agreement to that effect or not. Previously this had been so only when expressly so agreed[2].

not to a sale definitely agreed upon.

[1] So Schrader, ad Inst. loc. cit. It is rendered in the present tense—γίνεται—by Theophilus. The same view is taken by Pothier, 507.

[2] The passage in the Code is so understood by Pothier: ces arrhes qui se donnent lors d'un marché seulement proposé, et avant qu'il ait été conclu, forment la matière d'un contrat particulier, par lequel celui qui me donne des arrhes consent de les perdre, et de m'en transférer la propriété en cas de refus de sa part de conclure le marché proposé, et je m'oblige de mon côté à les rendre au double en cas de pareil refus de ma part : 497. The doctrine seems in effect to be reproduced in the Code Civil, Art. 1590: Si la promesse de vendre a été faite avec des arrhes, chacun des contractans est maître de s'en départir : celui qui les a données, en les perdant, et celui qui les a reçues, en restituant le double. This is thus explained by Demante, Cours analytique de Code Civil, p. 25: 'on entend par arrhes un certain objet que l'une des parties remet à l'autre au moment de la convention, soit en signe que le marché est conclu, soit comme *dédit*. [In the latter case] les parties ont voulu réserver à chacune d'elles le droit de se rétracter, de retirer

Mode of expressing agreement.

The modes in which the agreement is expressed, or the evidences of the fact of agreement, are of course manifold. Paulus says that the contract might be concluded not only by word of mouth, as may be supposed to have been most commonly the case with the Romans, but 'inter absentes per nuntium et per litteras[1]'. Where the parties are negotiating personally and by word of mouth, the contract is binding on both as soon as each is aware that the other is at one with him on the essentials, and on such non-essentials as have been the subject of discussion. But assent may be expressed by conduct no less than by words. Nothing is more common than for a contract of sale to be concluded by performance on one side in reply, rather than by an explicit expression of assent, to the proposal made by the other. For instance, a bookseller exposes a book in his window, marked 'five shillings': I put the money down on the counter and demand the book: or I write and ask a wine merchant to send me a dozen of claret of a particular vintage at forty-eight shillings per dozen, and he sends them. In either case, and in all such cases, the act is the evidence of assent to a proposal, or of acceptance of an offer, made by the other party [2].

sa promesse, de se *dédire*, mais elles ont subordonné cette faculté à la nécessité de donner à l'autre une certaine indemnité dont le chiffre est fixé par la valeur des arrhes remises. Celui qui a donné les arrhes les perd, les abandonne, s'il renonce au contrat : celui qui les a reçues, les rend au double, rend les arrhes, plus une valeur égale à celle qu'il a reçue, car s'il ne rendait que les arrhes reçues, il ne perdrait rien, il ne donnerait à celui qui les a fournies aucune indemnité, et la faculté de se dédire ne serait pas subordonnée à des conditions établissant l'égalité entre les deux parties . . . . . La présomption établie par le Code est que la convention d'arrhes est une convention de dédit.'

[1] Dig. 18. 1. 1. 2.

[2] Quidam ex parte dimidia heres institutus universa praedia vendidit, et coheredes pretium acceperunt : evictis his quaero, an coheredes ex empto actione teneantur. Respondi, si coheredes praesentes adfuerunt nec dissenserunt, videri unum quemque partem suam vendidisse : Dig. 21. 2. 12. See Blackstone's Comm. Bk. ii. ch. 30. p. 443. In *Brogden* v. *Metropolitan Ry. Co.* (2 App. Ca. 666) the parties had acted

There is very little textual authority on the question, at *Contracts made by correspondence.* what time a contract of sale is to be deemed to be irrevocably concluded, when the communications between the parties are carried on by messenger or letter, and the texts which have any bearing on the point are in fact so inconclusive that the holders of every modern theory on the subject claim to find support in them for their own doctrine. It may indeed be called the happy hunting-ground of theorising Romanists.

It must first be made clear that an actual proposal for a purchase or a sale has been sent: that is to say, the sender of the letter or messenger must have expressed a clear intention and readiness to make the contract in question [1]. The Roman texts most distinctly support the theory that such a proposal is converted into a contract by the communication of an acceptance to the proposer—communication implying knowledge by him that his offer has been accepted [2]. There can be no consensual contract unless and until both of the parties are aware of their agreement [3].

upon the terms of a draft proposed agreement, which was intended to form the basis of a formal contract, to be afterwards executed by them both. Cf. *Hart* v. *Mills*, 15 M. & W. 85.

[1] E. g. Will you sell me your horse for £50? is not an offer to buy him for that sum. It is otherwise if one writes 'I understand you are willing to sell me your horse for £50, and if that is so I am ready to buy him.'

[2] This 'Vernehmungstheorie,' as it is called, is held by Hasse. Rhein. Museum. ii. p. 371 sq.: Regelsberger, Civilrechtliche Erörterungen, p. 23: Bekker, Jahrbuch des gem. Rechts, iii. pp. 116 sq., 295 sq.: Vangerow, Pandekten, § 603, note 1: Brinz, Pandekten, § 362: Wächter, Pandekten, ii. § 185, p. 357. It is possible that an exception to it must be allowed outside the sphere of consensual contract. If a proposal is for the exclusive benefit of the person to whom it is addressed, it is generally held that knowledge by the proposer of its acceptance may be dispensed with: Dig. 39. 5. 10: ib. 26.

[3] E. g. where the proposer does not understand the language of the other party, Inst. iii. 15. 1, or is deaf and does not hear it, Dig. 44. 7. 1. 15: 45. 1. 1. pr.: the understanding, the 'being aware,' is stated as essential in Dig. 44. 7. 48. 'Je me trouve en présence d'un sourd, qui

The objection that on this hypothesis it would be necessary for the sender of the acceptance to hear that it had reached the proposer, and so on ad infinitum, so that no contract could ever be made by correspondence, falls to the ground if it be remembered that both offers and acceptances hold good until withdrawn (by communication) as against those to whom they are addressed, and that consequently if no revocation has reached either party before the moment at which the proposer becomes aware of acceptance, both at that moment know that they are agreed, and the contract is concluded[1].

The proposer may revoke his proposal, and the acceptor may revoke his acceptance, provided that knowledge of such revocation reaches the other party not later than the moment at which the proposer is notified of acceptance[2].

me dit : voulez-vous m'acheter telle chose, moyennant tel prix? Je lui réponds, je le veux bien : mais il ne m'entend pas, il me déclare ne m'avoir pas entendu, et il me prie de lui mettre par écrit la réponse qu'il juge d'après le mouvement de mes lèvres lui avoir été faite par moi. Alors je prends une plume, et je lui trace ces mots : je vous ai dit, que je voulais bien, mais, toutes réflexions faites, votre proposition ne me convient pas. Cet homme pourra-t-il prétendre, que par la réponse, que je conviens lui avoir faite de vive voix, je me suis lié irrévocablement envers lui? Non, certainement : et s'il me poursuit, le juge le déboutera sans hésiter :' Merlin, Répertoire, s. m. Vente, xiv. p. 308.

[1] The objection was made, and answered in exactly the same way for the first time in England in 1818 : *Adams* v. *Lindsell*, 1 B. & Ald. 681.

[2] Arg. Dig. 17. 1. 15 : 17. 2. 17. 1 : 14. 6. 12. The passage in Dig. 40. 2. 4. pr., which is so often cited in support of the theory that a revocation is good without being communicated, has no relation to contracts giving rise to bilateral obligation. In English Law, if the person to whom the offer is made is authorised, either expressly or by implication, to send a reply by post, the posting of a letter of acceptance concludes the contract, whether it ever reaches the proposer or not : *Household Fire Insurance Co.* v. *Grant*, 4 Ex. D. 216. C. A. : the revocation of a proposal is ineffectual unless it becomes known to the person to whom that proposal was made before he has accepted it : *Byrne* v. *Van Tienhoven*, 5 C. P. D. 344 : and there can be little doubt that if a letter of acceptance is once posted, it cannot be revoked,

Nevertheless, if a party to whom an offer has been made, and who believes that he has by acceptance converted it into a contract, loses an opportunity of profit, or so acts as eventually to incur a loss in that belief, and the offer is revoked as against him before his acceptance becomes known to the proposer, the latter is bound to indemnify him [1].

A promise to keep an offer open for a certain time is binding, and it cannot be revoked before that time has elapsed [2]: and a promise not to withdraw an offer is implied if the person to whom it is made is authorised in the event of his acceptance to proceed at once to execution of the contract, as where one writes offering to buy goods at a certain price, and directs the other, if he accepts the offer, to send them to a named third person [3].

even by a telegram arriving before it, for no contract can be dissolved by the act of one of the parties only : Benjamin, p. 57.

[1] He must indemnify him for the loss of any profit which he would have made, or for any damage which he would not have suffered, had he not been led to believe that the contract would be actually concluded. E. g. a purchaser, in view of the expected contract, omits to provide himself with goods from elsewhere : or a vendor misses the opportunity of disposing of his goods on favourable terms. See the illustration in Pothier, 32, cited and criticised by Benjamin, p. 77.

[2] In English Law of course it is otherwise unless the promise is made either under seal, or for valuable consideration : *Cooke* v. *Oxley*, 3 T. R. 653.

[3] Arg. Dig. 17. 1. 27. pr.: ib. 16.

Other views as to the Civil Law upon contracts made by correspondence are : that the contract is concluded by some act clearly indicating intention to accept the offer, such as writing a letter of acceptance: that (in addition) despatch of the letter is essential : that it must not only be despatched, but reach the proposer, though it is not necessary that he should have made himself acquainted with its contents; and some of those who hold the contract to be concluded by despatch of a letter of acceptance still think that the acceptance can be revoked by another letter or telegram which reaches the proposer not later than the letter of acceptance itself (cf. the Scotch case of *Dunmore* v. *Alexander*, 9 Shaw & Dunlop, 190). Finally, Windscheid (Lehrbuch, § 306, note 10) holds that the proposer is bound as soon as

and through agents.

It is not necessary to consider at any length the question of contracts of sale made through agents. It is well known that according to the Civil Law the contract was properly the contract of the agent, not of the principal. It was his will by which it was concluded, and therefore the rights and duties arising from it affected him alone. The principal could acquire rights against the other party only by an assignment (on which he could of course insist) from his own agent: and although under the later law he was suable by the other party, it was not by actio ex empto or ex vendito, but only by actions specially designed by the Practor to meet cases of agency, and so to obviate as much as possible the difficulty of double litigation.

Arra or earnest.

There is one kind of evidence of final agreement to which the Romans attached much importance, viz. the giving of earnest (arra) by one or other of the parties, most usually by the purchaser[1]. This indeed seems to have been so common that the language of Gaius[2] and Justinian[3] almost warrants one in believing that there was a vulgar opinion to the effect that arra was an essential condition of the contract, without which it was not binding on the parties: a heresy repudiated by Gaius in the Digest[4]. Unless given in part payment of the purchase money, the arra had to be

his proposal is accepted, the acceptor, as soon as his acceptance is known to the proposer. These different theories are clearly set forth in Vering, Geschichte und Pandekten des römischen und heutigen gemeinen Privatrechts, § 190, and Arndts, Pandekten, § 231, note 1 (d).

[1] Arra confirmatoria as distinct from arra contractu imperfecto data. High evidentiary value is attached to the giving of earnest in the 17th section of the Statute of Frauds (29 Car. II. c. 3), under which it ranks, in the alternative, with writing, payment of part of the purchase money, or acceptance and receipt of part of the goods, as a condition precedent to the enforceability of the contract: examples in *Bach* v. *Owen*, 5 T. R. 409, and *Goodall* v. *Skelton*, 2 H. Bl. 316.

[2] iii. 139. [3] Inst. iii. 23. pr.

[4] Dig. 18. 1. 35. pr. Among the things most commonly given 'arrae nomine' was a ring: Dig. 19. 1. 11. 6: 14. 3. 5. 15.

restored when the contract had been executed[1], or if its execution was prevented by accident, or if the parties agreed to be off their bargain.

According to the interpretation of the passage in the Institutes which has been followed in the earlier part of this chapter[2], no change was made by Justinian in the law relating to arra of this kind. Those however who understand that passage to relate to an actually completed contract, rather than to preliminary negotiations accompanied by the giving of earnest, contend that that Emperor enacted that in every actual sale in which earnest (arra confirmatoria) was given, a party who refused to execute should be liable (in addition to the ordinary action for damages) to forfeiture of the arra, or of double its value, according as he had given or received it. It is even thought by some writers that the effect of his law was to entitle either party to a sale in every case to rescind the contract on these terms, without being liable to an action for breach at all[3]: but there is no evidence for this opinion[4], which seems to be entirely erroneous[5].

[1] Dig. 19. 1. 11. 6 : 14. 3. 5. 15 : Pothier, 506.
[2] P. 42 supr.
[3] La Loi, disent ces Auteurs, ayant fixé les dommages et intérêts résultans de l'inexécution de l'obligation de l'acheteur, à la perte des arrhes du côté de l'acheteur, et à la restitution des arrhes au double du côté du vendeur, les parties ne peuvent pas en prétendre d'autres. En donnant et recevant les arrhes, elles doivent être censées s'être contentées de cette espèce de dommages et intérêts, et avoir renoncé à tous autres, même à toutes autres actions qu'elles pourroient avoir l'une contre l'autre pour l'inexécution du contrat : Pothier, 507.
[4] Il seroit absurde que les arrhes étant dans ce cas intervenues pour la confirmation du contrat, pour le rendre plus certain et plus connu, on voulût leur donner l'effet de détruire le contrat en détruisant les obligations qui en naissent, et les droits et actions qui en résultent : Pothier, ibid. Eine sogenannte arra poenitentialis beim Kauf ist dem römischen und gemeinen Recht unbekannt : Bechmann, Kauf, § 232.
[5] The error is shared by Benjamin, p. 177.

CHAPTER VI.

MISTAKE. FRAUD. DURESS.

General principles. Mistake as to the nature of the transaction: as to the subject-matter of the contract: identity: existence: quantity: quality. Mistake as to the price. Mistake of motive. Mistake as to the identity of the other party. Dolus or fraud: what it includes: active concealment: reckless ignorance as to truth of representations: innocent non-disclosure. Effect of these on the validity of the contract. Metus or duress, and its effects. Metus has a wider operation than Dolus.

General principles.

A TRANSACTION which presents all the external indicia of a valid contract may be void or voidable: (1) because the consent of the parties or of one of them has been given in ignorance of circumstances which, had they been known, would have prevented the contract from being made at all, or at any rate from having been made in the form in which in fact it has; or (2) because the consent of one party has been obtained by misrepresentations made, or violence used, or improper pressure exercised, by the other party. We have here to consider the effect on a contract of sale of those vitiating circumstances usually denoted by the terms Mistake, Fraud, and Duress [1].

As to mistake, three preliminary observations must be made. Firstly, we are speaking here of mistake or misconception not brought about by any wilfully false representations (or their equivalent) made by the other party to the contract. For where that is the case, one can regard either the mistake or the fraud: and inasmuch as

[1] They are coupled together in the Code Civil, Art. 1109: il n'y a point de consentement valable, si le consentement n'a été donné que par erreur, ou s'il a été extorqué par violence ou surpris par dol.

where there has been dishonesty, it is only reasonable that the guilty party should be made to suffer, the law as a rule does not compel the one deceived to rely upon the mistake, but allows him the option of either adopting the contract or rescinding it on the ground of the fraud which has been practised on him, because cases may occur in which it will be to his interest that the contract should be upheld. In the second place, we must distinguish between error which humanly speaking is unavoidable, and error which might have been avoided if the party labouring under it had taken reasonable care, or made reasonable enquiries: for while the former is in many cases a reason for holding the contract entirely void, the latter does not in any way relieve the negligent party from his liabilities except where the other was aware of his mistake, and could easily have corrected it [1]. Thirdly, it is not all mistake which affects the validity of a contract, although there are loosely worded dicta in the authorities [2] which might seem to warrant such a proposition. The following pages will make it clear that mistake, as such, has no effect except where it is of such a kind as presumably to exclude the hypothesis of real consent [3]. Such mistake is termed essential or fundamental: non-essential mistake is usually termed by writers on the Civil Law error concomitans.

Mistake may relate to the nature of the transaction: to the subject-matter of the agreement, more particularly to its identity, existence, quantity, or qualities: to the amount of the purchase money: to the motives by which one is

[1] Dig. 18. 1. 15. 1. The rule that error attributable to one's own negligence is no excuse is there stated only in reference to the purchaser: but the reasons for it in his case are even stronger in the case of the vendor.

[2] Dig. 2. 1. 15 : 5. 1. 2 : 39. 3. 20 : 50. 17. 116. 2 : Cod. 1. 18. 8 and 9.

[3] L'erreur n'est une cause de nullité de la convention que lorsqu'elle tombe sur la substance même de la chose qui en est l'object : Code Civil, Art. 1110.

induced to enter into the contract: and to the person of the other party.

<small>Mistake as to the nature of the transaction:</small> (1) If the parties are entirely mistaken as to the nature of the transaction, the one thinking of and meaning a sale, the other thinking of and meaning some other sort of contract, it is absolutely void [1].

<small>as to the subject-matter of the contract: its identity:</small> (2) Mistake as to the subject-matter of the contract.

(*a*) Identity (error in corpore). If the two parties are thinking of entirely different objects, the contract is void [2], and no property passes by a conveyance made by either, nor even such possession as can be converted into ownership by usucapion [3]. A mistake as to species, when the terms of the contract refer to a thing only generically (as where e.g. *A* agrees to buy a hundred sacks of corn, meaning wheat, while *B* intends to sell him barley), is deemed to be an error in corpore. If there is no doubt or confusion as to the main object of the contract, but there is a mistake as to the identity of an accessory, though it is certain that both intended some accession or other, the contract stands, and that accession must be delivered and taken which was intended by the vendor [4]. It is hardly necessary to observe

---

[1] Si in ipsa emptione dissentient .... emptio imperfecta est: Dig. 18. 1. 9. pr.: cf. Dig. 12. 1. 18: 44. 7. 3. 1. ib. 57. E. g. *A* wishes to buy a horse of *B*'s for the hunting season. *B* says he does not care to sell the horse, but will let him for the season for £50. After some negotiations it is agreed that *A* shall have the horse for that sum: *A* believes he has bought him: *B* has only intended to let him: cf. Pothier, 37.

[2] Si igitur ego me fundum emere putarem Cornelianum, tu mihi te vendere Sempronianum putasti, quia in corpore dissensimus, emptio nulla est: Dig. 18. 1. 9. pr. The English law is the same: *Thornton* v. *Kempster*, 5 Taunt. 786: *Raffles* v. *Wichelhaus*, 2 H. & C. 906.

[3] Dig. 41. 2. 34. pr.: 41. 4. 2. 6.

[4] Si in emptione fundi dictum sit accedere Stichum servum, neque intellegatur quis ex pluribus accesserit, cum de alio emptor, de alio venditor senserit, nihilominus fundi venditionem valere constat: sed Labeo ait cum Stichum deberi quem venditor intellexerit. Nec refert, quanti sit accessio, sive plus in ea sit quam in ipsa re cui accedat an minus: plerasque enim res aliquando propter accessiones emimus,

that if the disagreement relates merely to the name of the thing sold, the mistake is immaterial[1].

(*b*) Existence. The case in which the parties contract for the purchase and sale of a specific article which, unknown to both, has ceased to exist, either wholly or in part, at the time at which the contract was made, has already been discussed in a previous chapter[2], where the nullity of the agreement was put upon a different ground. The validity of the contract however is not affected if the object of it ceases to exist only after it is entered into, for there is no mistake whatever: the risk is with the purchaser, and he has to bear the loss, for he might have protected himself by some such stipulation as that, in the event of the object being destroyed before conveyance, the bargain should be off[3].

A thing which the law says cannot be the subject of a contract of sale may, for that purpose, be deemed nonexistent. But in respect of free men and things which are extra commercium the contract is saved from absolute nullity by ignorance of the parties, or of the purchaser only, as to the legal character of the object which they are

its existence:

---

sicuti cum domus propter marmora et statuas et tabulas pictas ematur; Dig. 18. 1. 34. pr. Many authorities, however, are of opinion that for 'venditor' we should read 'emptor,' e.g. Treitschke, Kaufcontract, p. 73, note 2: contra Vangerow, § 604, note.

[1] Plane si in nomine dissentiamus, verum de corpore constet, nulla dubitatio est quin valeat emptio et venditio: nihil enim facit error nominis, cum de corpore constat: Dig. 18. 1. 9. 1: cf. Dig. 5. 1. 80: 45. 1. 32.

[2] P. 21 supr.

[3] The English rule is the same. 'Where a contract of sale is made, amounting to a bargain and sale, transferring presently the property in specific chattels, which are to be delivered by the vendor at a future day, there, if the chattels without the fault of the vendor perish in the interval, the purchaser must pay the price, and the vendor is excused from performing his contract to deliver, which has thus become impossible. That this is the rule of English law is established by the case of *Rugg* v. *Minet* (11 East. 210):' per Blackburn, J. in *Taylor* v. *Caldwell*, 3 B. & S. 826: 32 L. J. Q. B. 164: cf. *Howell* v. *Coupland*, L.R. 9 Q.B. 462: 1 Q. B. D. 258. C. A.

attempting to buy and sell. Where, for instance, both are unaware that a supposed slave is in fact free, the better opinion was that the contract was good[1], at any rate so far as to entitle the purchaser to damages in the event of the man's freedom being established[2]: *a fortiori* if the vendor knew that he was a slave, and the purchaser did not[3]. That the law was the same in respect of res sacrae, religiosae and publicae, is shown by another passage[4], in which it is said that a person who sold such things to an ignorant purchaser was liable to him ex empto for such damages as he had sustained.

<small>its quantity:</small> (c) If the parties are thinking of different quantities, and the vendor intends to sell a less quantity for the stipulated price than the purchaser thinks he is buying, the contract is void: in the converse case it holds good for the smaller of the two quantities[5]. There may also be a mistake as to quantity in the performance of the contract. The vendor may erroneously deliver more than he was bound to, in which case he can recover the excess by condictio indebiti[6]. Or a man may buy a thing as a whole, the price to be paid depending on the number of its constituent parts: if its bulk has been stated erroneously, but in good faith, by the vendor, restitution must be made of the excess, if possible: if impossible or highly inconvenient, the vendor must put up with an increase in the purchase money proportionate to that excess, while if it is less than was stated, the purchase money will be abated[7]. But if a man buys a thing as a whole, and the price is to be paid for it as a whole, a mistake of either party as to its bulk or extent is im-

---

[1] Dig. 18. 1. 70. [2] Dig. 21. 2. 39. 3.
[3] Dig. 18. 1. 70: Inst. iii. 23. 5. [4] Dig. 18. 1. 62. 1.
[5] Arg. Dig. 19. 2. 52: si decem tibi locem fundum, tu autem existimas quinque te conducere, nihil agitur. Sed et si ego minoris me locare sensero, tu pluris te conducere, utique non pluris erit conductio quam quanti ego putavi.
[6] Dig. 12. 6. 26. 4–6. [7] Dig. 18. 1. 40. 2.

material, though of course if the vendor has represented its bulk as greater than it really is, he fails to perform his contract by delivering less[1]. If he has understated its quantity, he cannot recover the excess: and if a third person establishes a superior title to a portion of the thing sold, the vendor is liable to the purchaser on account of the eviction, even though the part which the latter still has is not less than what he stated the amount of the whole thing to be[2].

(*d*) Material, qualities or properties. If through a mistake for which he cannot be held to blame a man agrees to buy a thing which is of a different material, or which possesses different qualities or properties from what he supposed, the mistake is deemed fundamental, and nullifies the contract, only if, according to ordinary commercial usage in relation to the article in question, the absence of the quality or material wrongly supposed to exist places that article in a different category from those which really possess it[3]. There are numerous illustrations of this principle in the authorities. Thus, for instance, if one buys an article made of nickel under the impression that it is silver, and which the vendor also believes to be silver, the contract is void, and the purchase money, if paid, can be recovered back: the same is the case where the article is plated[4]. If

its material, qualities or properties.

---

[1] Dig. 19. 1. 13. 14: 21. 2. 69. 6.   [2] Dig. 21. 2. 45.
[3] Savigny, System, III. pp. 276 sqq.
[4] Pothier, 34: Dig. 18. 1. 41. 1: cf. ib. 9. 2. From Dig. ib. 10 it would appear that if the metal is merely an inferior quality of that which the purchaser intended to buy, the contract is not affected. Dig. ib. 14 is at variance with 41. 1, already cited, unless we can take 'inauratum' to mean not plated, but an alloy of gold. Dig. ib. 45 creates some difficulty, for it seems to lay down a rule quite irreconcileable with that stated in 41. 1, unless (with Vangerow) we suppose that Marcian was not considering the effect of mistake, but the question how far the vendor was liable if he warranted the material or quality of the thing he was selling, apart from the further question whether the contract was void on the ground of mistake or not. For different interpretations see Savigny, System, II. pp. 295 sqq.: Treitschke, Kaufcontract, p. 85.

one buys vinegar, believing it to be wine, the case is the same, but otherwise if the wine be merely sour[1]: and similarly if one buys a female slave, believing her to be a male, or vice versâ: though the contract is good if she was believed to be virgo, and is actually mulier[2]. A mistake as to the species of wood of which furniture is made is deemed to be non-essential[3]; but an action will lie for damages if the vendor represented it to be of a particular wood, of which it is not, even though he did so in good faith. Similar principles are applied if it is the vendor who is under the mistake instead of the purchaser. If both are in error, and the error is essential, it is obvious that the contract is entirely void.

Mistake as to the price. (3) A mistake of either party as to the price makes the contract void[4], provided that it could not have been avoided by ordinary care, and that it operates to the disadvantage of the party who is in error. That is to say, the purchaser cannot be compelled to buy at a higher price than he intended, nor can the vendor be compelled to sell at a lower: on the other hand, if the vendor believed the purchaser was offering him less than he really was, and agreed to sell at the price erroneously supposed to be offered, he is bound to do so[5].

Mistake of motive. (4) The validity of a contract is not (except in one case) affected by the fact that one is induced to enter into it by

[1] Dig. 18. 1. 9. 2.   [2] Dig. 18. 1. 11. 1.
[3] Dig. 19. 1. 21. 2. Some MSS., however, by reading emptionem *non* esse state an exactly opposite rule.
[4] Dig. 18. 1. 9. pr.: cf. 19. 2. 52: Pothier, 36.
[5] Arg. Dig. 19. 2. 52. In *Phillips* v. *Bistolli*, 2 B. & C. 511, the defendant, a foreigner, not understanding our language, was sued as purchaser of some ear-rings, at auction, for the price of eighty-eight guineas, and alleged in defence that he thought the bid made by him was forty-eight guineas, and that there was a mistake in knocking down the articles to him at eighty-eight guineas: Abbott, C. J. left it to the jury to find whether the mistake had actually been made, as a test of the existence of a contract of sale: Benjamin, p. 61.

what may be best described as a mistake of motive [1]. No one, for instance, would think it reasonable that a purchaser of a particular stock should be allowed to say that his purchase was void merely because the stock had fallen instead of having risen in the market, or because he erroneously believed that the vendor had rendered him a service. There is, however, an exception where on reasonable grounds one believes that one is legally compellable to sell a particular thing: for in that case, though if he does sell it a man is technically bound by his contract, he can resist an action when sued upon it, and can himself take proceedings to procure his release [2].

(5) If one believes one is buying from or selling to a particular person, when he really is some one entirely different, the mistake, according to some eminent authorities [3], is non-essential. But this can only mean that such mistake is, in perhaps the majority of sales, of absolutely no consequence. There is authority for saying [4] that when one has a special reason for contracting with a particular person, such, for instance, as one's confidence in his honesty, solvency, or business capacity, the law will not involve one against one's will in a contract with some one else, and it is difficult to believe that this rule had no application to the contract of sale. The point is not discussed in the Roman authorities on the subject [5]. *Mistake as to the identity of the other party.*

Deceit negatives the implied condition of good faith *Dolus or fraud.*

[1] Arg. Dig. 12. 4. 3. 7 : 12. 6. 65. 2.   [2] Dig. 19. 1. 5. 1.
[3] E. g. Treitschke, Kaufcontract, § 27 : Glück, Pandekten, 16. p. 18.
[4] E. g. Dig. 12. 1. 32.
[5] In English law 'a mistake as to the *person* with whom the contract is made may or may not avoid the sale according to circumstances. In the common case of a trader who sells for cash, it can make no possible difference to him whether the buyer be Smith or Jones, and a mistake of identity would not prevent the formation of the contract. But where the identity of the person is an important element in the contract of sale, as if it be on credit, where the solvency of the buyer is the chief motive which induces the assent of the vendor : or when the purchaser

upon which sale is founded along with the consensual contracts in general. It is well known that until the time of Cicero fraud was no defence whatever to an action on an agreement expressed in solemn form, such as stipulation, but that straightforward dealing was deemed essential to the perfect validity of those other contracts which were sued upon by actiones bonae fidei: thus it is said that a covenant 'dolum malum a venditore abfuturum' was superfluous and unnecessary [1], and that the vendor (and no doubt the purchaser equally) was unable to contract himself out of the consequences which his fraud would entail, because 'dolus semper abesse oportet in iudicio empti, quod bonae fidei sit [2].'

What dolus includes:
So far as the subject contains any difficulties, they relate to two questions: what kinds of conduct are to be included under the notion of dolus, and what is the effect upon the contract induced by it.

wilful mis-statements:
Fraud in the narrower sense may be defined as a false statement made with knowledge of its falsehood, for the purpose of inducing the other party, and actually inducing him [3], to make the contract to his detriment [4]. Thus it is fraudulent for the vendor knowingly to state that the

buys from one whom he supposes to be his debtor, and against whom he would have the right to set off the price: a mistake as to the person dealt with prevents the contract from coming into existence for want of assent': Benjamin, p. 63: *Boulton v. Jones,* 2 H. & N. 564: *Lindsay v. Cundy,* 3 App. Cas. 459.

[1] Dig. 18. 1. 68. 1: cf. 4. 3. 7. 3.
[2] Dig. 19. 1. 6. 9.: ib. 1. 1.
[3] Dolus causam contractui dans is distinguished from dolus incidens. The first is fraud without which the contract would not have been made at all: the second is fraud which induces the contracting party to make it in a particular form or with particular terms, though he would have made it in any case, fraud or no fraud. Le dol est une cause de nullité de la convention lorsque les manœuvres pratiquées par l'une des parties sont telles, qu'il est évident que sans ces manœuvres l'autre partie n'aurait pas contracté : Code Civil, Art. 1116.
[4] If the false representation causes no detriment, it does not affect

article which he is selling possesses qualities which it does not[1], though statements made merely by way of puffing, as to the truth of which the purchaser could easily inform himself by examination, are not deemed dishonest[2]: to give a false description of the acreage of[3] or charges on land[4], or to misrepresent the proportions of it which are meadow, vineyard, or arable[5]: to hold himself out as the owner of the property, when it is really not his at all[6]: to falsely state that land is under lease to a tenant[7], and so forth. Moreover, what is termed 'active concealment' is no less fraudulent than wilful misrepresentation: *active concealment:*

> dolum malum a se abesse praestare venditor debet, qui non tantum in eo est qui fallendi causa obscure loquitur, sed etiam qui insidiose obscure dissimulat[8]:

for instance, concealing from a purchaser the fact that land is subject to a servitude[9]: with which may be classed the conduct of a vendor who, knowing that a would-be purchaser is under a serious misconception as to the nature or character of what he is buying, does nothing to remove it[10]. Moreover, on the broad principle that, so far as civil liability is concerned, gross negligence is to be treated as equivalent to fraud[11], it is deemed fraudulent for a vendor to make untrue statements about the subject-matter of the contract in reckless ignorance as to their truth or falsehood[12]: *reckless ignorance as to truth of statements:*

the validity of the contract, Dig. 19. 1. 7. 'Fraud without damage gives no cause of action': per Croke, J. 3 Bulst. 95: cf. *Pasley* v. *Freeman*, 3 T. R. 51.

[1] Dig. 18. 1. 43. pr.: 19. 1. 13. 4: ib. 34.
[2] Dig. 18. 1. 43. pr.   [3] Dig. 19. 1. 13. 4.
[4] Dig. ib. 13. 6.   [5] Dig. ib. 22.   [6] Dig. ib. 30. 1.
[7] Dig. ib. 49. pr.   [8] Dig. 18. 1. 43. 2.
[9] Dig. 19. 1. 1. 1: ib. 39.   [10] Dig. 19. 1. 11. 5.
[11] Dig. 11. 6. 1. 1.: 17. 1. 29. pr.: 47. 4. 1. 2.
[12] 'I conceive that if a man, having no knowledge whatever on the subject, takes upon himself to represent a certain state of facts to exist, he does so at his peril: and if it be done either with a view to

quid tamen si ignoravit quidem [servum] furem esse, adseveravit autem bonae frugi et fidum et caro vendidit? videamus an ex empto teneatur. et putem teneri. atqui ignoravit: sed non debuit facile quae ignorabat adseverare ... non debuit facilis esse ad temerariam indicationem [1].

And the same maxim finds an application in the rule, that wherever the purchaser has such inadequate means of informing himself as to the qualities, liabilities, and so forth of the article which he is purchasing that he has no alternative but to rely upon the statements of the vendor, the latter is bound to give him the fullest possible information within his own knowledge of these matters, so that even an entirely innocent non-disclosure of things known, and which ought to have been communicated, will give the purchaser rights very similar to those which he would have had if the case had been one of absolutely fraudulent misrepresentation [2]. But this is a subject to which we shall recur in considering the purchaser's rights of rescinding in the chapter relating to modes of discharge [3].

innocent non-disclosure.

secure some benefit to himself, or to deceive a third person, he is in law guilty of a fraud, for he takes upon himself to warrant his own belief of the truth of that which he so asserts,' per Maule, J. in *Evans v. Edmonds*, 13 C. B. 786: cf. *Western Bank of Scotland v. Addie*, L. R. 1 Sc. App. 145: *Reese River Co. v. Smith*, L. R. 4. H. L. 64. 79: *Weir v. Bell*, 3 Ex. D. 238. C.A.

[1] Dig. 19. 1. 13. 3.

[2] E.g. Dig. 19. 1. 21. 1: ib. 41. For the question how far the principal is affected by the fraud of his agent see Dig. ib. 13. 7: in English Law, Benjamin, pp. 449-456.

[3] En faisant l'application de ces principes au contrat de vente, il s'ensuit que le vendeur est obligé de déclarer tout ce qu'il sait touchant la chose vendue à l'acheteur qui a intérêt de le savoir, et qu'il pèche contre la bonne foi qui doit régner dans ce contrat, lorsqu'il lui en dissimule quelque chose: Pothier, 233. In 241 Pothier refers to Cicero's question on the duty of a merchant who, arriving at Rhodes during a famine, and having a number of other ships laden with corn on the way, exposed his corn for sale: ought he to have informed

The effect of any of these circumstances comprised under the general head of fraud varies with the nature of the case. The contract is never void on the ground of fraud alone, unless the mistake brought about by the misrepresentation is essential or fundamental, for in that case there has been no consent: fraud in itself does not exclude consent, but merely supplies an erroneous motive for entering into the contract[1]. But if the party deceived would not have made the contract at all had he known the truth of the matter, he is entitled to avoid it, either by waiting until the other sues him and resisting the action, or by bringing the ordinary action ex empto or ex vendito for its rescission, for restitution of the goods or the purchase money, as the case may be[2], and for compensation for any ulterior damage which the fraud may have entailed on him:

> si quis virginem se emere putasset, cum mulier venisset, et sciens errare eum venditor passus sit, redhibitionem quidem ex hac causa non esse, verumtamen ex empto competere actionem ad resolvendam emptionem, et pretio restituto mulier reddatur[3].

It is clear, too, that if he may avoid the contract, he may, without taking this course, content himself with an action to recover such damages as he has sustained[4]. And this action under the contract for damages is his only remedy where the deceit has not actually and in itself induced him

---

buyers that a plentiful supply was close at hand? Cicero appears to have thought that he should do so, for to conceal his knowledge was contrary to good faith. He adds 'la décision de Cicéron souffre beaucoup de difficulté, même dans le for de la conscience. La plupart de ceux qui ont écrit sur le Droit Naturel ont regardé cette décision comme outrée.'

[1] For the proof see Vangerow, Pandekten, iii. § 605, note 1.
[2] Dig. 19. 1. 13. 27.
[3] Dig. 19. 1. 11. 5: cf. Cod. 4. 44. 5: ib. 10.
[4] Dig. 18. 1. 43. 2: ib. 68. 1 & 2: 19. 1. 4. pr.: ib. 6. 9: ib. 13. 4 & 5.

to enter into it, but merely relates to subordinate points which are matters for compensation, because he would still have made the contract had he known the truth about them (dolus incidens)[1]: as where, for instance, one is induced to give a higher price for an article than one would have given otherwise by a false statement by the vendor as to some non-essential quality or property.

If both parties have been guilty of fraud towards one another, neither can sue the other with any effect[2]: and if there has been performance by either he cannot, on the principle 'in pari delicto potior est conditio defendentis,' claim a return of either the goods or the purchase money, or any kind of compensation[3].

Should the fraud be practised on one by another person who is not a party to the contract at all, it is void if the mistake which it produces is essential, and he can recover for any damage which he may have sustained by bringing an actio doli against the guilty person[4]. If the mistake is non-essential, the contract is not even voidable against the other party, he being entirely innocent, though an actio doli for damages will lie against the one who practised the fraud[5]: and sometimes even the wrong may be redressed by an action on the contract against the other party[6].

---

[1] Dig. 19. 1. 13. 4, &c. The rules of the Civil Law seem to be clearly stated in the Saxon bürgerliches Gesetzbuch, §§ 833–835, cited by Treitschke, Kaufcontract. p. 101. note 1 : 'if a contracting party is induced to enter into a contract by fraud on the part of the other, he can either ratify the contract or impeach its validity. If the fraud relates to subsidiary matters, which are not essential in determining him to make the contract, he is entitled only to sue for damages.'

[2] Dig. 18. 1. 57. 3 : cf. ib. 34. 3.   [3] Dig. 50. 17. 154.
[4] Dig. 4. 3. 7. pr.   [5] Dig. 4. 3. 8.
[6] E. g. a merchant borrows some weights for the purpose of weighing out a certain quantity of goods (say potatoes) which another person has agreed to buy from him, and the lender knows them to be light: the purchaser can sue ex empto for such an additional quantity as will make up the right weight : Dig. 4. 3. 18. 3.

MISTAKE. FRAUD. DURESS.

Where a contract is procured by threats of some evil to be inflicted on the person whose consent it is desired to obtain (Duress), the consent is deemed to be voluntary, or at any rate an actual consent[1]: but the conduct of the party using such threats being contrary to the bona fides which we have seen to be an essential condition of the consensual contracts, the other has rights similar to but more extensive than those which arise from fraud. The conditions of those rights are twofold. In the first place, the threat must have been of something unlawful[2] and something sufficiently serious, and the chance of its being actually inflicted must have been sufficiently near, to have influenced a person of courage and resolution: for instance, threats against one's life, one's chastity, or one's personal liberty or security: threats to destroy valuable property, and so forth:

Metus or duress, and its effects.

> metum autem non vani hominis, sed qui merito et in homine constantissimo cadat, ad hoc edictum pertinere dicemus[3]:

and it is immaterial whether the person threatened is the one whose consent it is desired to extort, or the husband, wife, or some near relation[4]. In the second place, the threats must have been used for the very purpose of inducing the person directly or indirectly threatened to make

---

[1] Dig. 4. 2. 21. 4 & 5: 23. 2. 22.
[2] Arg. Dig. 47. 10. 13. 1: iuris enim executio non habet iniuriam.
[3] Dig. 4. 2. 6: cf. ib. 2-4: 4. 6. 3: Cod. 2. 20. 4 & 7. Il y a violence lorsqu'elle est de nature à faire impression sur une personne raisonnable. et qu'elle peut lui inspirer la crainte d'exposer sa personne ou sa fortune à un mal considérable et présent. On a égard, en cette matière, à l'âge, au sexe et à la condition des personnes: Code Civil, Art. 1112.
[4] The authorities mention only children (Dig. 4. 2. 8. 3), but no doubt as an example only. La violence est une cause de nullité du contrat, non seulement lorsqu'elle a été exercée sur la partie contractante, mais encore lorsqu'elle l'a été sur son époux ou sur son épouse, sur ses descendans ou ses ascendans: Code Civil, Art. 1113.

the contract which he seeks to repudiate; in other words, one cannot avoid a contract which one may have made as an ulterior consequence of threats used for a different purpose [1]. Assuming that these conditions are satisfied, the person whose consent to a contract of sale has been thus wrongfully obtained has the following remedies:—
(1) he can bring the ordinary action on the contract for its rescission and for damages, or if sued upon it, he can defeat the action by the exceptio metus: or, if he prefers it, he can let the contract stand, and content himself with an action for damages only [2]: (2) he can apply to the courts for an in integrum restitutio on the ground of the duress, the effect of which is to undo the contract with all its consequences, and to replace him in statu quo ante as regards third persons as well as the other contracting party [3]: (3) in some cases he will obtain heavier damages than by an action on the contract by bringing the actio quod metus causa against the person who had used the threats, and this is sometimes the more appropriate remedy, especially in cases where one is induced to contract with one person by duress practised by another: but being in substance an action ex delicto it does not require further mention in this connection.

Metus has a wider operation than Dolus.

It will thus be seen that duress confers more extensive rights than fraud. The latter is said to operate *in personam* only, the former *in rem*. That is to say, where one has been induced to make a contract by threats of the kind described, one can avoid its consequences even as against innocent third parties who have acquired rights through or under it; and even where the compulsion, though used with the direct object of inducing one to make the contract, is exercised by a person who is not a party to it at all, and without the knowledge of the

---

[1] Dig. 4. 2. 9. 1.   [2] Cod. 4. 44. 1 & 8 : 2. 20. 12.
[3] Cod. 2. 20. 3 : Dig. 4. 2. 9. 4-6.

person who is, one can nevertheless avoid it by an actio quod metus causa against the latter, and claim restitution of any benefit which he has obtained by its means [1].

It is perhaps hardly necessary to say that if a person who had been induced to make a contract by duress ratified it, either expressly or by implication, on becoming released from the influence, the right of rescission was lost [2].

If the threats by which a man is induced to make a contract are not of the serious character indicated above, he cannot avail himself of these remedies. If sued, however, he can usually defeat the action by exceptio doli: he can recover the purchase money or property transferred under the agreement by condictio ex iniusta causa: and he can get compensation for such other damages as he has suffered by an actio doli [3].

[1] Dig. 4. 2. 14. 3 : 44. 4. 4. 33 : Cod. 2. 20. 3 & 5. La violence exercée contre celui, qui a contracté l'obligation, est une cause de nullité, encore qu'elle ait été exercée par un tiers autre que celui au profit duquel la convention a été faite : Code Civil, Art. 1111.

[2] Cod. 2. 20. 2 & 4. Un contrat ne peut plus être attaqué pour cause de violence, si, depuis que la violence a cessé, ce contrat a été approuvé, soit expressement, soit tacitement, soit en laissant passer le temps de la restitution fixé par la loi : Code Civil, Art. 1115.

[3] Dig. 12. 5. 6 & 7 : 4. 2. 14. 3. It must not be inferred from what has been said above that there are no cases in which a man can be compelled to sell particular property. Sometimes this is done in pursuance of obligatory directions, as where a testator imposes on his heir a trust to sell the inheritance, or some particular portion of it or thing belonging to it, to a third party, or to buy something which he does not want from a beneficiary under the will (e.g. Dig. 30. 49. 8 & 9 : ib. 66 : Pothier, 510). So too in time of famine people might be compelled to sell grain of which they had no personal need at a fair price (Cod. 10. 27. 2 : Pothier, 511), and other compulsory sales for public purposes, such as roads, are mentioned in the authorities (Pothier, l. c.). The rescript of Antoninus Pius, compelling inhuman masters to sell their slaves on advantageous terms, is familiar to readers of the Institutes (Gaius, i. 53 : Inst. i. 8. 2). Other illustrations will be found in Dig. 11. 7. 12. pr. : 20. 5. 2 : cf. Bechmann, Kauf, ii. §§ 187-195.

CHAPTER VII.

RULES AS TO THE PRICE.

The price must be fixed in money. Consideration consisting partly in money, partly in some other thing. The price must be fixed: no doctrine of a 'reasonable price.' Agreement that the price shall be fixed by an arbitrator or expert. Variation of the price. Fixing of the price where a number of things are bought together. The price must be intended as a bona fide equivalent for the goods. Fairness or adequacy of the price.

<small>The price must be fixed in money.</small> THE first requirement of the price is one to which reference has already been made, viz. that it must consist in money (pecunia numerata): the reason of the rule being stated by Paulus[1], that otherwise it would be impossible to tell which of the parties was vendor and which was purchaser. If what is agreed to be given for the goods is some other thing than money, the transaction is exchange, and is governed by some rules fundamentally different from those of sale[2]. The question whether the price must be fixed in current coin—coin, that is to say, which is legal tender—or whether it might not also be in the coinage of some other country, or in coins which have ceased to be current, is not dealt with in the authorities, no doubt because foreign money was rare, if not quite unknown, in the time of the classical jurists[3]. It is not, however,

---

[1] Dig. 18. 1. 1. 1 : Inst. iii. 23. 2.

[2] Cod. 4. 64. 7 : see p. 5 supr. So too in English law 'the price must be money, paid or promised, accordingly as the agreement may be for a cash or a credit sale : but if any other consideration than money be given, it is not a sale. If goods be given in exchange for goods, it is a barter': Benjamin, p. 2.

[3] Bechmann, Kauf, ii. § 152, is of opinion that on the principles of

RULES AS TO THE PRICE.

necessary to the contract that the purchaser should satisfy the vendor in coined money, if it be otherwise provided, for the difficulty of determining which was vendor and which purchaser was met by the agreement that one was to give money, and therefore they might, without in any way altering the nature of the contract, agree afterwards to substitute for the payment of the purchase money the giving of some other thing[1]: and there seems no reason in the nature of things why they should not agree upon this at the outset, though no authority can be found for this suggestion[2]. Nor is it strictly necessary that the consideration should consist entirely in money: the purchaser may promise, in addition to the price of an estate, to take a lease of other land from the vendor[3], or to give him a lease of the land which he has bought[4], or to repair a house for him[5]. But although it must be granted that so long as any part of the consideration agreed upon is money there is enough to differentiate the transaction from exchange, and to determine the rôles of the parties respectively as vendor and purchaser, it is not at all clear that it will on that account always be held to be a sale, and owing to the scantiness of the authorities on the point the views of the commentators are somewhat arbitrary and conflicting. According to one view, the answer depends (in the absence of express declaration by the parties) upon the relative

Consideration consisting partly in money, partly in some other thing.

---

the modern Civil Law the price might be fixed in a currency which admits of reduction to that which is legal tender, such as that of a foreign country with a regular known rate of exchange, but that payment must be in coins which are legal tender.

[1] Cod. 4. 44. 9 : 8. 45. 4 : Pothier, 30.

[2] E.g. if A and B agree to exchange two articles, as to the money price of which they are also quite in accordance, and the two prices exactly correspond, one might not unreasonably say that there are two sales made with the intention that the purchase money of each is to be set off against the other.

[3] Dig. 18. 1. 79.   [4] Dig. 19. 1. 21. 4.

[5] Dig. 19. 1. 6. 1.

F 2

value of the two parts of the consideration; for if that part of it which is not money preponderates, it will not be sale, but exchange[1], while if they are of equal value, or if their relative value is not precisely ascertainable, it will be sale[2]. But the passages upon which this view is based[3] are far indeed from establishing it, for all that they say is, that the nature of the contract of sale is not altered because the purchaser is to do something for the vendor besides paying the purchase money which has been agreed upon. These promises to do other things are pacta adiecta, or what an English lawyer would call terms in the contract, and (notwithstanding the adverse opinion of some of the earlier lawyers of the Empire[4]) are enforceable by the ordinary action ex empto or ex vendito. It is, however, worthy of notice, that none of the passages to which reference has been made class as sale a transaction in which some other *thing* is to be given in addition to money; they all relate to the doing of some act, or the rendering of some service. It would seem, on the whole, more in accordance with the Roman doctrine to say that it is sale only where money, and money alone, is agreed to be given for the merx or goods, though the nature of the contract is not affected if it is agreed by a pactum adiectum that either vendor or purchaser is to do something else for the other[5].

The price must be fixed: In the second place, the price must be fixed (certum)[6], and as a rule fixed by the agreement of the parties themselves: until so fixed there is no obligation, and therefore no contract[7]. The Roman law knows nothing of a 'reason-

---

[1] So Glück, Pandekten, 16. p. 69.
[2] Thibaut, Pandektenrecht, § 857.
[3] Dig. 18. 1. 79: 19. 1. 6. 1 : ib. 21. 4.   [4] Dig. 18. 1. 79.
[5] See Treitschke, Kaufcontract, § 114 : Bechmann, Kauf, ii. § 152.
[6] Inst. iii. 23. 1.
[7] Le prix de la vente doit être déterminé et désigné par les parties : Code Civil, Art. 1591.

able price, which it is presumed the parties intended if they did not explicitly agree as to what was to be paid. Consequently, contracts of sale of a kind with which we are so familiar, as where one goes to a shop and gets goods on credit without asking the price, or directs the shopkeeper to make one an article of a particular description without asking what it will cost, are in the Civil Law not contracts of sale at all, but innominate: the tradesman who supplies the goods, or who makes and delivers the article which has been ordered, sues for a money compensation not by actio ex vendito but by actio praescriptis verbis [1]. Consequently also it is no sale if it is agreed that the determination of the price shall be left absolutely to one or other of the parties themselves:

<blockquote>
illud constat imperfectum esse negotium, cum emere volenti sic venditor dicit : 'quanti velis, quanti aequum putaveris, quanti aestimaveris, habebis emptum [2].
</blockquote>

no doctrine of a 'reasonable price.'

[1] Arg. Dig. 19. 5. 22. In English law, if nothing has been said as to price when a commodity is sold or agreed to be sold, the law implies an understanding that it is to be paid for at what it is reasonably worth: see Chalmers, Sale of Goods, p. 12. This was settled in 1834 for executed contracts by *Acebal* v. *Levy*, 10 Bing. 376, and for executory contracts by *Hoadley* v. *McLaine*, ib. 482. What is a reasonable price is a question for the jury, and will not necessarily be the current price as it was at the date of the contract. The Scotch law appears to have started with the Roman principle, but to have adopted the English one, at any rate so far as executed contracts are concerned : 'Where the contract has been conclusively settled by delivery of the goods sold, the parties will be presumed in law to have had in contemplation the reasonable value of the thing sold': Bell on Sale, p. 19 : Principles of the Law of Scotland, § 92.

[2] Dig. 18. 1. 35. 1 : Cod. 4. 38. 13 : Pothier, 23. 29. Some eminent authorities, among the more recent being Windscheid, Lehrbuch, § 386, note 6, dispute this rule, holding that such a contract is good, but that if the party who is left to fix the price fixes it altogether unreasonably, it can be rectified by reference to the judgment of a competent and impartial man (boni viri arbitratus). The passages upon which this view is based are Dig. 50. 17. 22. 1 : 18. 1. 7. pr. : 17. 2. 6 : ib. 77 : ib. 79 : 19. 2. 24. pr. : Cod. 5. 11. 3. It is to be observed that in Dig. 18. 1. 35. 1. cited the negotium is not said to be 'nullum,' but 'imperfectum.'

Agreement that the price shall be fixed by an arbitrator or expert.

Whether the contract was invalid because they agreed to leave the fixing of the price to a determinate third person or persons had been disputed from the commencement of the Empire, if not earlier. Labeo and Cassius were of opinion that such an agreement was void as a sale, while the Proculians held it to be a valid sale subject to the suspensive condition that the person named should as a fact fix what the price should be [1]. The controversy does not appear to have been set at rest until the time of Justinian, who enacted that the contract should bind both parties at the price named by the third person, but that if he declined or was unable to fix it, it should be void [2]. If, while agreeing that the price should be fixed by a third person, the parties did not or could not settle who he should be, the contract was void [3], and could not be validated by consulting the opinion of anyone else, however competent and impartial he might be [4]: and if the valuer named fixed an outrageously unfair price, it is very generally held that it could be rectified by recourse to an action [5]. On the principle 'id certum est quod certum reddi potest,' a temporary subjective uncertainty of the parties

---

[1] Gaius, iii. 140. There seems to be no authority whatever for a view which might have been suggested, that the price could be fixed boni viri arbitratu if it was not fixed at all by the valuer agreed upon.

[2] Inst. iii. 23. 1: Cod. 4. 38. 15. (Le prix) peut cependant être laissé à l'arbitrage d'un tiers : si le tiers ne veut ou ne peut faire l'estimation, il n'y a point de vente : Code Civil, Art. 1592. It is held that under this provision it is a good agreement that the price should be fixed by experts, although none are named when the contract is made: Demante, Cours analytique de Code Civil, vii. p. 32 : see the next note.

[3] Arg. Dig. 19. 2. 25. pr.: si merces promissa sit generaliter alieno arbitrio, locatio et conductio contrahi non videtur: for by Justinian's enactment in the Code last referred to there was to be no difference in this respect between Sale and Hire.

[4] Cod. 4. 38. 15.

[5] Arg. Dig. 17. 2. 79 : unde si arbitrium ita pravum ut manifesta iniquitas eius appareat, corrigi potest per iudicium bonae fidei: so Pothier, 24. *Contra* Bechmann, Kauf, ii. § 217, laying stress on Justinian's

as to the amount of the price was immaterial, if what they intended admitted of immediate[1] ascertainment:

> huiusmodi emptio 'quanti tu eum emisti,' 'quantum pretii in arca habebo,' valet: nec enim incertum est pretium tam evidenti venditione: magis enim ignoratur quanti emptus sit, quam in rei veritate incertum est[2]:

though if the assumed possibility of fixing it was based on a misconception as to something in the past the contract fell to the ground:

> si quis fundum iure hereditario sibi delatum ita vendidisset—'erit tibi emptus tanti, quanti a testatore emptus est'—mox inveniatur non emptus, sed donatus testatori, videtur quasi sine pretio facta venditio, ideoque similis erit sub conditione factae venditioni, quae nulla est, si conditio defecerit[3].

---

language . . . . omnimodo secundum aestimationem eius . . . . venditionem ad effectum pervenire. The English law as to agreements for the fixing of the price by third persons is much the same as the Civil Law where the contract is executory (*Thurnell* v. *Balbirnie*, 2 C. B. 786, and other cases cited by Benjamin, p. 90). But if the agreement has been executed by the delivery of the goods, the vendor will be entitled to recover the value estimated by the jury, if the purchaser should do any act to obstruct or render impossible the valuation, as in *Clarke* v. *Westroppe*, 18 C. B. 765, where the defendant had agreed to buy certain goods at a valuation and the valuers disagreed, and the defendant thereupon consumed the goods, so that a valuation became impossible: Benjamin, loc. cit.

[1] The word 'immediate' is emphatic, for it would not seem to be allowable to have the price fixed by reference to some uncertain event in the future, as e. g. in a purchase of stock 'at the carrying over price at the next account': see Dig. 18. 1. 7. 2, and Bechmann, Kauf, § 216. There is an apparent exception to the general rule established by a rescript of Severus and Antoninus: 'potest ita fieri pignoris datio hypothecaeve, ut, si intra certum tempus non sit soluta pecunia, iure emptoris possideat rem iusto pretio tunc aestimandam,' Dig. 20. 1. 16. 9: but this is explained by regarding the agreement as a pactum adiectum to a contract of pledge, not as an independent contract of sale. Pothier, 27. 28.

[2] Dig. 18. 1. 7. 1. [3] Dig. 18. 1. 37.

Variation of the price.

Similarly, a minimum price might be agreed upon, with a covenant that it should be increased in the event of the purchaser selling the goods at a profit; for here, as Ulpian says[1], the requirement of a 'fixed' price is satisfied. There was no reason why the price should not be altered by mutual consent of the parties after the contract was concluded, so long as there had not yet been performance, though this was really the discharge of the original agreement by the making of another whose terms were inconsistent with it:

> Paulus notat: si omnibus integris manentibus de augendo vel deminuendo pretio rursum convenit, recessum a priore contractu et nova emptio intercessisse videtur[2].

Fixing of the price where a number of things are bought together.

Where the subject-matter of a sale consists of, or may be regarded as consisting of, a number of things, such as an estate of so many acres, a herd of cattle of so many head, a vintage of so many barrels, &c., there are two methods of fixing the amount of the purchase money. It may be agreed either that a lump sum shall be paid for the whole, or that so much shall be paid for each acre, head, barrel, and so forth. In the first case the sale is called emptio in aversione or per aversionem[3], and the purchase money is unaltered whether the number of individuals comprised in the aggregate prove more or less than was expected, though of course if the vendor had stated what the number was, and he cannot make it up, he must allow of an abatement in the price[4]. In the second case, which is called emptio ad mensuram, the purchase money is deemed to be 'certum' from the moment that the parties

---

[1] Dig. 18. 1. 7. 2.   [2] Dig. 18. 1. 72. pr.
[3] Dig. 18. 1. 62. 2 : 18. 6. 4. 1.
[4] Dig. 19. 1. 2. pr.: ib. 4. 1: ib. 6. pr.: ib. 38. pr. The apparent contradiction in Dig. ib. 13. 4. disappears if one distinguishes between two cases, in one of which there is a fraudulent misrepresentation of acreage, in the other one which is made in good faith.

have agreed as to what is to be paid for each acre, head, barrel, &c., because it admits of practically immediate ascertainment, and neither party can after that moment repudiate the bargain: the sum actually due depends on the number ascertained by counting, weight, or measurement, and a statement made by the vendor as to that number, unless fraudulent, is not taken as a warranty, but rather as a rough and ready estimate for the information of the purchaser[1]. There is a further difference between the two cases in respect of the moment from which the goods bought are at the purchaser's risk, which will be considered in the next chapter.

No transaction will be held a sale in which the price agreed upon is not intended by the parties to be a real and bona fide equivalent for the thing pretended to be purchased[2], or in which it is not intended that it shall be paid at all[3]. Such simulated sales are not unfrequently resorted to in order to evade the law (e.g. as to gifts between husband and wife[4], and conveyances in fraud of creditors): but even where there is no such object in view,

The price must be intended as a bona fide equivalent for the goods.

[1] Dig. 18. 1. 40. 2. Cf. the use of 'about,' 'say about,' 'more or less,' in English contracts. These terms mean that the quantity is not restricted to the exact number or amount specified, but that the vendor is to be allowed a moderate and reasonable latitude or margin in performance: *Cross* v. *Eglin*, 2 B. and Ad. 106 : *Moore* v. *Campbell*, 10 Ex. 323 : *McConnell* v. *Murphy*, L. R. 5 C. P. 203.

[2] Ce que la doctrine entend par un prix non sérieux, c'est une somme d'une modicité dérisoire par comparaison à la valeur de la chose : Demante, Cours analytique de Code Civil, vii. p. 33.

[3] It is commonly said the pretium must be 'verum,' but this seems to be hardly a Roman use of the epithet. Le prix doit être un prix sérieux, et convenu avec intention qu il pourroit être exigé : c'est pourquoi si une personne me vendoit une chose pour une certaine somme, et que par le contrat il m'en fit remise, un tel acte ne seroit pas une vente, mais une donation ... il en seroit autrement si la remise du prix n'avoit été faite que *ex intervallo* : car il y a en ce cas un prix que l'acheteur s'est véritablement obligé de payer : Pothier, 18.

[4] Pothier, 39.

although the contract may be held a gift, a deposit, a mortgage, or (in short) whatsoever the parties may have really intended, it cannot produce the effects which the law says shall result from a sale[1]. Such sales as those of an inheritance 'nummo uno' under a trust before the enactment of the Sc. Trebellianum[2], and sales for a price which it was never intended to demand, were gifts, and were governed by the rules applying thereto[3]: no action would lie for the pretended purchase money[4]. There was, however, no reason why one should not sell a thing at a lower price than one could get for it in the open market to oblige a friend[5], though this would not be allowed if the real object was to evade such rules as those prohibiting gifts between husband and wife: a sale between them at half price, for instance, is half gift, half sale, and valid only in respect of the latter[6]. It would also seem that if at the time when the contract was made it really was intended to be a bona fide sale, and not a gift, its character would not be altered by the vendor's subsequently remitting a portion or even the whole of the purchase money[7], for, as Ulpian says, it is not the payment of the purchase money, but the intention of the parties, which makes the contract, and determines its true nature[8].

Fairness or adequacy of the price. So far as the fairness or adequacy of the price goes, the fundamental principle of the law is to leave the parties to make their own bargain. It is of the very nature of the contract that they shall be at liberty to sell and buy cheap or dear, provided of course that there is no fraud :

in emendo et vendendo naturaliter concessum est quod

---

[1] Dig. 18. 1. 36 : ib. 55 : Cod. 4. 38. 3 & 9.   [2] Gaius, ii. 252.
[3] Cod. 8. 53. 34 : ib. 36. 3 : Pothier, 19. 39.   [4] Cod. 4. 38. 9.
[5] Dig. 18. 1. 38 : Pothier, 21.
[6] Dig. 24. 1. 5. 5 : ib. 31. 3.
[7] Arg. Dig. 19. 2. 5 : si tibi habitationem locavero, mox pensionem remittam, ex locato et conducto agendum erit.
[8] Dig. 18. 1. 2. 1.

pluris sit minoris emere, quod minoris sit pluris vendere, et ita invicem se circumscribere [1].

An early exception to this rule was the regulation of the price of corn on grounds of public policy [2]: another is found in Justinian's enactment [3] providing that if one of two or more joint owners of a slave one desires to manumit him the others shall be compellable to sell him their shares, and fixing the compensation to be paid according to the slave's age and capacities [4]. But the most important departure from the original principle was the enactment in A. D. 285 of Diocletian and Maximian, by which it was laid down that if one sold a thing for less than half its real value one could rescind the sale unless the purchaser would make the price up to a fair one [5]. Here, however, the sale is not void, but merely voidable, and the subject will be dealt with more fully, under the head of the vendor's right of rescission, in the chapter relating to modes of discharge.

[1] Dig. 19. 2. 22. 3 : cf. 4. 4. 16. 4.
[2] E. g. by the lex Sempronia, B. C. 24.
[3] Inst. ii. 7. 4 : Cod. 7. 7.
[4] Cod. 7. 7. 1. 5 : 6. 43. 3.
[5] Cod. 4. 44. 2

CHAPTER VIII.

THE EFFECTS OF THE CONTRACT.

(a) *Periculum and Commodum rei.*

General rule as to the passing of the risk to the purchaser. Meaning of periculum rei. It passes when the emptio is 'perfecta.' Grounds on which it may be 'imperfecta:' (i) agreement not yet completely binding, because the price is not fixed, or there is a suspensive condition, or the purchaser has reserved the right of examining the goods: various cases of this: (ii) the goods not yet specifically determined: meaning of 'weighing, counting, or measuring' the goods: vendor's negligence in such cases. Rule as to the risk when the vendor has the right of selection: in sales in the alternative: and in sales of res alienae. Vendor's obligation to assign rights of action where the goods are at the purchaser's risk. Exceptions to the rule as to risk. Theories as to its rationale. Meaning of commodum rei: the purchaser is entitled to fruits, and accessions, from the moment the contract is concluded.

General rule as to the passing of the risk to the purchaser.

THE general principle is that on an absolute sale (and we may add on a sale subject to a resolutive condition) of a specifically determined and existing thing, that thing is at the risk of the purchaser from the moment that the contract is concluded, even before it has been made his by conveyance, and quite apart from the transfer of title: in other words, if after the contract is once made, the thing is lost, stolen, destroyed, or damaged without any fault of the vendor, the latter is nevertheless entitled to the purchase money, and the loss falls on the purchaser[1]. Conversely,

[1] Cum autem emptio et venditio contracta sit, periculum rei venditae statim ad emptorem pertinet: Inst. iii. 23. 3: cf. Dig. 18. 1. 34. 6: 18. 5. 5. 2: 18. 6. 1. pr., ib. 4. 1: ib. 8. pr.: Cod. 4. 48. 2. 1., ib. 5. In Pothier's time the law of France was the same: c'est un principe établi au titre du digeste *de peric. et comm. rei rend.* qu'aussitôt que le contrat de vente est parfait, la chose vendue devient aux risques de

the profits, emoluments, fruits and benefits generally derivable from it belong to the purchaser from the same moment[1]. The more precise meaning of these expressions, and the bearing of this important and somewhat singular principle on conditional sales, and sales in which the goods or the amount of the purchase money are not yet exactly determined, requires some further elucidation.

'Periculum' denotes any damage or injury, including entire loss or destruction, which may befall the subject-matter of the contract after its conclusion: whether it is due to natural causes or accident, or to human action, is immaterial, though most of the illustrations which are given of it are of the first kind[2]. It is important further to distinguish between the risk of destruction or entire loss (periculum interitus) and the risk of mere damage or depreciation not amounting to destruction (periculum deteriorationis[3]), for, as we shall see, there are exceptional cases in which one of the parties has to bear risk of the one kind, and the other that of the other. As a rule, however, they go together. *Meaning of periculum rei:*

The property purchased is at the purchaser's risk as soon as the emptio is 'perfecta.' The word 'perfecta' here means something more than that the parties are bound by the contract because they are agreed upon the goods to be sold and the price to be paid: the contract may be quite complete for the purpose of producing the *it passes when the emptio is 'perfecta.'*

l'acheteur, quoiqu'elle ne lui ait pas encore été livrée. 307. By the Code Civil, Art. 1583, an agreement to sell or buy 'lorsque la vente est pure et simple, et qu'elle a pour objet un corps certain' ipso facto transfers property in the goods sold to the purchaser 'à l'égard du vendeur,' and they are at his risk on the simple ground that ' damnum sentit dominus.'

[1] Nam et commodum eius esse debet cuius periculum est: Inst. loc. cit.

[2] Dig. 18. 6. 1. pr. and 1 : ib. 8 : ib. 12 : ib. 16. In Dig. ib. 15. 1 there is a case of theft.

[3] Dig. 18. 6. 1. pr. : ib. 4. pr. and 1 : ib. 8. pr.

obligations which ordinarily result from it, and yet not 'perfect' for the purpose of transferring the risk from the vendor to the purchaser[1]:

> necessario sciendum est, quando perfecta sit emptio: tunc enim sciemus, cuius periculum sit: nam perfecta emptione periculum ad emptorem respiciet. et si id quod venierit appareat, quid, quale, quantum sit, sit et pretium, et pure venit, perfecta est emptio[2].

Grounds on which it may be 'imperfecta': i, agreement not yet completely binding, because the price is not fixed, or there is a suspensive condition,

The contract may be imperfecta, and the risk be still with the vendor, on two grounds.

I. Because the agreement is not yet completely binding in itself. For instance, the parties may have come to terms about the goods to be bought, but have differed in opinion as to what would be a fair price, and agreed to refer this to a third party, who has not yet said what ought to be paid[3]: or the contract may have been made subject to a suspensive condition, or condition precedent, which has not yet been satisfied[4], as where one agrees to buy a particular horse at a certain price if he shall win a particular race: for until satisfaction of the condition there is no obligation[5]. In this case, if the subject-matter of the sale is entirely destroyed before the condition is satisfied, the loss falls on the vendor, and the purchase money, if paid, can be recovered back, because the contract has never come to anything: whereas if it is merely damaged by accident, or becomes less valuable through the operation of natural causes or by the act of man without the vendor's fault, the loss falls on the purchaser if the condition is in fact satisfied, and he cannot refuse to pay the purchase money in full, or recover back any portion of it, if it has

---

[1] See Code Civil, Art. 1585, cited infra.
[2] Dig. 18. 6. 8. pr.: Pothier, 308.   [3] p. 70 supr.
[4] Cod. 4. 48. 5.
[5] Ante conditionem non recte agi, cum nihil ad interim debeatur: Dig. 20. 1. 13. 5.

been paid, because the condition relates back to the moment at which the provisional agreement was concluded[1]:

> quod si sub conditione res venierit, si quidem defecerit conditio, nulla est emptio, sicuti nec stipulatio : quod si exstiterit, Proculus et Octavenus emptoris esse periculum aiunt : idem Pomponius libro ix probat. quod si pendente conditione ... res tradita sit, emptor non poterit eam usucapere pro emptore, et quod pretii solutum sit repetetur: et fructus medii temporis venditoris sunt, sicuti stipulationes et legata conditionalia perimuntur, si pendente conditione res extincta fuerit. Sane si exstet res, licet deterior effecta, potest dici esse damnum emptoris[2].

It need hardly be pointed out, that if the contract is made subject in the alternative to two suspensive conditions which are absolutely contradictory and admit of no third possibility[3], it is deemed to be an absolute contract, on the principle that 'qui sub conditione stipulatur quae omnimodo exstatura est pure videtur stipulari[4].' If the sale is unconditional, and by a subsequent agreement a suspensive condition is annexed, this does not make the original contract 'imperfect' by relation back, so that if before the annexation of the condition the goods have perished unknown to the parties, the loss has to be borne by the purchaser[5]. Lastly, the contract may not be as yet absolutely binding because the purchaser has reserved the right of examining, testing, or sampling the goods[6], so that its

or the purchaser has reserved the right of examining the goods:

---

[1] Conditio existens ad initium negotii retrotrahitur: retrotrahitur impleta conditio ad conventionis diem : Dig. 20. 4. 11. 1 : 46. 3. 16 : 30. 69. 1 : 50. 17. 18.

[2] Dig. 18. 6. 8. pr. : cf. Dig. 23. 3. 10. 5 : Pothier, 311.

[3] Dig. 18. 6. 8. 1.   [4] Dig. 46. 2. 9. 1.

[5] Dig. 18. 5. 7. pr.

[6] This condition is implied in sales of certain descriptions of goods by the Code Civil, Art. 1587 : à l'égard du vin, de l'huile et des autres choses que l'on est dans l'usage de goûter avant d'en faire l'achat, il n'y a point de vente tant que l'acheteur ne les a pas goûtées et agréées. In the French law of Pothier's time (310) it would seem that, following

various cases of this.

perfection may be said to depend on the condition of his approval. The precise form of this condition varies in different cases according to the language or the presumed intention of the parties, and the answer to the question at whose risk the goods are, in respect both of destruction and of deterioration, turns on the form in which it is expressed or intended by them. There are three possible alternatives. The goods may be agreed to be bought (*a*) subject to the fulfilment of a suspensive condition (e. g. 'si placuerit, erit tibi emptus[1]'): or (*b*) subject to a resolutive condition proper (e. g. 'si displicuerit, erit tibi inemptus[2]'): or (*c*) subject to a pactum displicentiae (e. g. 'ut res si displicuerit redderetur[3]'), that is, a resolutive condition not operating *ipso facto* to avoid the sale, but entitling the purchaser to return the goods and so avoid it if he shall so choose.

In the case of (*a*) a suspensive condition, the goods, as has been pointed out, are at the vendor's risk in respect of deterioration no less than of destruction pendente conditione, until the purchaser signifies his approval of them, and his discretion in this matter is absolute[4]. If, however, a time has been fixed within which he must express himself satisfied with the goods, if he wishes to do so at all, and he is disabled from doing so by the vendor's fault, the goods remain at the risk of the latter:

si quis vina vendiderit et intra diem certum degustanda

---

the Civil Law, the right of testing must be expressly reserved, though no doubt in sales of this kind very slight expressions would be construed as indicative of the required intention.

[1] Inst. iii. 23. 4: Dig. 19. 5. 20. 1.
[2] Dig. 18. 1. 3.   [3] Dig. 18. 5. 6.
[4] The Code Civil, Art. 1588, enacts 'la vente faite à l'essai est toujours présumée faite sous une condition suspensive': and a 'vente à l'essai' is defined by Demante (Cours analytique de Code Civil, vii. p. 15) as 'une vente faite avec cette clause que l'acheteur usera de la chose pendant un certain temps, et qu'il déclarera ensuite si la chose lui convient ou ne lui convient pas.'

dixerit, deinde per venditorem steterit, quominus degustarentur, ... arbitror debere dici emptionem manere, periculum autem ad venditorem respicere etiam ultra diem degustando praefinitum, quia per ipsum factum est [1].

If, on the other hand, the fault in such a case is with the purchaser himself, the prevailing view is that the risk is transferred to him as soon as the day has passed, but it would certainly seem more in consonance with the general theory of suspensive conditions to say that the whole contract falls to the ground through failure of the condition [2]: and if the goods have been delivered to the purchaser for inspection or trial, and he fails to express his disapproval and return them within the period fixed, his conduct will apparently be deemed an acceptance by implication [3]. If no time has been fixed at all within which the purchaser is to try or examine the goods, he must try them as soon as an opportunity to do so is given him by the vendor: and if when such opportunity is given he does not do so and declare himself within a reasonable time, the condition is taken to have failed, and the vendor may sell them to some one else or otherwise dispose of them as he may please [4]. The putting of a seal upon goods, or marking them in any other way, is not construed as evidence of approval by the purchaser, but is to be taken merely as a means of identification [5], and in itself does not suffice to transfer the risk to him from the vendor [6].

---

[1] Dig. 18. 6. 4. pr.   [2] So Vangerow, iii. p. 437.
[3] Arg. Dig. 19. 5. 20. pr.
[4] Arg. Dig. 18. 6. 4. 2 : Treitschke, Kaufcontract, p. 196.
[5] Dig. 18. 6. 1. 2.
[6] Dig. 18. 6. 1. pr. A similar question has arisen in England, whether marking goods with his name by the purchaser, or by some one else with his consent, is a sufficient acceptance to satisfy § 17 of the Statute of Frauds : it is held to be an 'acceptance' but not a 'receipt,' *Bill* v. *Bament*, 9 M. & W. 36, and other cases cited by Benjamin, p. 157. Does marking goods with the buyer's name divest the

a resolutive condition proper:

In the case of (*b*) a resolutive condition proper, the goods are at the purchaser's risk, so far as entire loss or destruction goes, from the moment the contract is concluded, while the risk of damage or deterioration remains with the vendor, because in the event of such damage or deterioration the purchaser may say that he will not have them, and so rescind the contract. If a term has been fixed within which he must (if at all) avoid the contract by expressing his disapproval, and the time elapses without his doing so, and there is no default in the vendor, the condition is deemed to have failed, and the contract ceases to be voidable: if no such term has been fixed, the failure of the purchaser to test the goods, or (if he has tested them) to express his dissatisfaction within a reasonable time, produces the same effect.

a pactum displicentiae.

In the case of (*c*) a pactum displicentiae, if a term has been fixed within which the purchaser may return the goods and cancel the sale, he is at liberty to do so and redemand his purchase money (if paid) at any moment until such term has elapsed, and during that period the goods are entirely at the risk of the vendor[1]. If no such term has been agreed upon, the law allows one of sixty days, after the lapse of which, unless the goods have been

---

vendor's lien? *Goodall* v. *Skelton*, 2 H. Bl. 316: *Dixon* v. *Yates*, 5 B. & Ad. 313: Benjamin, p. 817.

It is obvious that if the purchaser reserves no right of examining or testing the goods, they are entirely at his risk from the moment of the purchase (Dig. 18. 6. 1. pr.: ib. 4. 1), though the passages referred to say that there is an exception to the rule if the vendor has expressly undertaken the risk (1. pr.). In this case it is said that the risk is with him for so long as has been agreed upon, or until the goods have been approved by the purchaser. But why, when there has been no condition of approval, should the perfection of the contract depend on such approval being signified? One solution consists in supposing that in a purchase of wine in bulk such approval is an implied term in the contract: but this seems irreconcileable with Dig. 18. 6. 15.

[1] Dig. 21. 1. 31. 24: cf. ib. 47. 1 & 48.

returned, the contract ceases to be voidable, and the risk passes to the purchaser [1].

II. The risk may still be with the vendor because the goods which are the subject matter of the contract are not specifically ascertained or defined, or because the exact amount of the purchase money is not yet determined. The simplest illustration is an agreement to buy such or such a weight, measure, or number of a certain article at present defined only generically, and the goods have not yet been weighed, measured, or counted. The distinction has been drawn in the preceding chapter between a purchase of a number of things in the aggregate for a single price (emptio per aversionem) and a purchase of a number of things, or even of a single thing consisting of similar parts (such as a cask of wine or an estate) at so much for each thing or part [2]. In the first case the whole is at the purchaser's

The goods not yet specifically determined:

---

[1] Dig. 21. 1. 31. 22 & 23. Most of the illustrations given in the authorities of this 'emptio ad gustum' are drawn from the wine trade, and Cato (de re rust. 148) says that purchases of wine in bulk were seldom made without some such condition. According to Vangerow (iii. p. 434), following Goldschmidt, this particular case of wine was governed by special rules, which he states thus:

(i) The presumption is in favour of the 'gustus' being a resolutive condition (Dig. 18. 1. 34. 5), so that in the absence of evidence to the contrary the periculum interitus is with the purchaser.

(ii) The purchaser may not reject the wine arbitrarily, but only because the trade would pronounce it to be of inferior quality (Dig. 18. 6. 1. pr.; ib. 4. pr. & 1: ib. 15: cf. Cato, loc. cit.: 'viri boni arbitratu degustato').

(iii) If a time is agreed upon within which the wine is to be tasted, and through the vendor's fault it is not done, the contract is not avoided, and the vendor has still to bear the risk of deterioration (Dig. 18. 6. 4. pr.). If the fault is with the purchaser, or if he tastes the wine but still does not signify his disapproval within the time fixed, the contract ceases to be voidable, and the whole risk is with him. If no time has been fixed at all, he must taste the wine and make up his mind as soon as the vendor gives him an opportunity: if he does not do so, the condition is taken to have failed.

[2] Pothier, 309, lays down three rules for determining whether a sale

risk as soon as they are agreed upon the amount of the purchase money:

> in his quae pondere, numero, mensurave constant, veluti frumento, vino, oleo, argento, modo ea servantur, quae in ceteris, ut, simul atque de pretio convenerit, videatur perfecta venditio ... nam si omne vinum, vel oleum, vel frumentum, vel argentum, quantumcunque esset, uno pretio venierit, idem iuris est quod in ceteris rebus[1].

In the second case it is otherwise: the sale is imperfect, so far as the transfer of the risk to the purchaser is concerned, until the counting, weighing, or measuring has taken place ('quia venditio quasi sub hac conditione videtur fieri[2]).' It is immaterial whether the purchase is of the whole estate, or of the whole stock of goods, at so much

---

is per aversionem or ad mensuram. It is ad mensuram (*a*) lorsque le prix est expressément convenu pour chaque mesure : soit que le contrat porte qu'on vend tant de muids de bled qui sont dans tel grenier, à raison de tant par muid : soit qu'il porte qu'on vend un tas de bled qui est dans un tel grenier qui contient dix muids, à raison de tant le muid : (*b*) lorsqu'on vend tant de mesures d'une telle chose, comme lorsqu'il est dit qu'on vend dix muids de bled pour cinq cent livres, ce prix étant censé n'être que le total des prix pour lesquels chaque muid est vendu. It is per aversionem lorsqu'on vend pour un seul prix, non tant de mesures d'une telle chose, mais une telle chose qu'on dit contenir tant de mesures, comme lorsqu'il est dit qu'on vend pour la somme de mille livres un tel pré qu'on assure être de la contenance de vingt arpens.

[1] Dig. 18. 1. 35. 5 : Cod. 4. 48. 2. Mais si ces choses n'ont pas été vendues au poids ou à la mesure, mais *per aversionem*, c'est-à-dire, en bloc, par un seul et même prix, en ce cas la vente est parfaite dès l'instant du contrat, et dès ce temps ces choses, de même que toutes les autres, sont aux risques de l'acheteur : Pothier, 308.

[2] Lorsque des marchandises ne sont pas vendues en bloc, mais au poids, au compte ou à la mesure, la vente n'est point parfaite, en ce sens que les choses vendues sont aux risques du vendeur jusqu'à ce qu'elles soient pesées, comptées ou mesurées, mais l'acheteur peut en demander la délivrance ou des dommages et intérêts, s'il y a lieu, en cas de l'inexécution de l'engagement. Si au contraire, les marchandises ont été vendues en bloc, la vente est parfaite, quoique les marchandises n'aient pas encore été pesées, comptées, ou mesurées : Code Civil, Arts. 1585, 1586.

per unit[1] (so much an acre, so much a gallon, so much a quarter, &c.), or of so many units out of the whole (as 'sixty gallons of your stock of brandy') either at a lump sum or at so much per unit. For instance, in the latter case one may buy a hundred quarters of wheat from a stock in a given granary, but the whole stock is at the vendor's risk until the hundred quarters have been measured out and appropriated to the purchaser (unless the latter hinders the vendor from doing it), for until that has been done it is uncertain what particular part of the stock the purchaser is to have[2]. Thus the rule is, that whenever

---

[1] In this case, under the Code Civil, the goods belong to the purchaser from the moment the contract is concluded, and yet they are at the vendor's risk until measured, weighed, or counted. 'La vente est faite sous une condition suspensive, c'est-à-dire, subordonnée à l'opération du pesage, du compte ou du mesurage. Les risques alors retombent, en vertu des principes, sur le vendeur débiteur du corps certain promis, et cela n'empêche pas l'acheteur de devenir propriétaire sous cette condition': Demante, Cours analytique de Code Civil, vii. p. 10.

[2] Dig. 18. 1. 35. 7: Pothier, 308. Demante is of opinion that if the whole stock perishes without the vendor's fault before the selection has been made, the periculum interitus ought to fall on the purchaser in the ratio of the proportion of what he agreed to buy to the whole: 'que les risques soient pour le vendeur tant qu'il n'a péri qu'une partie des marchandises parmi lesquelles devaient être prises celles qu'il fallait livrer, c'est l'application à l'espèce des théories sur les dettes de quantité. Pourquoi le créancier ne perd-il pas sa créance quand le débiteur de quantité a perdu les choses qui lui appartenaient et qui faisaient partie du genre promis? C'est qu'il reste d'autres objets du genre promis, que le débiteur n'avait pas spécialement promis les choses qui lui appartenaient, et que son obligation peut encore être exécutée. Mais si le genre venait à périr tout entier, par exemple à être retiré du commerce, le débiteur serait libéré. Dans l'espèce qui nous occupe, la dette a pour objet une chose faisant partie d'un genre limité, non pas 10 moutons ou 10,000 kilogrammes de charbon *in genere*, mais 10 des moutons qui font partie de telle bergerie, 10,000 kilogrammes de charbon qui se trouvent dans telle cave. Le genre, ce n'est pas tous les moutons ou tout le charbon existant sur la terre, c'est une petite collection restreinte de moutons ou de charbon, ceux qui sont dans telle bergerie ou dans telle cave : c'est un genre limité. Si donc tous les moutons de la bergerie ont péri, ou tout le charbon de la

a contract of sale requires for its perfection the counting, weighing, or measuring of the article bought, for the purpose of determining either what part of a given whole the purchaser is to have, or what is the size or quantity of the aggregate or portion of an aggregate bought, and how much consequently has to be paid, the risk of deterioration no less than of destruction is with the vendor until that has been done [1].

Another possible case, which does not appear to have occurred to the Roman lawyers, is the sale of a determinate quota of the goods in a given stock or warehouse for a lump sum—e. g. of one quarter of all the wines now in my cellar for the sum of £100. It may be conjectured that this would be regarded as a purchase per aversionem of an undivided share: the sale would be 'perfecta,' and the risk with the purchaser in the ratio which the share he has bought bears to the whole stock [2].

meaning of 'weighing, counting, or measuring' the goods:

When it is said that the sale is not perfect until the goods have been weighed, counted, or measured, the meaning of these expressions is not entirely obvious. The view that it is enough for the vendor himself and alone to weigh, count, or measure them, without the presence of the purchaser or of any one acting on his behalf, has little to recommend it: the authorities speak of the article being *ad*numerata, *ad*pensa, *ad*mensa, and against it also is the mention of 'mora emptoris in mensura facienda [3].'

cave, les risques doivent peser sur l'acheteur comme dans l'hypothèse de la vente en bloc': Cours analytique de Code Civil, vii. pp. 11. 12.

[1] Cod. 4. 48. 2.

[2] La perte d'une partie des marchandises serait subie pour moitié par l'acheteur, car la chose vendue ayant été non pas telle ou telle partie matérielle du bloc de marchandises, mais la moitié abstraite de ce bloc, la perte d'une partie des objets contenus dans le magasin doit produire par rapport à l'acheteur le même effet, proportion gardée, que s'il avait acheté en bloc toutes les marchandises : Demante, Cours analytique de Code Civil, vii. p. 13.

[3] Dig. 18. 6. 5 : Cod. 4. 48. 2.

Almost equally untenable is the theory that the vendor must have performed his part of the contract by sending or delivering the goods to the purchaser, though this is supported by the word 'tradantur' in the passage of the Code last referred to: and the true meaning of the texts appears to be that they must be weighed, counted, or measured in the presence of the purchaser or of some one acting on his behalf, so that he is enabled to examine them and see whether they are free from defects, and are of the kind contemplated by the contract.

The vendor is not excused from the obligation of taking care of the thing because it is not yet at the purchaser's risk [1], for the contract, even though not 'perfect' in the sense of this chapter, imposes on both parties the usual duties which arise from it: in other words, if it is damaged or destroyed in the meanwhile, and the vendor is in any way to blame, he not only loses his claim to the purchase money (as in the case of damage or destruction brought about by accident or the operation of natural causes), but he must also indemnify the purchaser for all loss which his misconduct or negligence may have occasioned him: and the degree of care which he must show is that ordinarily required from vendors and purchasers alike. If, however, the purchaser, by his own delay or negligence, has hindered the due weighing, measuring, or counting which would transfer the risk to him from the vendor, the latter is no longer required to display such care: he becomes answerable only for wilful misconduct and gross negligence [2]. The purchaser must also indemnify him for all loss or damage which he may suffer through such delay or negligence: full illustrations of this principle are cited below from the authorities [3].

vendor's negligence in such cases.

[1] Dig. 18. 6. 1. 1.: ib. 2. 1.   [2] Dig. 18. 6. 5 : ib. 18.
[3] Licet autem venditori vel effundere vinum, si diem ad metiendum praestituit, nec intra diem admensum est: effundere autem non statim poterit, priusquam testando denuntiet emptori, ut aut tollat vinum,

Rules as to the risk when the vendor has the right of selection, in sales in the alternative.

The principles are the same in purchases of a thing determined only by genus, which has to be specifically ascertained by the vendor's selection[1], and in purchases concluded in the alternative. In the latter the vendor's right of selection continues only so long as the exercise of it remains possible, and if the various articles from which one was to be chosen are reduced by natural causes, or otherwise without the vendor's fault, to one, that one is forthwith at the purchaser's risk; and the rules are precisely the same if the selection had been given by agreement to the purchaser himself:

> si emptio ita facta fuerit: 'est mihi emptus Stichus aut Pamphilus,' in potestate est venditoris, quem velit dare, sicut in stipulationibus, sed uno mortuo qui superest dandus est. Et ideo prioris periculum ad venditorem, posterioris ad emptorem respicit, sed et si pariter decesserunt, pretium debebitur: unus enim utique periculo emptoris vixit. idem dicendum est etiam, si emptoris fuit arbitrium quem vellet habere[2].

aut sciat futurum ut vinum effunderetur. Si tamen, cum posset effundere, non effundit, laudandus est potius. Ea propter mercedem quoque doliorum potest exigere, sed ita demum, si interfuit eius inania esse vasa, in quibus vinum fuit, veluti si locaturus ea fuisset, vel si necesse habuit alia conducere dolia. Commodius est autem conduci vasa, nec reddi vinum, nisi, quanti conduxerit, ab emptore reddatur: aut vendere vinum bona fide, id est, quantum sine ipsius incommodo fieri potest operam dare, ut quam minimo detrimento sit ea res emptori. Si doliare vinum emeris, nec de tradendo eo quicquam convenerit, id videri actum, ut ante evacuaretur, quam ad vindemiam opera eorum futura sit necessaria: quod si non sint evacuata, faciendum, quod veteres putaverunt, per corbem venditorem mensuram facere, et effundere. Veteres enim hoc propter mensuram suaserunt, si quanta mensura esset non appareat, videlicet, ut appareret, quantum emptori perierit. hoc ita verum est, si is est venditor, cui sine nova vindemia non sint ista vasa necessaria, si vero mercator est, qui emere vina et vendere solet, is dies spectandus est, quo ex commodo venditoris tolli possunt: Dig. 18. 6. 1. 3 & 4: ib. 2.

[1] If such contracts are really sales at all on Roman principles: see p. 29 supr.

[2] Dig. 18. 1. 34. 6: Pothier, 312.

Nor, except in one case, is there any deviation from the general rule where the property which the vendor has sold was not his to sell. If it is destroyed without any fault on his part before delivery to the purchaser, the loss falls on the latter, and he must nevertheless pay the purchase money. For if the article had been in fact delivered, and then had been destroyed before the rightful owner proved his title to it, it is well established that he would have had to pay it[1], and the vendor's rights are not prejudiced by a postponement in delivery for which he is not to blame. But where he has fraudulently represented the property to be his own, this rule does not apply[2]. *and in sales of res alienae.*

Vendor's obligation to assign rights of action where the goods are at the purchaser's risk. If, while the goods are at the purchaser's risk, they are lost, destroyed, or damaged by the acts of third persons for which the vendor cannot be in any way held answerable, the latter is bound to assist the purchaser to the best of his ability in recovering them if lost, or in obtaining damages in cases of destruction or injury, and therefore to assign to him all rights of action, whether *in rem* or *in personam*, which may be vested in him and by which any of those objects is attainable[3]. If he cannot bring such actions through not having been owner of the goods, and had not informed the purchaser of this fact, he must indemnify the latter as fully as if he had been evicted by legal process[4] though if they are confiscated by the State before delivery he is bound only to return the purchase money[5].

Supposing the vendor sells the same article to two persons in succession, and it is accidentally destroyed before delivery to either, the loss falls on the second purchaser, and he must pay the purchase money, because

---

[1] Dig. 21. 2. 21. pr. & 1 : Cod. 8. 45. 3 & 26.
[2] Dig. 21. 2. 21. pr. : 19. 1. 30. 1.
[3] Inst. iii. 23. 3 : Dig. 18. 6. 14 : 19. 1. 31. pr.
[4] Dig. 18. 1. 35. 4.   [5] Dig. 19. 2. 33.

the vendor cannot assert any rights against a first purchaser after selling to a second, whether the second sale was fraudulent as against the first, or was made in good faith[1]. But if the sale to the second purchaser is fraudulent as against him, the loss will fall on the vendor[2].

Exceptions to the rule as to risk. The general rule which throws the risk on the purchaser from the moment that the contract is 'perfect' may be overridden by express agreement to the effect that it shall remain with the vendor up till the moment of delivery[3]: and it has no application where the loss, destruction, or depreciation of the goods might have been avoided if the vendor had taken due care of them[4], or where the vendor makes delay in delivery, and the damage or loss results from such delay[5].

Theories as to its rationale. The reason why the civil law made such a departure from fundamental principles[6] in casting the risk, as a general rule, on the purchaser from the moment that the contract was concluded, has been much debated. According to one view[7], the basis of the rule was Equity. If the vendor is bound to show the greatest possible care in the charge of the property from the moment that the contract is binding, so that he is answerable for any loss, damage or deterioration which the exercise of such care could have prevented, it is only reasonable that if it is lost, destroyed, or damaged before delivery without his fault, he should nevertheless be entitled to the purchase money. Pothier's[8]

---

[1] So Windscheid, Lehrbuch, § 390, note 17. Vangerow, iii. p. 439, thinks he may demand the purchase money from either at his option, but not from both.

[2] Arg. Dig. 21. 2. 21. pr.: 19. 1. 30. 1.

[3] Dig. 18. 1. 35. 4: 18. 6. 1. pr.

[4] Inst. iii. 23. 3: Dig. 18. 6. 12: 19. 1. 36.

[5] Cod. 4. 48. 4 & 6.

[6] Usually expressed in the maxims, damnum sentit dominus: res perit domino.

[7] Glück, Pandekten, 17. p. 132 sq.   [8] Pothier, 307.

explanation is the consensual character of the contract: the purchaser promises to pay the price in exchange, not for the vendor's conveyance, but for his promise to convey, and if the vendor is disabled from performing that promise by causes beyond his control, there is no reason why the purchaser also should be released from a duty whose performance remains perfectly possible. Others[1] regard the rule as a survival of the time when the contract of sale is believed by them to have been Real, not Consensual, or base it on a fiction that the property has actually been delivered[2], which looks very like giving the rule as a reason for itself. Probably Windscheid[3] is correct in attributing it to the alienatory character of the contract: so far as the parties are concerned, the goods even before delivery are deemed to have ceased to be the vendor's, and to have become the purchaser's, for (as between the parties) a man is regarded in law as already having that for which he can bring an action: id 'apud se' quis 'habere' videtur, de quo habet actionem: habetur enim quod peti potest[4].

[1] E.g. Pernice, Labeo, i. p. 457 sq.
[2] Mommsen, Beiträge zum Obligationenrecht, i. p. 349.
[3] Lehrbuch, §§ 321, 390.
[4] Dig. 50. 16. 143. The English law as to the question at whose risk the goods are is in substance much the same as the Civil Law, but the principle is different. In respect of sales, as of other matters, we follow the maxim 'res perit domino,' and whether the goods are at the risk of the purchaser depends on whether (quite apart from delivery) the property in them has passed to him—a point which will be dealt with in connection with the next chapter. In *Simmons* v. *Swift* (5 B. & C. 862) Bayley J. said 'generally, where a bargain is made for the purchase of goods, and nothing is said about payment or delivery, *the property passes immediately*, so as to cast upon the purchaser all future risk, if nothing remains to be done to the goods.' For examples of buyer's risk see *Rugg* v. *Minet*, 11 East, 210 : *Sweeting* v. *Turner*, L. R. 7 Q. B. 310: of seller's, *Simmons* v. *Swift*, cit. : *Head* v. *Tattersall*, L. R. 7 Ex. 14: *Elphick* v. *Barnes*, 5 C. P. D. 326. But in the sale of a specific chattel conditionally, the property and the risk remain with the vendor till the condition is satisfied, unless the purchaser either expressly or by implication assumes the risk from an

Meaning of commodum rei:

It remains to consider more precisely what is meant by the term 'commodum' when it is said, for instance,

> post perfectam emptionem omne commodum ac incommodum, quod rei venditae contingit, ad emptorem pertinet[1].

The purchaser's rights in respect of 'commodum rei venditae' may be dealt with under the heads of fruits and accessions.

the purchaser is entitled to fruits and accessions from the moment the contract is concluded.

He is entitled to all the fruits of the property which he has purchased. Fruits which have acquired an independent existence by separation before the perfection of the contract are the property of the vendor[2]: fruits not yet separated, such as unborn lambs or calves, or standing crops, or hanging grapes, belong, whether ripe or unripe, to the purchaser[3], so that if he is disabled from gathering them through the vendor's delay in making delivery he is entitled to damages[4]. The right to what are termed 'fructus

earlier moment, as in *Martineau* v. *Kitching*, L. R. 7 Q. B. 436: and where delivery has been delayed through the default of either buyer or seller the goods are at the risk of the party making default as regards such loss as would not have occurred but for such default: *Martineau* v. *Kitching*, cit. at p. 456: Chalmers, Sale of Goods, p. 35.

Scotch law on the subject is practically in all respects the same as that of Rome. 'That the risk of the thing is with the buyer does not, as in England, proceed on the ground that the property is transferred: but the engagement of the seller being to deliver the thing sold, and the right of the buyer being *ad rem specificam*, the engagement is discharged, and the right extinguished, by the thing perishing without fault . . . . But the risk is continued on the seller, where there is undue delay in making delivery without fault on the buyer's part, where there is an express or implied undertaking of the risk by the seller, as to deliver at a certain place, or where anything remains to be done in completing, ascertaining, or identifying the thing to be delivered': Bell's Principles of the Law of Scotland, §§ 87, 88.

[1] Cod. 4. 48. 1 : Inst. iii. 23. 3, cited p. 77 supr.
[2] Cod. 4. 49. 2. 2.
[3] Cod. 4. 49. 13, ib. 16 : Dig. 19. 1. 13. 10.
[4] Arg. Dig. 19. 1. 21. 3.

civiles'—money paid for the use of a thing corporeal or incorporeal, moveable or immoveable—is not so simple a matter. If at the time at which the contract was made the property was under lease or hire to a third person, it would seem that a distinction must be drawn, according as the thing is one which can be used always and at any time, such as a house, a slave, or a carriage, or one which produces its fruits from which the rent is paid at regular intervals, such as a vineyard or land otherwise under cultivation. In the first case apparently the hire money will belong to the vendor before, and to the purchaser after, the perfection of the contract[1]. In the second case the authorities strongly support the view that the rent belongs to the vendor throughout the currency of the lease[2], though the reason given for this by the commentators[3], viz. that the purchaser can break the lease, obviously applies to the one case no less than to the other. Others[4] hold that if the contract was perfected after the gathering of the fruits, the rent belongs to the vendor, but that all rent accruing thereafter in the future belongs to the purchaser. It seems to be assumed by these writers that in the passage cited Ulpian is speaking only of rent actually due[5], and that in no case could rent subsequently accruing belong to the vendor: but there would be no injustice in this if the purchase money were reduced in consideration of the land being subject to a lease, upon which the purchaser would naturally insist if he was aware of the facts; while if he was not, and was kept

[1] Arg. Dig. 19. 1. 13. 13 : cf. 7. 1. 26.
[2] Si in locatis ager fuit, pensiones utique ei cedent qui locaverat . . . nisi si quid nominatim convenisse proponatur: Dig. 19. 1. 13. 11.
[3] E. g. Cujacius, Obss. xxv. c. 31.
[4] E. g. Glück, Pandekten, 17. p. 196.
[5] Denn das Pachtgeld ist als ein Surrogat der natürlichen Früchte zu betrachten, Glück, l. c.

in the dark by the vendor, the latter would be liable to him in damages[1]. It may be the case that Ulpian was not considering to whom the rent will really belong, but who can sue for it; and though no doubt no one but the lessor-vendor can do this, still it is quite possible that he may be bound to hand it over, or to assign his rights to be paid or to sue for it if unpaid, to the purchaser[2].

The purchaser is also entitled to all accessions which may accrue to the property which he has bought from and after the moment at which the contract is perfect so as to throw the risk on him. Among these are included all benefit of increased value, all additions of soil by alluvion to land[3], children born of female slaves, and all property acquired through slaves of either sex[4], such as the inheritance of anyone who has died since the making of the contract, and who has appointed the slave his heir[5]. Whether treasure which has been found on land before it has been conveyed to the purchaser, but after the perfection of the contract, belongs to him or to the vendor is a much-disputed question. Some authorities hold that it would go to the vendor, as being still owner of the property, relying upon the enactment of Hadrian, which was confirmed by Justinian[6], and by which it was provided that treasure should belong to the owner of the land, if found by him, and should be divided between him and the finder if accidentally found by anyone else. But after the conclusion of the contract the vendor is owner only in relation to third parties, and consequently it would seem more correct to say that even if the vendor found the treasure himself

---

[1] P. 59 supr.

[2] The words 'nisi si quid nominatim convenisse proponatur' are, however, very much against this hypothesis.

[3] Dig. 18. 6. 7.
[4] Dig. 22. 1. 4. 1.
[5] Dig. 19. 1. 13. 18.
[6] Inst. ii. 1. 39.

he was entitled only to half as finder, and to none as owner[1].

[1] In English law the commodum, like the periculum, is with the party who has the property in the goods. 'Any calamity befalling the goods after the sale is completed must be borne by the purchaser, and, by parity of reasoning, any benefit to them is his benefit, and not that of the vendor': per Blackburn J. in *Sweeting* v. *Turner*, L. R. 7 Q. B. at p. 313.

CHAPTER IX.

THE EFFECTS OF THE CONTRACT.

(b) Duties of the Parties. The Vendor.

Performance by each party is a concurrent condition of performance by the other. Duty of the vendor to deliver. What constitutes delivery. Time and place of performance by the vendor. The possession delivered must be 'vacua.' Vendor under no obligation to give a title as owner: strictness of this rule, and theories as to its rationale. Effect of discovery that land is subject to servitudes or charges undisclosed by the vendor. Vendor's obligation to take due care of the goods pending delivery. Delay in delivery. No property passes by the contract. Vendor's implied covenant of quiet enjoyment. History of the obligation to compensate the purchaser on eviction. Meaning of 'eviction.' Modes in which it may take place. The flaw in the purchaser's title must have existed when the contract was made. Eviction must not be attributable to purchaser's own fault. Eviction by a third person proving rights less than ownership. Necessity of the purchaser's notifying the vendor that the title is called in question: exceptions to this rule. Variation by contract of the vendor's liability for eviction: stipulatio duplae: pactum de evictione non praestanda. Measure of the vendor's liability. Purchaser's right to retain the purchase money when the title is disputed. Partial eviction. Summary of cases in which there is no right to compensation on eviction. Subsidiary remedies of the purchaser. Note A: Scotch, English, and French Law as to the effect of the contract in passing the property. Note B: Scotch and English Law as to implied warranty of title on a sale of goods.

Performance by each party is a concurrent condition of performance by the other.

IN the absence of agreement to the contrary (exemplified in the common case of a sale on credit), each of the parties is bound to perform his side of the contract immediately it is concluded: performance by one is not conditional on performance by the other [1]. At the same time, as it would

[1] The rule is the same in the laws of England, Scotland, and France. For England: 'unless otherwise agreed, delivery of the goods and payment of the price are concurrent conditions, that is to say, the seller must be ready and willing to give possession of the goods to the buyer

be unreasonable to compel either to execute before the other, if either is sued for non-performance before he has received the consideration, he can defend himself by the exceptio doli (in this case called by the moderns exceptio non adimpleti contractus) whereby he is enabled to refuse performance on his side [1] unless the plaintiff can show by replication that he has either performed, or has been ready and willing to perform throughout [2], or has been disabled from performance by impossibility arising from causes entirely beyond his control. In brief, neither party can succeed in an action against the other for non-performance unless he has either performed himself, or has been willing to perform on receiving performance from the other party.

The duties of the vendor may be what the parties may please to agree, so long as they are not at variance with

in exchange for the price, and the buyer must be ready and willing to pay the price in exchange for possession of the goods: Chalmers, Sale of Goods, p. 46: Benjamin, p. 580, sqq.: *Morton* v. *Lamb*, 7 T. R., 125: *Rawson* v. *Johnson*, 1 East, 201: *Wilks* v. *Atkinson*, 1 Marshall, 412. For Scotland, 'When the bargain is simple and without special stipulation, the buyer's obligation is to pay immediately, and the seller is entitled to demand and have action for payment on offering delivery of the thing, or proving the delivery made, or on showing that the thing has perished by accident. The delivery must be immediately on the buyer performing all the conditions stipulated:' Bell's Principles of the Law of Scotland, §§ 100, 115. For the French Law see Demante, Cours analytique de Code Civil, vii. p. 70.

[1] Si argentarius pretium rei, quae in auctione venierit, persequatur, obicitur ei exceptio, ut ita demum emptor damnetur, si ei res, quam emerit, tradita esset, quae est iusta exceptio: Gaius, iv. 126: qui pendentem vindemiam emit, si uvam legere prohibeatur a venditore, adversus eum petentem pretium exceptione uti poterit: si ea pecunia, qua de agitur, non pro ea re petitur, quae venit, neque tradita est: Dig. 19. 1. 25.: cf. Dig. 44. 4. 5. 4: Cod. 8. 44. 8.

[2] Offerri pretium ab emptore debet, quum ex empto agitur, et ideo, si partem pretii offerat, nondum est ex empto actio (i.e. he cannot sue with effect): venditor enim quasi pignus retinere potest eam rem, quam vendidit: Dig. 19. 1. 13. 8.

the fundamental and unalterable principles of the contract[1]: but here we shall deal more particularly with those liabilities which it imposes on him of its very nature, and without the necessity of express stipulation:

> et imprimis sciendum est in hoc iudicio id demum deduci, quod praestari convenit: cum enim sit bonae fidei iudicium, nihil magis bonae fidei congruit quam id praestari quod inter contrahentes actum est: quod si nihil convenit, tunc ea praestabuntur quae naturaliter insunt huius indicii potestate [2].

Duty of the vendor to deliver. The first of these duties is to deliver the goods to the purchaser: imprimis ipsam rem praestare venditorem oportet, id est, tradere [3]. With it he must deliver all its belongings and appurtenances [4], even though no mention

---

[1] E.g. Dig. 12. 4. 16.   [2] Dig. 19. 1. 11. 1.

[3] Dig. 19. 1. 11. 2. Le vendeur a deux obligations principales, celle de délivrer et celle de garantir la chose qu'il vend : Code Civil, Art. 1603.

[4] La chose doit être délivrée en l'état où elle se trouve au moment de la vente. Depuis ce jour, tous les fruits appartiennent à l'acquéreur. L'obligation de délivrer la chose comprend ses accessoires et tout ce qui a été destiné à son usage perpétuel : Code Civil, Arts. 1614, 1615: cf. Pothier, 47 : 'l'obligation de livrer une chose renferme aussi celle de livrer toutes les choses qui en font partie, ou en sont des accessoires.' The appurtenances which pass on a sale are denoted by the term *causa*: alienatio cum fit, cum sua causa dominium ad alium transferimus, quae esset futura si apud nos ea res mansisset, idque toto iure civili ita se habet, praeterquam si aliquid nominatim sit constitutum : Dig. 18. 1. 67. They include (1) all the natural appendages of the property bought, such as standing crops (Dig. 19. 1. 13. 10), shrubs, trees, underwood, hedges, and alluvial deposits. (2) Things which though they can be separated from the property without injury or change of nature are clearly designed to further its proper use and enjoyment, and (in short) to belong to it; e.g. the metallic fastening of tiles on a roof (Dig. 50. 16. 242. 2), bolts and keys (Dig. 19. 1. 17. pr.), manure, vine stakes, &c., intended for use on the land sold (ib. 2), water pipes (ib. 8), the buckets and windlasses of wells (Dig. 18. 1. 40. 6), &c. (3) Servitudes appendant to land or houses (Dig. 18. 1. 47-49). Whether the 'instrumentum' of a landed estate, i.e. the stock, implements, vehicles, and other things used in its cultivation (Dig. 33. 7. 8. pr.)

THE VENDOR'S DUTIES. 99

may have been made of them in the contract, except so far as they have been expressly reserved by the vendor[1]. He is bound to put the purchaser in actual possession of the property, and he is deemed to do so by giving him the means of immediately appropriating it[2], as in the well-known instance of delivering to him the keys of a warehouse in which it is secured[3]; and where the articles are of great bulk they are deemed to be delivered by the vendor's allowing the purchaser to put his mark upon them[4]. The obligation of delivery is an obligation to deliver so as to

What constitutes delivery.

pass with it on a sale has been disputed, but the better opinion seems to be in the negative. On the whole subject reference may be made to Wächter, Pandekten, § 65, appendix 2 : Dig. 18. 1. 29-31 : ib. 40. 5 & 6 : ib. 47-49 : ib. 51 : ib. 67 : ib. 76 : Dig. 19. 1. 13 (10. 11. 13. 16. 18) : ib. 14-17. 5 : ib. 17. 7-10 : ib. 18 : ib. 38. 2 : ib. 52. 3 : ib. 53.

[1] Among such things not uncommonly reserved are standing crops (Dig. 18. 1. 80. pr.): minerals (Dig. 19. 1. 17. 6): quarries (Dig. 18. 1. 77): the right of dwelling in a house (Dig. 19. 1. 13. 30: ib. 21. 6: ib. 53. 2), and the right of interring dead bodies in a burial ground (Dig. 19. 1. 53. 1).

[2] Le vendeur satisfait pleinement à son obligation de livrer la chose, lorsqu'il a fait ce qui dépendoit de lui de sa part, pour que l'acheteur pût, quand il voudroit, enlever la chose : l'enlèvement est l'affaire de l'acheteur : Pothier, 46. La délivrance est le transport de la chose vendue en la puissance et possession de l'acheteur. L'obligation de délivrer les immeubles est remplie de la part du vendeur lorsqu'il a remis les clefs s'il s'agit d'un bâtiment, ou lorsqu'il a remis les titres de propriété. La délivrance des effets mobiliers s'opère ou par la tradition réelle, ou par la remise des clefs des bâtiments qui les contiennent, ou même par le seul consentement des parties, si le transport ne peut pas s'en faire au moment de la vente, ou si l'acheteur les avait déjà en son pouvoir à un autre titre : Code Civil, Arts. 1604-1609. Under English law the seller's duty to deliver the goods is satisfied by his affording to the buyer reasonable facilities for taking possession of them at the place where they are at the time the contract of sale is made, or, in the case of goods to be manufactured, at the place of manufacture : Chalmers, Sale of Goods, p. 47 : *Wood* v. *Tassell*, 6 Q. B. 234 : Benjamin, p. 683 sq.

[3] Dig. 18. 1. 74: Pothier, 45.

[4] Videri autem trabes traditas, quas emptor signasset : Dig. 18. 6. 14. 1. It is otherwise with articles as small as wine casks or jars, Dig. ib. 1. 2.

H 2

enable the purchaser to have and hold the property as his own in perpetuity, so that, if he is deprived of it by some one who has a better title than the vendor, the latter is bound[1] to indemnify him—a liability which will be considered in detail in a later part of this chapter. Moreover, although he may have the possession, the purchaser may not be able to derive from the property all the advantages which an owner would, and, if this is so, he is entitled to compensation from the vendor: thus, if he buys a slave whom the latter had no right to sell, and whom he had himself intended to manumit, he can recover damages for the loss of rights of patronatus[2]; or if a woman gives a slave, whom she had bought from a vendor who had no right to sell him, to the real owner by way of dowry, she can sue the vendor because she becomes dowryless[3].

Time and place of performance by the vendor. The rule that, in the absence of agreement to the contrary, the time of performance is the time at which the contract is made[4], is of course subject to the necessary exception, that where the goods bought are not yet ready for delivery, as where one employs a goldsmith to make one a ring, or where the vendor still has something to do to them, the vendor is entitled to such time as is reasonably required for the work which has to be done[5]. If a place has been agreed upon for performance, it should take place there: the purchaser is not obliged to accept it, nor the vendor to make it, anywhere else[6]. Otherwise, as is obvious in the case of land, the proper place of performance is the place where the property is at the time when the contract is concluded[7], and nowhere else[8]: and if the vendor is sued

---

[1] Quae res, si quidem dominus non fuit venditor, tantum evictionis nomine venditorem obligat: Dig. 19. 1. 11. 2.
[2] Dig. 19. 1. 43: ib. 45. 2.   [3] Dig. 21. 2. 24.
[4] Dig. 50. 17. 14.
[5] Dig. 50. 17. 186: Inst. iii. 15. 5: ib. 19. 27: Pothier, 49.
[6] Pothier, 51.   [7] Pothier, 52: Benjamin, p. 684.
[8] Dig. 19. 1. 3. 4.

at some other place for non-delivery, this is taken into account in fixing the damages [1].

The possession delivered must be undisturbed (vacua): not only in the sense that there must be no third person who alleges a contrary right to the immediate possession, but in the sense also that the purchaser must be able to establish his own possessory title to it as superior to that of all other persons: *The possession delivered must be 'vacua.'*

> vacua possessio emptori tradita non intelligitur, si alius in ea legatorum fideive commissorum servandorum causa est, aut creditores bona possideant. idem dicendum est, si venter in possessione est: nam et ad hoc pertinet vacui appellatio [2].
>
> idem Neratius ait, venditorem in re tradenda debere praestare emptori, ut in lite de possessione potior sit, sed Julianus libro xv Digestorum probat nec videri traditum, si superior in possessione emptor futurus non sit. erit igitur ex empto actio, nisi hoc praestetur [3].

Consequently, if the goods are in mortgage or pawn, the vendor must redeem them:

> praedium aestimatum, in dotem a patre filiae suae nomine datum, obligatum creditori deprehenditur: quaesitum est an filius, qui hereditatem patris retinet, cum ab ea se filia abstinuisset dote contenta, actione ex empto teneatur, ut a creditore lueret, et marito liberum praestaret? respondit, teneri [4].

If the vendor is disabled from delivering the goods through no fault of his own, as where he is violently dispossessed by a third person, he is bound to assign to the purchaser

---

[1] Dig. 13. 4. 2. pr.
[2] Dig. 19. 1. 2. 1.   [3] Dig. 19. 1. 11. 13.
[4] Dig. 19. 1. 52. 1. Here an estate is conveyed to a husband by way of dos, appraised at a certain value, and therefore he is deemed a purchaser: aestimatio enim pro venditione est, Dig. 23. 3. 10. 4 & 5, so that he can require his father-in-law's heir to redeem it on its being found to be mortgaged: cf. Cod. 8. 44. 5: Pothier, 42.

his rights of action against the wrongdoer, so as to enable him to recover the possession for himself by legal process[1]. Delivery of incorporeal things being impossible, its place is taken, in the case of servitudes, by a special and independent covenant entered into by the vendor that he would do nothing to hinder the purchaser in the exercise and enjoyment of them[2], and in the case of other rights or choses in action by a simple assignment coupled with delivery of the documents, if any, by which they are proved[3].

Vendor under no obligation to give a title as owner:

Being bound to give only undisturbed possession of the property, the vendor is under no obligation to give a title as owner: the purchaser cannot refuse to take the goods on discovering that they are not his, nor can he sue him, or claim to rescind the contract, merely because the property has not become his, though, as has been observed, he can do so if he is rightfully deprived of possession by some other person having a superior title:

> qui vendidit, necesse non habet fundum emptoris facere, ut cogitur qui fundum stipulanti spopondit[4]:

and a purchaser to whom the goods had been delivered had no remedy against his vendor on discovering that he had no right to sell them until the true owner had proved his title:

> qui rem emit et possidet, quamdiu evicta non est, auctorem suum propterea, quod aliena vel obligata res dicatur, convenire non potest[5].

---

[1] Dig. 19. 1. 31. pr.   [2] Dig. 19. 1. 3. 2.
[3] Pothier, 316.
[4] Dig. 18. 1. 25. 2: cf. Dig. 19. 1. 11. 2: ib. 30. 1: 19. 4. 1. pr.: Cod. 8. 44. 3. C'est pourquoi, si quelqu'un m'a vendu de bonne foi un héritage qui ne lui appartient pas, dont il m'a mis en possession : quoique je vienne à découvrir par la suite qu'il n'en étoit pas le propriétaire, néanmoins je n'ai aucune action contre lui, tant que je ne suis troublé par personne : Pothier, 48.
[5] Cod. 8. 44. 3.

THE VENDOR'S DUTIES. 103

No doubt the intention of the parties almost invariably is that the property shall pass [1], and delivery of possession will ipso facto pass it if the vendor as a fact is owner [2], or has authority to sell: indeed, if there were an agreement that property should not vest in the purchaser at all, the contract could not be sale [3]. So strong, however, is the rule that the vendor's obligation is to give undisturbed possession only, that, according to Celsus, if one party gave money as the consideration for the vesting of ownership in him by the other, the agreement was to be deemed not sale, but exchange [4]. *strictness of this rule,*

To English lawyers this rule of the Roman system seems so anomalous that an explanation of it is demanded: but to continental exponents of the Civil Law, or of modern systems based upon the Civil Law into which it has been adopted, it would seem to so commend itself as natural and reasonable that its rationale is seldom if ever enquired into. In its mature form it is probably a rule resting on the convenience of commerce, though in origin it is more likely to have been connected with the uncertainties of title which are inevitable under a highly complex and formal method of transfer or alienation. It is beyond the scope of a work like the present to discuss the source of the vendor's liability in duplum if he sold a thing by mancipation to which he had no title, and which was recovered from the buyer by the rightful owner: but that there was such a liability under the Twelve Tables is *and theories as to its rationale.*

---

[1] See Dig. 18. 1. 20. Si l'on consulte, en effet, l'intention probable des parties, dont il faut toujours tenir compte pour apprécier une convention, on peut dire que, presque toujours, l'acheteur prétend acquérir une créance de propriété, et que le vendeur sait qu'il s'oblige à transférer une propriété : Demante, Cours analytique de Code Civil, vii. p. 2.

[2] Dig. 19. 1. 11. 2.   [3] Dig. 18. 1. 80. 3.

[4] Dig. 12. 4. 16. Paulus hardly seems to agree on this point: he says (in Dig. 19. 5. 5. 1) et si quidem pecuniam dem ut rem accipiam, emptio et venditio est : but he probably does not mean 'ut alter rem meam faciat.'

beyond all question[1]. Too little is known of the gradual substitution in actual practice of simple delivery for mancipation to enable one to say more than that any reason there was for establishing such a liability in mancipatory sales was tenfold greater if the goods were merely delivered. It is doubtful whether one could always pass the property in res nec mancipi by simple delivery, even though they were one's own: it is certain that one could not do so if the thing happened to be 'mancipi.' If the law held a sale to be void, or even voidable, simply because the vendor did not give a good title as owner to the buyer, it is clear that many transactions would not be entered into at all, because the vendor had a reasonable doubt as to his title, and that still more would be avoided because the vendor subsequently discovered that he had not become owner of the goods by their delivery. By the rule which the Romans actually followed commerce was no doubt helped forward and facilitated. In effect, the law said that the object of a purchase was to vest the enjoyment and use of the goods in the purchaser, and that therefore until he was disturbed by some one having a better title he could do nothing to the vendor: it protected him against all substantial loss or injustice, while at the same time it prevented litigation, and removed the obstacles which the opposite rule must have placed in the way of free and ready trading[2].

[1] Cic. pro Mur. 2. 3: Paul., sent. rec. 2. 17. 3: Voigt, Zwölf Tafeln, § 87: Muirhead, Roman Law, pp. 280. 281.

[2] 'Est ist das offenbar eine Begünstigung des Waarenumlaufs in Handel und Wandel,' Kuntze, Cursus des römischen Rechts, § 682. A somewhat different explanation is given by Unterholzner (Schuldverhältnisse, ii. p. 294, § 481), who holds that the distinction drawn between the vendor, who is not bound to give a good title to the goods, and the purchaser, who is bound to do so in respect of the purchase money, is 'natural': for the money can properly be used only by being paid away, and if the vendor learns that the money did not belong to the purchaser, and therefore is not his either, he dare not make any use of it in that way, for it would be theft (Inst. ii. 6. 3). But the purchaser is not in this predicament: what he wants is to keep

Whether the vendor of land is liable to the purchaser if it be found to be subject to praedial servitudes of which no information was given by the former is not quite clear. There can of course be no doubt of his liability if he has expressly represented the land as 'optimus maximus'—free from such burdens [1]—or if he knew of the existence of the servitude and dishonestly concealed his knowledge from the purchaser with a view to getting a better price [2]. But where there has been nothing in the nature of a representation or warranty, and nothing which amounts to fraud, two views are possible on the authorities. According to one the vendor is under no liability whatever; according to the other, he must pay damages equivalent to the sum by which the purchase money would have been abated had the existence of the servitude been known to the purchaser when he entered into the contract. Of these the first finds most support in the Roman texts. Celsus says [3] that unless there is a warranty on a sale of land, 'non liberum, sed qualis esset, fundum praestari oportere,' and this is confirmed by Venuleius [4] and by less unmistakeable passages from Pomponius [5] and Neratius [6]. In respect of personal servitudes the rule was different, for they involved a dis-

Effect of discovery that land is subject to servitudes or charges undisclosed by the vendor.

and use the goods rather than to dispose of them to some one else, and if he originally acquired possession in good faith, his right to use them is beyond all doubt, so that until he is evicted by some one with a superior title he is as well off as though he had been made owner.

Dr. Hunter (Roman Law, 2nd ed. p. 369) finds the reason of the rule in a desire to open the door to transactions by peregrini, 'who could not give a good title to the ownership.' But this suggestion raises historical questions touching the rights of aliens at Rome upon which it is impossible to enter here, and the simplest answer to it would seem to be that at any rate the alien could own the goods as completely as he could own the money with which he paid for them, and the purchaser was bound—whether citizen or alien—to make the money the vendor's property.

[1] Dig. 18. 1. 59: 21. 2. 75: 50. 16. 90 & 169.
[2] Dig. 19. 1. 1. 1: 21. 2. 69. 5.   [3] Dig. 18. 1. 59.
[4] Dig. 21. 2. 75.   [5] Dig. 18. 1. 66. pr.   [6] Dig. 21. 2. 48.

turbance of the possession, which could not be said to be 'vacua' if the property were subject to a usus or usus fructus[1]. Nor is the vendor bound to inform the purchaser of servitudes appurtenant to the land, so that if they are subsequently lost by non-exercise, owing to the purchaser's ignorance of his rights, he is free from liability, unless his silence amounts to fraud. Similarly, he is under no obligation to state the taxes or other charges on land of the same kind which are matters of ordinary knowledge[2], though he will be answerable if he sold it as free from them, or understated their amount[3]: but of extraordinary charges information should be given[4]: if he was aware of them, he must compensate the purchaser in full for all damages which his silence may have entailed upon him; if not, he must allow a proportionate abatement of the purchase money. A term in the contract that the vendor should be liable for all taxes charged on the property sold was void[5]. Where the subject matter of the sale is land, it is also the vendor's duty to point out its boundaries to the purchaser, unless they have been already defined in writing, or by the instrument of sale[6], and to deliver up to him such documents as receipts for land tax, without which he might be made liable for charges already satisfied[7].

Vendor's obligation to take due care of the goods pending delivery.
As it is part of the vendor's duty to deliver the property in the state and condition in which it was at the time when the sale was concluded, the rule is that he is liable in damages for any injury or deterioration which it may suffer thereafter, except so far as it is attributable to accident, to human action beyond his control, or to changes

---

[1] Dig. 18. 1. 66. pr. The passage upon which the opposite view is based are Dig. 45. 1. 38. 3: 8. 4. 6. 3: 21. 1. 61: 21. 2. 15. 1. For an examination of them see Vangerow, § 610, note 3: cf. Windscheid, Lehrbuch, § 391, note 28.

[2] See Pothier, 194-199.   [3] Cod. 4. 49. 9.
[4] Dig. 19. 1. 21. 1: ib. 41.   [5] Cod. 4. 47. 1-3.
[6] Dig. 18. 1. 63. 1: 19. 1. 48.   [7] Dig. 19. 1. 52. pr.

incident to its very nature : for these in general he has to answer only if he has been guilty of wrongful delay in making delivery [1]. Similarly, if he disables himself, either wilfully or by his own negligence, from performing his contract or any term in it, he is liable in damages [2]. He is, in short, responsible [3] for all loss, destruction, damage, or deterioration, which might have been prevented had he taken precautions which would have suggested themselves under the circumstances to a circumspect man of business, used to dealing with goods or property of the kind in question (diligentia boni patris familias [4]). It will perhaps suffice to give one concrete case in illustration. The vendor of a house, which is threatened with damage owing to the unsafe condition of an adjoining tenement, is bound to require from its owner a covenant for indemnification in the event of the anticipated damage actually occurring (cautio damni infecti [5]), because the purchaser cannot demand such security for himself before the house has been delivered to him. On the other hand, if the goods sold, being specific and ascertained, perish either in whole or part without the vendor's fault before delivery, he is pro tanto excused from performance [6]. If, however, the purchaser wrongfully delays acceptance of the goods, the

---

[1] Dig. 18. 6. 4. pr. : Cod. 4. 48. 4.
[2] Dig. 18. 1. 68. 2 : 19. 1. 13. 16.   [3] Pothier, 53.
[4] Dig. 18. 1. 35. 4 : 18. 6. 2. 1 : ib. 3 : 19. 1. 31. pr.: ib. 36 : ib. 54. pr.
[5] Dig. 19. 1. 36.
[6] In English law, when the property has passed, the buyer must pay the price according to the terms agreed on, even if the goods are destroyed in the vendor's possession. The goods are at the buyer's risk : the vendor simply holds them as bailee for him in such a case, Benjamin, p. 716 : and so it is said by Chalmers, Sale of Goods, p. 35, that though the goods are at the risk of whichever of the parties has the property in them, this will not affect the duties or liabilities of either seller or buyer as a bailee of the goods of the other party ; the cases referred to are *Head v. Tattersall*, L. R. 7, Ex. 7 : *Elphick v. Barnes*, 5 C. P. D. 321.

vendor is no longer bound to exhibit any high degree of care in the charge of them; he becomes answerable only for wilful misconduct and gross negligence [1]. Where the property is stolen while under his charge, the presumption is that he could have made it secure from theft by taking such precautions as his duty of diligence imposes on him, though he may rebut this by showing that he took all the care of it that the law could require [2]: if it is taken from him by force or robbery, the presumption is the other way [3], though it is open to the purchaser to prove that by his negligence he contributed to the result, which might have been avoided if he had taken proper precautions. Where he is not to blame, his duty is satisfied by his assigning to the purchaser any actions which he may have against other persons by whose act the property has been taken away, destroyed, or damaged [4].

[1] Dig. 18. 6. 15. pr.: ib. 18. Pothier says (55) 'par exemple, depuis que le marchand à qui j'ai vendu mon vin est en demeure de l'enlever: quoique le vin soit sur ses risques, et que je ne sois plus obligé de veiller à sa conservation, néanmoins si l'on vient m'avertir qu'il est en danger imminent de se perdre, et qu'étant sur le lieu, et ayant la facilité d'y faire apporter remède, je néglige de le faire : c'est de ma part une négligence crasse, une négligence affectée qui tient de la malice, qui me doit rendre responsable de la perte.' In English law, 'When the seller is ready and willing to deliver the goods, and requests the buyer to take delivery, and the buyer does not within a reasonable time after such request take delivery of the goods, he is liable to the seller for any loss occasioned by his neglect or refusal to take delivery, and also for a reasonable charge for the care and custody of the goods:' Chalmers, Sale of Goods, p. 55 : *Greaves* v. *Ashlin*, 3 Camp. 425 : cf. *Bloxam* v. *Sanders*, 4 B. & C. 941.

[2] Dig. 47. 2. 14. pr.   [3] Dig. 19. 1. 31. pr.

[4] Utique tamen vindicationem rei et condictionem exhibere debebit emptori, quia sane qui nondum rem emptori tradidit, adhuc ipse dominus est. idem est etiam de furti et de damni iniuriae actione: Inst. iii. 23. 3 : cf. p. 89 supr.

The authorities say generally (e.g. Dig. 18. 6. 2. 1) that the vendor is answerable for custodia *plena* between the conclusion of the contract and delivery. It is true that in Inst. iii. 23. 3. Justinian speaks as if the obligation of custodia would be incurred only by an express pro-

Delay in delivery by the vendor entitles the purchaser to such damages as he can show he has thereby sustained [1], either on account of depreciated value, or in the form of profit on a resale [2], or of any kind of use, benefit or enjoyment of which he may have been deprived [3]: and such damages may even sometimes exceed the amount of the purchase money [4]. Indirect and more problematical profits, however, such as gains which the purchaser might reasonably have calculated on making in other ways if he had had the money to be derived from a resale, and more remote damages, which are not the natural and ordinary consequence of the vendor's default, are not considered [5]. No damages of course are recoverable for delay in delivery if the purchaser cannot show that it has entailed any loss on him, though if he has paid the purchase money he is entitled to interest on it from the time at which delivery ought to have been made [6].

It is hardly necessary to say that the vendor is bound

Delay in delivery.

mise to that effect made by the vendor, and was not an ordinary incident of the contract : but it is plain that what he is considering is whether in any case the periculum rei remains with the vendor— whether, in other words, he would in any case have to suffer for pure accident. Treitschke (Kaufcontract, p. 305, note 1) holds correctly that in this passage custodia means periculum, but he is clearly wrong in supposing that the remark must be confined to the case of a runaway slave : Justinian expressly says, 'idem et in caeteris animalibus caeterisque rebus intelligimus.'

[1] Pothier, 58.   [2] Dig. 19. 1. 3. 3.
[3] Dig. 19. 1. 1. 1 : Cod. 4. 49. 4. 10 & 12.
[4] Dig. 19. 1. 1. pr. E.g. the goods may have risen over 100 per cent. in value, and then gone back to their original price before the purchaser can get hold of them.
[5] Cum per venditorem steterit, quominus rem tradat, omnis utilitas emptoris in aestimationem venit, quae modo circa ipsam rem consistit : neque enim si potuit ex vino puta negotiari et lucrum facere, id aestimandum est, non magis quam si triticum emerit et ob eam rem, quod non sit traditum, familia eius fame laboraverit : nam pretium tritici non servorum fame necatorum consequitur : Dig. 19. 1. 21. 3.
[6] Dig. 19. 1. 47.

to deliver the property sold according to its description as given by himself. It must be as large as he described it to be [1], and it must possess the qualities and accessions with which he undertook to sell it. This obligation of making his representations good, which has already been touched upon in a previous chapter, may indeed be regarded as a branch of the general liability to answer for nonperformance of his contract, whether it be due to wilful breach or to negligence: for he either knew that the goods were not of such a kind, or did not possess such appurtenances, as he represented, or in describing them as he did he must have been guilty of a carelessness for which the law holds him responsible [2].

No property passes by the contract.

At the risk of repetition it is well to point out that even where the vendor is owner of the goods, or otherwise has authority to dispose of them, property in them passes to the purchaser only by delivery, and not in virtue of the contract: traditionibus et usucapionibus dominia rerum, non nudis pactis transferuntur [3].

Vendor's implied covenant of quiet enjoyment.

We have still to consider a duty of the vendor which is treated at considerable length in the authorities [4], and which, as a complement of the rule that he is not bound

---

[1] Code Civil, Arts. 1616-1624: Pothier, 250-258.

[2] Applications: a statement that land is of a certain acreage, Dig. 19. 1. 2. pr.: that there are certain servitudes appurtenant to it, ib. 6. 6: that it is free from servitudes, ib. 8. 1: that a slave shall have his peculium, ib. 23: that the rent due from the tenant of land sold shall belong to the purchaser, 18. 1. 68. pr.: accessions promised, 19. 1. 11. 17, such as a specific number of casks in a vineyard, ib. 26 & 27: ib. 54. 1.

[3] Cod. 2. 3. 20. Le contrat de vente ne peut pas produire par lui-même cet effet : les contrats ne peuvent que former les engagements personnels entre les contractans: ce n'est que la tradition qui se fait en conséquence du contrat, qui peut transférer la propriété de la chose qui a fait l'objet du contrat: Pothier, 318. For the Scotch, English, and French law relating to the transfer of the property see note A at the end of this chapter.

[4] Dig. 21. 2 : Cod. 8. 45 : de evictionibus.

to give a title as owner, is of great practical importance. It has been pointed out more than once that the vendor is bound to guarantee the purchaser undisturbed possession [1], and that if the property is recovered from the latter by some third person on the strength of a superior title the vendor must fully indemnify him. In such a case the purchaser is said to be 'evicted,' and the vendor's duty is said to be to guarantee him against eviction [2]; as an English lawyer would say, he is under an implied covenant for quiet enjoyment. It is a duty which we find in other cases, besides that of sale: as a rule, in fact, it is an ordinary incident of every transaction whereby one creates or transfers legal rights for valuable consideration, such as marriage settlements, compromises, exchanges [3], partition of inheritances [4] and of other property held in common [5].

As an incident of the contract of sale, the obligation to compensate on eviction originated in the Ædilician Edict (itself, in this matter, based upon a still older rule relating to sales by mancipation [6]). By the provisions of this edict, the vendor was compellable in many cases [7] to enter, on the purchaser's demand, into a stipulation, that is a distinct

History of the obligation to compensate the purchaser on eviction.

---

[1] He is bound 'praestare emptori rem habere licere:' Dig. 21. 2. 8: 19. 1. 30. 1. So too we have the expression 'evictionem praestare,' Dig. 19. 1. 10. &c.

[2] Quoique lors de la vente il n'ait été faite aucune stipulation sur la garantie, le vendeur est obligé de droit à garantir l'acquéreur de l'éviction qu'il souffre dans la totalité ou partie de l'objet vendu, ou des charges prétendues sur cet objet, et non déclarées lors de la vente : Code Civil, Art. 1626. L'obligation de garantie se décompose en trois obligations : 1º s'abstenir de tout acte qui tendrait à évincer l'acheteur: 2º protéger l'acheteur contre les tentatives d'éviction, le défendre dans les procès qui peuvent lui être intentés, *prendre son fait et cause*: 3º si l'on n'a pas réussi à protéger l'acheteur, l'indemniser de la perte qu'il a faite : Demante, Cours analytique de Code Civil, vii. p. 83.

[3] Dig. 19. 4. 1. 1 : Cod. 4. 64. 1.   [4] Cod. 3. 36. 14.

[5] For the subject generally, and not in relation to sale only, see Glück, Pandekten, 20. § 1117.

[6] Paul. sent. rec. 2. 17. 3.   [7] Dig. 21. 2. 37.

and independent contract, to that effect, the obligation undertaken being usually to return double the purchase money if the purchaser had to surrender the property to a third person on the ground of superior title (stipulatio duplae [1]); and if the vendor refused to undertake the guarantee it would be implied [2]. Eventually it became a fundamental principle that, in the absence of express stipulation, he was bound by the nature of the contract to indemnify the purchaser in full if he were thus deprived of the possession [3].

> si in venditione dictum non sit, quantum venditorem pro evictione praestare oporteat, nihil venditor praestabit praeter simplam evictionis nomine, et ex natura ex empto actionis hoc quod interest [4].

Meaning of 'eviction.' The conditions of the vendor's liability require to be somewhat more precisely determined. There must have been an eviction: that is to say, as a general rule, some third person must have proved, by fair legal process, that he has a better right than the purchaser to the possession of the property sold: until he has been evicted, the latter cannot turn upon the vendor [5]. If, however, a man sells to an innocent and unwitting purchaser property from which

---

[1] Dig. 21. 2. 37. pr. & 1 : ib. 56. pr.

[2] Si dupla non promitteretur, et eo nomine agetur, dupli condemnandus est reus : Dig. 21. 2. 2.

[3] For the history of this development see Bechmann, Kauf, I. §§ 93-97 : Muirhead, Roman Law, pp. 282-286.

[4] Dig 21. 2. 60 : cf. Cod. 8. 44. 6 ; ib. 25.

[5] Qui rem emit, et post possidet, quamdiu evicta non est, auctorem suum propterea, quod aliena vel obligata res dicatur, convenire non potest : Cod. 8. 44. 3. By an enactment of the Emperor Zeno a person who claimed to be owner of or to have a hypothec over property sold or otherwise transferred by the Treasury was to have no rights against the purchaser or alienee, but was entitled to sue the Treasury for damages within four years of the transaction : Inst. ii. 6. 14 : Cod. 7. 37. 2. The rule was extended by Justinian to alienations by or on behalf of the Emperor or Empress.

he knows he is liable to be evicted, the purchaser is not bound, on discovering the fraud, to wait until the rightful owner has actually proved his title, but can sue at once for such damages as the eviction will entail upon him [1]. Nor is it necessary that the purchaser should have been put in possession: for he may have resold the property before delivery to him, and the vendor may by his instructions have delivered it to the subvendee, who is evicted [2], and wherever his own alienee can sue him for eviction, he can sue his own vendor [3].

The mode in which the eviction takes place is immaterial. In the majority of cases, no doubt the third person who claims title to the property will be plaintiff against the purchaser in possession, and will recover judgment against the latter, whereby he will have to surrender possession or pay damages as the price of retaining it [4]: but there is equally an eviction when a third person is in possession, who is sued for it by the purchaser, and whose superior title, as defendant and possessor, is proved in the action:

modes in which it may take place.

---

[1] Dig. 19. 1. 30. 1.   [2] Dig. 21. 2. 61.
[3] Dig. 21. 2. 39. 1 : ib. 61 : ib. 22. 1. Il n'importe que ce soit à l'acheteur lui-même, à qui la chose vendue soit évincée, ou à son successeur en la dite chose, pour que l'acheteur ait l'action de garantie. C'est pourquoi si je vous ai vendu un héritage, que vous l'ayez revendu à Pierre, et que Pierre en soit évincé : vous aurez action de garantie contre moi, comme si c'étoit vous-même qui en fussiez évincé : car je vous l'ai vendu pour vous et tous *vos ayant cause* ; je me suis engagé de vous en faire jouir, vous et tous vos ayant cause : et vous avez intérêt que je défende Pierre de cette éviction, dont vous êtes vous-même tenu de le garantir : Pothier, 97. For the measure of damages in such a case see Pothier, 146-148.

[4] It is possible that the vendor himself might be plaintiff, and then the purchaser will be able to defeat his action by pleading the facts in the form of an exceptio. For instance, after selling a res aliena the vendor may become its owner by inheritance or otherwise, and then sue his own purchaser to recover it : quem de evictione tenet actio, eundem agentem repellit exceptio : Pothier, 165. Similarly if after becoming its owner he sells it to a third party, who sues the purchaser in possession : the latter can set up the same plea : ib. 166.

I

duplae stipulatio committi dicitur tunc, cum res restituta est petitori, vel damnatus est litis aestimatione, vel possessor ab emptore conventus absolutus est[1].

In order, however, to ground the purchaser's claim for damages, it is further necessary that if he has been successfully sued he shall have delivered the property up, or otherwise satisfied the judgment, for until then he is not really deprived of the advantages which the vendor is bound by the contract to guarantee to him[2]. There is again an eviction if the true owner obtains possession without legal proceedings, so that he cannot be compelled to surrender the property again: as where a woman buys land in good faith and gives it to her husband by way of dowry, and then he is discovered to have in fact been its rightful owner throughout[3]. Similarly, if after purchasing a res aliena unawares a man acquires a title to it, either for valuable consideration, or by gift, legacy, or inheritance, although he could not sue the vendor under a stipulatio duplae, the action on which, being stricti iuris, would not lie except where there had been an actual eviction, he can bring an action ex empto to recover the purchase money[4]: and if before actual eviction and before having

---

[1] Dig 21. 2. 16. 1.   [2] Dig. 21. 2. 57. pr.: Pothier, 88.
[3] Dig. 21. 2. 24.
[4] Si alienum fundum mihi vendideris, et hic ex causa lucrativa meus factus sit, nihilominus ex empto mihi adversus te actio competit: Dig. 19. 1. 13. 15: cf. 21. 2. 9: ib. 41. 1. En voici la raison. Lorsqu'après avoir acheté de vous une chose qui ne vous appartenoit pas, ou qui ne vous appartenoit pas pour toujours, je succède à quelque titre que ce soit à celui à qui elle appartient, c'est en vertu de ce nouveau titre que je retiens désormais cette chose: ce n'est plus en vertu de la vente que vous m'en avez faite: vous cessez donc dès-lors de remplir envers moi votre obligation, non jam praestas mihi rem habere licere: et par conséquent vous me devez rendre le prix que vous avez reçu: Pothier, 96. L'acheteur devient héritier du vrai propriétaire, il conserve par conséquent la chose sans craindre d'être troublé à l'avenir. Mais ce n'est pas la vente qui lui fait cette situation. Elle résulte uniquement

paid the purchase money he enters into an arrangement with the true owner in order to retain possession, whereby the latter agrees to waive or abandon his action, the vendor cannot demand payment, for although there has been no technical eviction, because the purchaser retains possession, yet he has it in virtue not of his contract with the vendor, but of the second contract with the rightful owner [1].

The result of the investigation then, so far as we have proceeded, is that there must have been an actual eviction [2], and that that eviction, in order to ground an actio evictionis proper as distinct from an actio ex empto for recovery of purchase money, must have resulted from a fair and *bona fide* trial at law, or from some equivalent to which the purchaser could have been compelled [3]. Two other principles require to be stated. Firstly, it is essential that the flaw in the purchaser's title shall have existed at the time when the contract was made: in other words, the vendor will not be answerable for defects of title which arise subsequently, except for those which are due to his own act [4]. The necessity of this last qualification is obvious: otherwise the vendor might hypothecate the property to

The flaw in the purchaser's title must have existed when the contract was made.

de ce qu'il a acquis les droits de celui qui pouvait l'évincer: Demante, Cours analytique de Code Civil, vii. p. 82.

[1] Dig. 21. 2. 29. pr.

[2] Hence the purchaser has no remedy if through no fault of the vendor the property perishes before eviction: Dig. 21. 2. 21. pr. & 1: Cod. 8. 44. 26: but the vendor will be liable to an action for fraud if he knowingly sold the property as his own: Dig. 21. pr. cit.

[3] Therefore there is no remedy where the purchaser is not evicted by process of law, but is violently dispossessed by a third person (Cod. 4. 49. 17) or has the property taken from him by the State (Dig. 21. 2. 11. pr.). So too if the judgment against him is erroneous, owing to either the judge's dishonesty or incompetence (Dig. 21. 2. 51. pr.: Pothier, 94), for here the presumption is that he could have got it set aside by resorting to an appeal.

[4] Les évictions dont la cause n'a commencé d'exister que depuis le contrat, donnent lieu à la garantie lorsque cette cause procède du fait du vendeur: autrement elles n'y donnent pas lieu: Pothier, 90.

a third person after the sale, but before delivery, to the purchaser, without being liable to the latter on his being evicted by the hypothecary creditor. Secondly, there can be no claim against the vendor if the eviction is in any way attributable to the purchaser's own fault or negligence. It might be so attributable in a variety of ways. The purchaser might fail to defend[1] or to properly defend[2] the action brought against him by the adverse claimant, or to appeal from a judgment which there was good reason to believe might be reversed[3]. He might lose the possession by consenting to refer the question of title to a private arbitration instead of to a properly constituted court: for he was not bound to go to an arbitrator[4]. Similarly, if he voluntarily parted with the possession, and on being compelled to sue for its recovery failed to prove his title in the *rôle* of plaintiff, when if he had retained it he could not have been deprived of it by action brought against him[5]: or if in defiance of his vendor's instructions he brought the wrong action for recovery of the property[6]: or if he allowed an interruption in his usucapion, by which the rightful owner's title might have been extinguished[7], or suffered another to complete a usucapion commenced before the sale of the property to him[8]; or if he preferred to rely on some other title than that of his vendor[9], or failed in his action to recover it by reason of a plea in defence personal to himself, and which could not have been set up against his vendor[10].

---

[1] Dig. 21. 2. 56. 1. It seems clear however from Dig. 19. 1. 11. 12. that if the adverse claimant's title was indisputable the purchaser's resistance to it was not a necessary condition of his claim to indemnification: cf. Pothier, 95.
[2] Dig. 21. 2. 55. pr.
[3] Dig. 21. 2. 63. 1 & 2.
[4] Dig. 21. 2. 56. 1.
[5] Dig. 21. 2. 29. 1.
[6] Dig. 21. 2. 66. pr.
[7] Dig. 21. 2. 56. 4.
[8] Pothier, 93.
[9] Dig. 21. 2. 76.
[10] Dig. 21. 2. 27 & 28.

For the sake of simplicity it has hitherto been assumed that the vendor's liability arises only when a third person proves the property to be his, and deprives the purchaser of the possession on the ground of his dominion. But the law is the same when any similar right over the property, of whatever kind, is proved by such third person. The vendor guarantees by implication not only that the property is his to sell, but also that no one else has any adverse right by which the purchaser can be deprived of the possession, whether such right be a right of possession[1] merely, or a personal servitude[2], or mortgage[3], or a right to partition of property jointly owned[4], to in integrum restitutio[5], or to bring a noxal action[6]. But the proof by a third person of a servitude over the property which does not deprive the purchaser of the possession, such as a right of way or of ancient lights, is not sufficient to found a claim for eviction[7].

Eviction by a third person proving rights less than ownership.

A second condition of the vendor's liability, in addition to the actual eviction, is that he shall have received notice from the purchaser of the action in which he is involved (litis denuntiatio). If the latter embarked upon the litigation and allowed the case to be decided adversely to himself without giving such notice, he lost all remedy against the vendor:

The purchaser must notify the vendor that the title is called in question:

> si cum posset emptor auctori denuntiare, non denuntiasset, idemque victus fuisset, quoniam parum instructus esset,

---

[1] Dig. 19. 1. 11. 13.   [2] Dig. 18. 1. 66. pr.: 21. 2. 49: ib. 62. 2.
[3] Dig. 21. 2. 34. 2: ib. 35: ib. 63. 1.
[4] Dig. 21. 2. 34. 1.
[5] Dig. 21. 2. 39. pr.: ib. 66. 1.   [6] Dig. 19. 1. 11. 12.
[7] Si l'héritage vendu se trouve grevé, sans qu'il en ait été fait de déclaration, de servitudes non apparentes, et qu'elles soient de telle importance qu'il y ait lieu de présumer que l'acquéreur n'aurait pas acheté s'il en avait été instruit, il peut demander la résiliation du contrat, si mieux il n'aime se contenter d'une indemnité: Code Civil, Art. 1638. See p. 105 supr.: and Vangerow, Pandekten, § 610, note 3.

hoc ipso videtur dolo fecisse et ex stipulatu agere non potest[1].

emptor fundi, nisi auctori aut heredi eius denuntiaverit, evicto praedio, neque ex stipulatu, neque ex dupla, neque ex empto actionem contra venditorem vel fideiussorem eius habet[2].

The reason why such notice was a condition of the purchaser's remedy over is that he is not so likely as the vendor to know the past legal history of the property, or what defences may be set up against claims alleged in respect of it by third persons, so that it will be his own fault if he is deprived of the possession by defending such actions alone, when if he had known and relied upon a defence of which the vendor could have informed him they would probably have been decided the other way[3]. The object of the notice accordingly is to enable the vendor, if he wishes, to support or even to take upon himself the purchaser's case[4], and to protect himself against possible collusion between the latter and the adverse claimant: and

[1] Dig. 21. 2. 53. 1. In relation to this obligation to compensate the purchaser on eviction the vendor was called auctor (Dig. 50. 17. 175. 1 : 21. 2. 28 : ib. 51. pr.: ib. 64. 2) : any one who by contract made himself liable in the event of eviction, although not himself the alienor, was called auctor secundus (Dig. 21. 2. 4. pr.). The terminology is derived from mancipation, for if a purchaser was evicted from property which had been conveyed to him in this manner there was an actio auctoritatis to recover double the purchase money : Muirhead, Roman Law, p. 136 : Bechmann, Kauf, i, §§ 11-13. To call upon one's vendor to assist in defending one's title is called in the Corpus iuris 'auctorem laudare': Dig. 19. 1. 6. 5 : 21. 2. 63. 1 : Cod. 8. 44. 7 & 14.

[2] Cod. 8. 44. 8.

[3] La garantie pour cause d'éviction cesse lorsque l'acquéreur s'est laissé condamner par un jugement en dernier ressort, ou dont l'appel n'est plus recevable, sans appeler son vendeur, si celui-ci prouve qu'il existait des moyens suffisans pour faire rejeter la demande : Code Civil, Art. 1640.

[4] Interpellare venditorem, sive successorem eius debes, ut tibi assistant causamque instruant : Cod. 8. 44. 21. 1. The procedure closely resembles the vouching to warranty in a common recovery for the purpose of barring an entail before the Fines and Recoveries Act of 1833.

on this ground, saving some exceptions which will presently be stated, it is a necessary condition of the purchaser's remedy over in the event of the adverse claimant establishing his title [1]. The notice must be given to the immediate vendor, that is to say, to the person liable in law to the purchaser whose title is called in question [2]: but no notice need be given to his sureties [3], if he has any, because they are for the purchaser's security merely, and the reason of the doctrine of notice has no application to them. The purchaser whom it is sought to deprive of possession could not validly give notice to anyone except his own vendor, unless there had been an assignment to him of some

---

[1] Nam si denuntiasti ei qui tibi vendidit, intellegit evictionis periculum: Cod. 3. 19. 1. Pothier says (107) 'il y a à cet égard une différence entre le Droit Romain et notre pratique Françoise. Par le Droit Romain l'acheteur aussitôt qu'il étoit troublé, soit par une demande en révendication, soit par quelqu'autre demande, avoit seulement la faculté de dénoncer au vendeur cette action qui étoit intentée contre lui, pour que le vendeur prît sa défense sur cette action, s'il le jugeoit à propos : mais ce n'étoit qu'après la condamnation intervenue contre l'acheteur sur cette action, qu'il pouvoit intenter contre son vendeur l'action de garantie pour le faire condamner à l'indemniser de la condamnation, et c'étoit devant le Juge du domicile du vendeur que cette action devoit être intentée. Dans notre pratique Françoise on évite ce circuit : l'acheteur en même temps qu'il dénonce au vendeur l'action en révendication, ou autre par laquelle il est troublé en sa possession, et qu'il le somme de prendre son fait et cause sur cette action, et d'y défendre pour lui, peut aussi former en même temps son action en garantie contre son vendeur devant le Juge pardevant qui est pendante la demande originaire, quoiqu'il ne soit pas le Juge du domicile du vendeur, et conclure contre le vendeur, à ce que faute par lui de pouvoir le défendre, et dans le cas auquel le demandeur originaire obtiendroit à ses fins, le dit vendeur soit en même temps et par la même sentence condamné à l'indemniser.'

[2] So strict is this rule, that if a slave sells something out of his peculium, he, and not his master, must be notified : Dig. 21. 2. 39. 1. Notice to the vendor's agent suffices only if he himself is absent and it is given with his knowledge : Dig. ib. 56. 4. For sales by pupilli see ib. 56. 7.

[3] Cod. 8. 44. 7 : Pothier, 111.

intermediate person's remedy over, or unless the remoter auctor had given an hypothecary security against eviction[1]: and if the property had been sold by two or more persons as joint vendors, or if the vendor had died leaving two or more coheirs, notice must be given to all[2], and all were answerable in respect of their respective shares, although the obligation to defend the action after notice had been given was indivisible[3]. As to the time at or within which the notice must be given no precise rules are to be found. Pomponius[4] says that any time would suffice, provided that the vendor had a fair opportunity of defending the title and that the notice was not given 'prope ipsam condemnationem': and many authorities are of opinion that the vendor might be first notified on appeal, because evidence and arguments were allowed in the appellate court which had not been brought forward in the court below[5]. On the other hand Labeo[6] requires that the notice must be given 'ante iudicium acceptum,' that is to say, before the close of the preliminary proceedings (in Pomponius and his day before the Praetor) which ended with joinder of issue. The apparent contradiction between the two writers disappears if we remember that when they wrote the judge could listen to no pleas which were not inserted in the formula of the action, which was formally settled at the time of joinder of issue, so that notice given to the vendor 'post iudicium acceptum' would practically be given 'prope ipsam condemnationem.'

exceptions to this rule. The exceptional cases in which the purchaser could recover damages for eviction, notwithstanding his having given the vendor no notice that his title was disputed, are as follow:—

---

[1] Dig. 21. 2. 59.   [2] Dig. 21. 2. 62. 1.
[3] Dig. 45. 1. 85. 5: ib. 139. See Demante, Cours analytique de Code Civil vii. pp. 84 & 85.
[4] Dig. 21. 2. 29. 2.   [5] Cod. 7. 63. 4.   [6] Dig. 32. 29. 3.

(1) Where by a term in the contract the vendor has waived his right to such notice[1]. The purchaser is of course not disentitled by such waiver from requiring the vendor to defend his title, nor is the vendor himself disentitled from voluntarily undertaking it[2].

(2) Where it is through the vendor's fault that the notice is not given: for instance, if he is away, and the purchaser is unable to discover his whereabouts[3], or if he takes steps to prevent the notice reaching him[4].

(3) Where the vendor knowingly sells property which is not his own: for here he is liable in any case on account of his fraud[5].

(4) Where the title of the third party is so clear and indisputable that to call upon the vendor to dispute it would be quite useless: though the purchaser must be able to make out that no different result could have ensued had the vendor received the fullest and promptest notice[6].

If on receiving notice of the adverse claim the vendor professed himself willing to defend the title, he must be content to have the cause tried by the court before which it had been brought, and might not assert any privilege which would ordinarily have exempted him from its jurisdiction[7]. He was also bound to carry on the action in the stage in which it was when he was notified, whether he joined himself as a party with the purchaser, or took his place and acted as his attorney for the conduct of the defence[8], but he could not take his place absolutely without

---

[1] Dig. 21. 2. 63. pr.
[2] Cod. 8. 44. 20.
[3] Dig. 21. 2. 55. 1 : ib. 56. 6.
[4] Dig. 21. 2. 56. 5.
[5] Dig. 19. 1. 30. 1.
[6] Arg. Dig. 19. 1. 11. 12 : cf. 21. 2. 53. 1. Windscheid (Lehrbuch, § 391, note 12) denies the absolute necessity of notice as a condition of the purchaser's remedy over, mainly on the ground that there are cases in which the purchaser need not resist the third party's claim, p. 116, n. 1 supr.: but the weight of textual authority against him is almost overwhelming.
[7] Dig. 5. 1. 49. pr.
[8] Dig. 21. 2. 21. 2.

the other party's consent; if that were given the effect was a novation, and the purchaser was discharged as a party to the action whether he assented to it or not[1]. If judgment went against the vendor while representing the purchaser, he could not recover from the latter, his nominal principal, any damages which he might be ordered to pay in default of the property being delivered up to the successful claimant[2]. If, on the other hand, he paid no attention to the notice given him by the purchaser, or denied his obligation to assist him, his liability could be determined only by an action for damages after satisfaction of the judgment given in favour of the rightful owner.

Variation by contract of the vendor's liability for eviction:

Before proceeding to define more precisely the limits, under different circumstances, of the vendor's general liability in cases of eviction, it may be convenient to briefly consider how that abstract liability may be varied by contract between the parties.

stipulatio duplae:

It has been already stated that the purchaser was by law entitled to exact from the vendor a stipulatio duplae, double the market value, or dupli pretii, double the purchase money, to be paid to him if deprived of the possession by a third person having a better title to it than his own. This right might however be modified by evidence of local usage[3], and though the general law did not in any case require a promise of more than a double penalty[4], it might be made a term in the contract of sale itself[5] that the vendor should undertake a threefold or even fourfold liability if eviction actually took place.

The rights of the purchaser however must be taken with the qualification that even the stipulatio duplae could not be required in sales of articles of small value:

---

[1] Solutione vel iudicium pro nobis accipiendo et inviti et ignorantes liberari possumus: Dig. 46. 3. 23.
[2] Dig. 21. 2. 66. 2.   [3] Dig. 21. 2. 6.
[4] Dig. 21. 2. 37. pr.   [5] Dig. 21. 2. 56. pr.: ib. 37. pr.

quod autem diximus, duplam promitti oportere, sic erit accipiendum, ut non ex omni re id accipiamus, sed de his rebus, quae pretiosiores essent: si margarita forte, aut ornamenta pretiosa, vel vestis serica, vel quid aliud non contemptibile veneat [1].

It might, on the other hand, be made a term in the contract that the vendor should not be liable in case of eviction [2], and such a term was implied if the purchaser was aware at the time of the sale that the title to the property was disputed [3], and in certain cases of emptio spei [4]. If it were simply agreed that the vendor should be free from the ordinary liability (pactum de evictione non praestanda), Julian was of opinion that he was nevertheless bound to repay the purchase money if the purchaser was in fact evicted, because otherwise the equity which was of the essence of the contract would be offended against [5]: but this view was rejected by Ulpian [6], and is generally admitted to have been untenable [7]. If however the vendor

pactum de evictione non praestanda.

[1] Dig. 21. 2. 37. 1. Besides the articles mentioned in the passage cited, the res pretiosiores include land, slaves, and horses. In cases of doubt it would probably be for a Court to decide whether the value was sufficient to entitle the purchaser to the stipulation.

[2] L'obligation de garantie est bien de la nature du contrat de vente, elle y est toujours sous-entendue quoiqu'elle n'y soit point exprimée: mais quoiqu'elle soit de la nature de ce contrat, elle n'est pas de son essence: il peut y avoir un contrat de vente sans obligation de garantie, et elle peut par conséquent être exclue du contrat par une clause particulière: Pothier, 181.

[3] Cod. 8. 44. 27.

[4] Dig. 18. 1. 8. 1: Pothier, 186: Code Civil (cited inf.), Art. 1629: Demante, Cours analytique de Code Civil, vii. p. 89.

[5] Ibidem ait idem [Julianus] esse dicendum et si aperte in venditione comprehendatur nihil evictionis nomine praestatum iri, pretium quidem deberi re evicta, utilitatem non deberi: neque enim bonae fidei hac patitur conventione, ut emptor rem amitteret, et pretium venditor retineret: Dig. 19. 1. 11. 18.

[6] Sed in suprascriptis conventionibus contra erit dicendum, nisi forte sciens alienum vendit: Dig. loc. cit.

[7] See Glück, Pandekten, 20. p. 297. sqq.: Vangerow, Pandekten, §

knowingly sold property which was not his own, and attempted to protect himself by a pact of this kind, it was held not to bind the purchaser by reason of his fraud [1]; and consequently it is obvious that no such compact could discharge the vendor from liability for an eviction due to any act of his own, whether done before or after the making of the contract [2].

<small>Measure of the vendor's liability.</small>
In considering the precise extent of the vendor's liability, it will be best to consider first the general law by which it was determined in the absence of express stipulation.

He is bound to indemnify the purchaser for all loss which he may suffer through being deprived of the possession: and the measure of the damages in general is the market value of the property at the time of eviction:

> evicta re, ex empto actio non ad pretium duntaxat recipiendum, sed ad id, quod interest, competit [3].
>
> si in venditione dictum non sit, quantum venditorem pro evictione praestare oporteat, nihil venditor praestabit praeter simplum, evictionis nomine, et ex natura ex empto actionis hoc quod interest [4].

610, note 4: *contra* Pothier, 185: his view is adopted in the Code Civil, Art. 1629. cited inf.

[1] Dig. 19. 1. 6. 9: ib. 11. 18. ad fin.

[2] The provisions of the Code Civil on the subject, Arts. 1627-1629, are as follow: les parties peuvent même convenir que le vendeur ne sera soumis à aucune garantie. Quoiqu'il soit dit que le vendeur ne sera soumis à aucune garantie, il demeure cependant tenu de celle qui résulte d'un fait qui lui est personnel: toute convention contraire est nulle. Dans le même cas de stipulation de non-garantie, le vendeur, en cas d'éviction, est tenu à la restitution du prix, à moins que l'acquéreur n'ait connu, lors de la vente, le danger de l'éviction, ou qu'il n'ait acheté à ses périls et risques.

[3] Dig. 21. 2. 70.

[4] Dig. 21. 2. 60: cf. ib. 8: 19. 1. 43: Cod. 8. 44. 23. Lorsque la garantie a été promise, ou qu'il n'a rien été stipulé à ce sujet, si l'acquéreur est évincé, il a droit de demander contre le vendeur la restitution du prix, celle des fruits, lorsqu'il est obligé de les rendre au propriétaire qui l'évince, les frais faits sur la demande en garantie de l'acheteur, et ceux faits par le demandeur originaire: enfin les dom-

Thus if at the time of eviction the property was worth less than the sum which had been given for it, the actual value only, and not the whole of the purchase money, could be recovered [1]: if it was worth more, the vendor was liable in the enhanced value, because the purchaser could have got that for it if he had been able to retain possession [2]. Whether there was not some limit to the sum recoverable as damages in relation to the price actually paid is a matter of dispute. Let it be supposed that a man gives £5 for a copy *de luxe* of a particular book, and that owing to the accidental destruction of all the other copies it becomes worth £50 in the market, can he recover the whole of this from the vendor in the event of eviction? A passage of Paulus [3] would lead one to suppose that the enhanced value

mages et intérêts, ainsi que les frais et loyaux coûts du contrat : Code Civil, Art. 1630.

[1] Dig. 19. 1. 45. pr.: 21. 2. 70. This rule is disputed at great length by Pothier, 69, who in the face of the texts contends that the purchase money must certainly be restored entire, irrespective of loss of value in the property from which the purchaser is evicted, except so far as such loss of value has gone into the purchaser's pocket. He says : 'C'est pourquoi n'ayant contracté envers mon vendeur l'engagement de lui payer le prix, qu'autant qu'il ne manqueroit pas au sien, et mon vendeur y ayant manqué, par faute de me défendre de l'éviction que j'ai soufferte : l'obligation que j'avois contractée envers lui de lui payer le prix, de même que le droit qui résultoit à son profit de cette obligation, se résolvent : mon vendeur cesse dès-lors d'avoir aucun droit au prix que je me suis obligé de lui payer : d'où il suit qu'il ne peut en rien exiger, et que s'il a été payé, il n'en peut rien retenir, et que je le puis répéter en entier, *condictione sine causa*. D'ailleurs il est manifestement contre l'équité, que mon vendeur qui est en faute, en me vendant une chose qui ne lui appartient pas, et qui me trompe, profite de cela pour gagner sur moi une partie du prix.' His view is adopted in the Code Civil, Art. 1631 : lorsqu'à l'époque de l'éviction la chose vendue se trouve diminuée de valeur, ou considérablement détériorée, soit par la négligence de l'acheteur, soit par des accidens de force majeure, le vendeur n'en est pas moins tenu de restituer la totalité du prix.

[2] Pothier, 132.

[3] Plane si in tantum pretium excessisse proponas, ut non sit cogitatum a venditore de tanta summa, veluti si ponas agitatorem postea

was not wholly recoverable if it so far exceeded the purchase money that it could not be believed that the vendor had so great a liability present to his mind at the time of the sale, and Africanus[1] suggests the inference that the purchaser could in no case recover more than double the sum which he had paid for the property: an inference which is strengthened by a consideration of Justinian's own enactment as to the measure of damages[2]. On the other hand it is contended[3] that such passages as that of Africanus relate only to the stipulatio duplae, and that the suggested limitation can be accepted only in cases where the vendor sold the property for less than half its real value[4].

Where the value of the property has been in fact increased or even merely maintained by pecuniary outlay made upon it by the purchaser, such outlay must be reimbursed to him on eviction by the vendor, unless he is able to recover it, as will frequently be the case, on the ground of his bona fide possession from the rightful owner when the latter sues him[5]:

> illud expeditius videbatur, si mihi alienam arcam vendideris, et in eam ego aedificavero, atque ita eam dominus

factum vel pantomimum, evictum esse cum qui minimo veniit pretio, iniquum videtur, in magnam quantitatem obligari venditorem: Dig. 19. 1. 43.

[1] Dig. 19. 1. 44.

[2] Cum pro eo quod interest dubitationes antiquae in infinitum productae sunt, melius nobis visum est huiusmodi prolixitatem prout possibile est in angustum coartare, sancimus itaque in omnibus casibus, qui certam habent quantitatem vel naturam, veluti in venditionibus et locationibus et omnibus contractibus, hoc quod interest dupli quantitatem minime excedere: Cod. 7. 47. pr. & 1.

[3] E. g. Treitschke, Kaufcontract, p. 254, note 4.

[4] Pothier, 132. Si la chose vendue se trouve avoir augmenté de prix à l'époque de l'éviction, indépendamment même du fait de l'acquéreur, le vendeur est tenu de lui payer ce qu'elle vaut au-dessus du prix de la vente: Code Civil, Art. 1633.

[5] E. g. Inst. ii. 1. 30–32.

evincit: nam, quia possim petentem dominum, nisi impensam aedificiorum solvat, doli mali exceptione summovere, magis est ut ea res ad periculum venditoris non pertineat, quod et in servo dicendum est, si in servitutem, non in libertatem evinceretur, ut dominus mercedes et impensas praestare debeat. quod si emptor non possideat aedificium, vel servum, ex empto habebit actionem [1].

But where he is unable to recover from the true owner, for instance, through not having been in possession, or because the owner is insolvent, or because the outlay came under the head of impensae voluptariae, not those of impensae necessariae or utiles, or where a supposed slave whom he has bought has his freedom established by action —in all these and similar cases the purchaser can recover these damages from the vendor himself[2]: and the vendor is absolutely liable, whether the true owner is or not, if he sold the property knowing that he had no right to dispose of it[3].

If the increase in the value of the property is not due to the purchaser's outlay, but to the operation of natural causes (as in the favourite illustration of an addition of soil by alluvion) or is what is now called 'unearned increment,' the true owner is of course under no liability to the purchaser, who can recover from the vendor only[4]. The latter must also compensate him for any sums which he may have to pay the owner on account of fruits, and must pay interest on the purchase money from the date of the contract, unless (and except so far as) the purchaser has

---

[1] Dig. 19. 1. 45. 1: cf. Cod. 8. 44. 9 & 16: Pothier, 133.

[2] Pothier, 134, 135.

[3] Le vendeur est tenu de rembourser ou de faire rembourser à l'acquéreur, par celui qui l'évince, toutes les réparations et améliorations utiles qu'il aura faites au fonds. Si le vendeur avait vendu de mauvaise foi le fonds d'autrui, il sera obligé de rembourser à l'acquéreur toutes les dépenses, même voluptuaires ou d'agrément, que celui-ci aura faites au fonds: Code Civil, Arts. 1634, 1635: Pothier, 137.

[4] Dig. 21. 2. 16. pr.

derived an equivalent from fruits consumed, for which, as possessor in good faith, he would not be liable to the owner: he must compensate him for the loss of profits which, had he not been evicted, he would certainly have secured through and by means of the property[1], such as the inheritance of a deceased person to whom a slave, whom the vendor is found to have had no right to sell, has been made heir[2]; and he must pay all expenses and costs incurred by him in the action by which the question of title is determined[3]: but if he can procure the property from the third party after he has proved his title to it, and delivers it to the purchaser, he can relieve himself of all liability except that for the costs, and any other damage which the purchaser may have suffered through being temporarily deprived of the possession[4].

A purchaser who had bought two or more things simultaneously from the same vendor, from one or some only of which he was evicted, was entitled to recover damages precisely as if he had bought it or them alone, even though the residue from which he was not evicted had so much increased in value as to be worth as much as he had given for the whole:

> si duos servos quinis a te emam, et eorum alter evincatur, nihil dubii fore quin recte eo nomine ex empto acturus sim, quamvis alter decem dignus sit : nec referre, separatim singulos, an simul utrumque emerim[5].

Purchaser's right to retain the purchase money when the title is disputed. It need hardly be said that if the purchaser had not yet paid the purchase money at the time of the eviction, or even of receiving notice of the adverse claim, he might hold it as security for his own claim against the vendor[6]. Nor did he lose his rights against the latter if after eviction

---

[1] Pothier, 138.
[2] Dig. 21. 2. 51. 3.
[3] Cod. 8. 44. 17.
[4] Dig. 21. 2. 67 : 44. 4. 15.
[5] Dig. 21. 2. 47 : cf. ib. 72.
[6] Dig. 21. 2. 29. pr. : 18. 6. 19. 1 : Cod. 8. 44. 5 & 24.

the owner made him a present of the property, or if he succeeded to it as heir or legatee[1]. It has already been pointed out that if he acquired such new title before being evicted[2], he could not sue upon a stipulatio duplae, but could recover his purchase money by actio ex empto, an actual adverse judgment being an indispensable condition of the condictio on the penal stipulation[3].

The sum secured by such stipulation, whether twice, thrice, or four times the amount of the purchase money, could of course be recovered in case of actual eviction[4], without the necessity of taking into account any rise or fall in value which the property may have had since the contract was concluded[5]. If, however, the purchaser is not evicted from the whole of the property, but only from a portion of it, it is necessary to distinguish whether that portion is ideal (or undivided) or specific. It is ideal, for instance, when one of two joint-owners of an estate sells the whole of it, and then the other sues the purchaser to recover his undivided moiety. If, in this case, the property has diminished in value since the time at which it was sold, the vendor is liable under his stipulation only for the lower value[6]: if it has increased, he is liable only for the value as it was when the contract was made[7]: if part has

Partial eviction.

---

[1] Dig. 19. 1. 13. 15: 21. 2. 9: ib. 41. 1 & 2.
[2] Dig. 21. 2. 57. 1.   [3] P. 114 supr.: Pothier, 96.
[4] Except where the Treasury was the vendor: the Treasury being under no obligation ever to repay more than the purchase money actually received, even though its officials had expressly promised more: Dig. 49. 14. 5. pr.
[5] Dig. 21. 2. 64. pr.
[6] E. g. A sells B an estate of 1000 acres, four-fifths of which really belong to him, and the rest to C. After the conveyance, 200 acres are washed away by a flood, and then C claims and recovers his undivided fifth (e. g. 160 acres). A is liable for these 160 only: duplae stipulatio pro parte quinta, non quarta praestabitur: Dig. 21. 2. 64. pr.: Pothier, 154–157.
[7] Quod si modo terrae integro, qui fuerat traditus, ducenta iugera per alluvionem accesserunt, ac postea pro indiviso pars quinta totius

become more valuable and part less, the diminution in value is taken into account, while the increase is not[1]. The portion is specific, where it is ascertained by metes and bounds, or where the part claimed by the evicting owner is clearly distinguished by marks from the rest, so that its own precise market value is determinable: and here the vendor's liability on eviction is ascertained not by the ratio of size, but by reference to its actual quality and consequent value as at the time of the sale[2]:

> ceterum quum pro diviso pars aliqua fundi evincitur, tametsi certus numerus iugerum traditus sit, tamen non pro modo, sed pro bonitate regionis praestatur evictio[3].

It is otherwise, however, if the property was not bought in the aggregate for a lump sum, but so much was given for each portion of it separately: for here the compensation due to the purchaser depends on the price actually paid for the portion from which he is evicted[4]. Finally, it should be pointed out that where the purchaser sues on account of the eviction ex empto, under the general law,

evicta sit, perinde pars quinta praestabitur, ac si sola ducenta de illis mille iugeribus, quae tradita sunt, fuissent evicta, quia alluvionis periculum non praestat venditor: Dig. 21. 2. 64. 1 : Pothier, 158.

[1] Dig. 21. 2. 64. 2 : Pothier, 159, 160.
[2] Dig. 21. 2. 13 & 14: Pothier, 142, 143.
[3] Dig. 21. 2. 64. 3.
[4] Si fundo tradito pars evincatur, si singula iugera venierint certo pretio, tunc non pro bonitate, sed quanti singula venierint quae evicta fuerint praestandum, etiam si ea quae meliora fuerint evicta sint: Dig. 21. 2. 53. pr. This question of eviction from part of the property bought is thus regulated by the Code Civil, Arts. 1636, 1637 : Si l'acquéreur n'est évincé que d'une partie de la chose, et qu'elle soit de telle conséquence, relativement au tout, que l'acquéreur n'eût point acheté sans la partie dont il a été évincé, il peut faire résilier la vente. Si, dans le cas de l'éviction d'une partie du fonds vendu, la vente n'est pas résiliée, la valeur de la partie dont l'acquéreur se trouve évincé lui est remboursée suivant l'estimation à l'époque de l'éviction, et non proportionellement au prix total de la vente, soit que la chose vendue ait augmenté ou diminué de valeur.

THE VENDOR'S DUTIES.

and not upon an express stipulation, the damages are assessed on the principle of putting the plaintiff, so far as possible, in the position in which he would have been had the eviction not taken place, so that increase and decrease of value between the sale and the eviction are uniformly taken into consideration [1].

It may be convenient here to summarise the cases in which, contrary to the general rule, the purchaser is not entitled to compensation from the vendor on eviction, though some of them have been incidentally mentioned already. They are as follow:—(1) Where the action brought to determine the right to the possession is decided against the purchaser in consequence of his own fault or negligence, for instance, by his suing in the wrong form [2]. (2) If he is deprived of the possession by a decision of the court which is clearly wrong [3]: the onus of proving this is on the vendor, who cannot escape his ordinary liability if he omitted to appeal, having the opportunity of doing so [4]. (3) If the property perishes or is destroyed through no fault of the vendor before eviction, even though judgment be subsequently given against the purchaser [5]. (4) If the roperty is bought with knowledge that the vendor intends to use the purchase money for gambling purposes [6]. (5) Where the sale comes under the description of venditio spei [7]. (6) Where it has been provided by a term in the contract that the vendor shall not be liable: for the limits within which such a term will bind the purchaser it is sufficient to refer to what has been said already [8]. (7) If mortgaged property is sold by the mortgagee in order to satisfy the debt, and the purchaser is evicted, the latter has no remedy against his immediate vendor, because he sells

<small>Summary of cases in which there is no right to compensation on eviction.</small>

[1] Dig. 21. 2. 8 : ib. 15. 1 : Pothier, 139-141.
[2] Examples in Dig. 21. 2. 66. pr. : ib. 55. pr.: ib. 63. 2 : p. 116 supr.
[3] Dig. 21. 2. 51. pr. : Cod. 8. 44. 15.   [4] Dig. 21. 2. 63. 1.
[5] Dig. 21. 2. 21. pr.   [6] Dig. 44. 5. 2. 1.
[7] Dig. 18. 4. 10 & 11 : p. 123 supr.   [8] P. 123 supr.

as agent for the mortgagor: the same principle applies to all sales by agents if the relation of agency is disclosed. (8) If the purchaser had been informed by the vendor or otherwise was aware that he had no right to sell the property, or that other persons had rights over it which might entitle them to deprive him of the possession, the vendor was not liable [1]: for they were in pari delicto [2], and in any case it must be assumed that in fixing the amount of the purchase money the chance of being evicted was taken into consideration. If, however, though the property is not subject to the rights of third persons at the time of the sale, there is a possibility of such rights subsequently attaching, as e.g. where the vendor, being an heir, sells a thing which is bequeathed to another subject to the fulfilment of a suspensive condition, and this is known to the purchaser, he is entitled on eviction to recover his purchase money, but no more [3]: and if at the time of the sale the vendor informs him that the property is subject to a mortgage, but understates its amount, the difference can be recovered in the event of eviction [4]. (9) If the subject-matter of the sale is a universitas iuris, such as a peculium or an inheritance, the vendor, though liable to the vendor if he is evicted from the universitas, is not liable in respect of separate pieces of property which he has delivered in the erroneous belief that they were part and parcel of it [5]. If, however, some definite share or quota of the inheritance is recovered from the purchaser by a joint-heir, his right to damages is beyond question. On the sale of what is termed a universitas facti or rerum — an aggregate which has no existence apart from the corporeal units of which it is composed, such as a flock of sheep — the rule is different, the vendor being liable to an action ex empto for the

---

[1] Cod. 8. 44. 27 & 30.
[2] Dig. 12. 5. 3.
[3] Cod. 6. 43. 3. 4.
[4] Arg. Dig. 21. 2. 54. 1 : ib. 69. 3.
[5] Dig. 21. 2. 5 : Cod. 8. 44. 1.

eviction of any such unit which he delivers[1], though not to an action on a stipulatio duplae[2].

Although, as has been already observed, the purchaser is not entitled to sue the vendor for damages until all the conditions of eviction have been satisfied[3], he may avail himself of certain subsidiary means of protection, if it becomes certain that his title to quiet possession will be called in question, as, for instance, by the commencement of an action[4].

Subsidiary remedies of the purchaser.

Thus, if the property has been delivered to the purchaser, but he has not yet paid the purchase money when notice reaches him of the impending litigation, he may hold it back until the vendor gives him substantial sureties for payment of damages if eviction actually ensues[5]: and if sued for it by the vendor he can reply by the exceptio doli or imminentis evictionis. Nor is his right of retaining the whole of the purchase money affected by the fact that he is threatened with eviction from only a part of what he has bought, if it was a sale of the whole for a lump sum, per aversionem. If, on the other hand, the sale was of a number of things, or of a single thing capable of being regarded as consisting of a number of similar units (e.g. an estate of so many acres) at a price of so much for each[6], he may hold back the purchase money which is due in respect of that part only to which the adverse claim relates, unless he expressly bought the rest only in order to get that particular part, in which case he may retain the whole[7],

---

[1] Dig. 41. 3. 23. 1.

[2] For the subject of Implied Warranty of Title in the Law of England and that of Scotland, see note B at the end of this chapter.

[3] Cum res restituta est possessori, vel damnatus est [emptor] litis aestimatione, vel possessor ab emptore conventus absolutus est: Dig. 21. 2. 16. 1: venditori sufficit, ob evictionem se obligare, possessionem tradere, et purgari dolo malo: itaque, si evicta res non sit, nihil debet: Dig. 19. 4. 1. pr.: cf. Cod. 8. 44. 3.

[4] Cod. 8. 44. 24.   [5] Dig. 18. 6. 19. 1: Cod. 8. 44. 24.

[6] Dig. 21. 1. 34. pr. & 1.   [7] Dig. 21. 1. 34. 1.

because then the vendor is liable to have the whole contract avoided.

If, on the other hand, the property was discovered, before delivery, to be subject to a mortgage, the purchaser could compel the vendor to redeem it[1], though after delivery, provided there had been no fraud, he had no such right, and could do nothing until actually deprived of the possession by the mortgagee[2], except refuse to pay the purchase money until, as in the case last considered, the vendor gave him solid sureties: unless indeed he bought with knowledge of the mortgage, and there was a term in the contract that it should be redeemed by the vendor.

If the contract had been fully executed on both sides, the purchaser had no remedy pending eviction, except in the case, so often mentioned, of a man selling to an innocent purchaser property of which he knew that he had no right to dispose. Under these circumstances he might sue ex empto[3] before eviction, though not on a stipulatio duplae[4]: and it seems to be generally held that similarly, if a man fraudulently sold property which to his knowledge was mortgaged, and the mortgage was unknown to the purchaser, and the vendor had received the purchase money, he could be compelled to redeem it.

The vendor's implied warranty that the goods are free

---

[1] Cod. 8. 44. 5.

[2] Cod. 8. 44. 3. Dig. 19. 1. 52. 1. might seem to contradict this, but in that case there is nothing to show that the dotal estate had been delivered to the husband (cf. Dig. 23. 3. 14: 23. 5. 16), and even if it had it is possible that a sale made dotis causa was exceptionally treated.

[3] Si sciens alienam rem ignoranti mihi vendideris, etiam priusquam evincatur, utiliter me ex empto acturum putavit in id, quanti mea intersit meam esse factam : quamvis enim alioquin verum sit, venditorem hactenus teneri, ut rem emptori habere liceat, non etiam ut eius faciat, quia sciens alienam non suam ignoranti vendidit : Dig 19. 1. 30. 1.

[4] Dig. 19. 1. 4.

from undisclosed defects which the purchaser could not discover on inspection is reserved for a later chapter, in which we shall consider the circumstances under which either party might avoid the contract in whole or part.

NOTE A.

In respect of the transfer of property upon a sale, the common law of Scotland is in accordance with that of Rome. 'Sale, as a *contract*, is contradistinguished from sale as a *transference*. The contract of sale, when completed, is in the law of Scotland nothing more than the titulus transferendi dominii, with obligations on either part to pay the price and deliver the things sold. No property passes till delivery: nothing but the ius *ad rem specificam*': Bell, Principles of the Law of Scotland, § 86. But it is now provided by the Mercantile Law Amendment Act, Scotland, 1856 (19 & 20 Vic. c. 60) §§ 1 and 2, that when goods have been sold but not delivered, the seller's creditors cannot attach them (on this point cf. Pothier, 320) and a subvendee is entitled to demand the goods subject to satisfying the seller's lien for the price.

Scotch, English, and French Law as to the effect of the contract in passing the property.

The English law, under which, as is well known, the property often passes without delivery in virtue of the contract, may be briefly stated thus:

(i) An unconditional sale of a specific chattel, to which nothing further is to be done by the vendor, passes the property in it to the purchaser without delivery: 'Where there is a sale of goods generally, no property in them passes till delivery, because until then the very goods sold are not ascertained. But where by the contract itself the vendor appropriates to the vendee a specific chattel, and the latter thereby agrees to take that specific chattel and to pay the stipulated price, the parties are then in the same situation as they would be after a delivery of goods in pursuance of a general contract. The very appropriation of the chattel is equivalent to delivery by the vendor, and the assent of the vendee to take the specific chattel and to pay the price is equivalent to his accepting possession. The effect of the contract, therefore, is to vest the property in the bargainee': per Parke, B. in *Dixon* v. *Yates*, 5 A. & E. 313, 340: Chalmers, Sale of Goods, p. 28. But this rule will be overridden if it can be shown that the parties had a different intention: per Sir Cresswell Cresswell in *Gilmour* v. *Supple*, 11 Moo. P. C. 556: Blackburn on Sale, pp. 147, 167.

(ii) Where by the agreement the vendor is to do anything to the goods for the purpose of putting them into that state in which the purchaser is to be bound to accept them (or into a deliverable state), the performance of those things shall, in the absence of circumstances indicating a contrary intention, be taken to be a condition precedent to the vesting of the property, Blackburn on Sale, pp. 151, 152, and the property does not pass until they are done, Chalmers, Sale of Goods, p. 28: *Rugg* v. *Minet*, 11 East 210, and other cases cited by Benjamin, pp. 282-88.

(iii) Where anything remains to be done to the goods, for the purpose of ascertaining the price, as by weighing, measuring, or testing the goods, where the price is to depend upon the quantity or quality of the goods, the performance of these things also shall be a condition precedent to the transfer of the property, although the individual goods be ascertained, and they are in the state in which they ought to be accepted: Blackburn on Sale, loc. cit.: Chalmers, loc. cit.: *Furley* v. *Bates*. 33 L. J. Ex. 43: *Hanson* v. *Meyer*, 6 East 614: *Simmons* v. *Swift*, 5 B. & C. 857. The close parallelism between these rules, and those of the civil law for determining when the risk passes to the purchaser, will strike every reader.

(iv) Where there is a term in the contract that the buyer shall do anything as a condition of the passing of the property, the property will not pass till the condition be fulfilled, even though the goods may have been actually delivered into the buyer's possession: *Bishop* v. *Shillito*, 2 B. & Ald., 329: *Brandt* v. *Bowlby*, 2 B. & Ad. 932.

(v) Where there is a contract for the sale by description of unascertained goods, or of goods to be made or manufactured, and goods of that description and in a deliverable state are unconditionally appropriated to the contract, either by the seller with the assent of the buyer, or by the buyer with the assent of the seller, the property in the goods thereupon passes to the buyer: such assent may be express or implied, and may be given either before or after the appropriation is made: Chalmers, Sale of Goods, p. 29: Blackburn on Sale, p. 127: Benjamin, Bk. II, chap. 5. ('Of subsequent appropriation'): *Heilbutt* v. *Hickson*, L. R. 7 C. P. 449.

(vi) When goods are delivered for sale 'on approval' or 'on sale or return,' the property passes on the buyer's doing any act conclusively showing that he adopts the transaction (*Swain* v. *Shepherd*, 1 M & Rob. 223): and if he does not signify his approval or acceptance to the seller, but retains the goods without giving notice of rejection, then, if a time has been fixed for the return of the goods, on the expiration of such time, or if no time has been fixed, on the expiration of a reasonable time: Chalmers, Sale of Goods, p. 29: Benjamin, pp. 592, 593: *Moss* v. *Sweet*, 16 Q. B. 493.

(vii) Even where, according to the principles already stated, the property would have passed to the purchaser, the vendor may, by the terms of the contract or appropriation, reserve his right of disposal of

the goods until certain conditions are fulfilled : and where this is the
case, even though the goods are delivered to the purchaser, or to a
bailee for the purpose of transmission to him, the property does not
pass until such conditions are fulfilled : Chalmers, p. 33 : Benjamin,
Bk. II, chap. 6 ('Reservation of the ius disponendi,' particularly pp.
366-371) : see judgment of Cotton, L. J. in *Mirabita* v. *Imperial Ottoman Bank*, 3 Ex. D. C. A., at pp. 171, 172.

The origin of the English rule, under which the property usually
passes by the contract, is incidentally discussed in *Cochrane* v. *Moore*
(1890, 25 Q. B. D. 57), where Fry, L. J., delivering the judgment of
himself and Bowen, L. J., pointed out (p. 65) that in Bracton's time
'the law recognised seisin as the common incident of all property
in corporeal things, and tradition or the delivery of that seisin from
one man to another as essential to the transfer of the property in that
thing, whether it were land or a horse, and whether *by way of
sale* or gift, and whether by word of mouth or by deed under
seal . . . . It was in the reigns of the early Tudors that the action
on the case in indebitatus assumpsit obtained a firm foothold in
our law: and the effect of it seems to have been to give a greatly
increased importance to merely consensual contracts. It was probably a natural result of this that, in time, the question whether
and when property passed by the contract came to depend, in cases
where there was a valuable consideration, upon the mind and consent
of the parties, and that it was thus gradually established that in the
case of bargain and sale of personal chattels the property passed according to that mind and intention, and a new exception was thus
made to the necessity of delivery. This doctrine that property may
pass by contract before delivery appears to be comparatively modern.
It may, as has been suggested, owe its origin to a doctrine of the civil
law that the property was at the risk of the purchaser before it passed
from the vendor : but at any rate the point was thought open to argument as late as Elizabeth's reign (see Plowd., 11. 6., and a learned
Note 2 Man. & Ry., 566).'

The question of Transfer of Title in English Law has been briefly
examined on p. 27 supr.

The French Law originally agreed with that of Rome and Scotland :
but M. Viollet ('Précis de l'histoire du droit français,' p. 519) observes
that in the medieval law of France the Roman rule was undergoing transformation, the actual delivery being symbolical only, or being recited
in a deed ('clause de saisine'), or represented by the appearance of the
parties before a court. The next development was the 'clause de constitut ou de précaire,' by which the vendor made himself detainer merely
of an immovable in the purchaser's name, until the latter had actually
taken possession : and by many of the Coutumes it is declared that
land may in some cases pass to the purchaser 'par le consentement

du vendeur.' The jurists follow suit: Domat says that the 'clause de précaire' is implied in contracts of sale where it is not expressed, 'car la vente (écrit-il), transférant la propriété, elle renferme le consentement du vendeur que l'acheteur se mette en possession': and similarly Grotius and Pufendorf, writing 'au point de vue du droit naturel.' Pothier, 318, who is 'plus Romain,' states the rule in accordance with that of the Civil Law, p. 110. n. 3 supr. The way was thus paved for the enactment of the Code Civil, Art. 1583, which brings French law into accordance with that of England: 'la propriété est acquise de droit à l'acheteur à l'égard du vendeur dès qu'on est convenu de la chose et du prix, quoique la chose n'ait pas encore été livrée ni le prix payé.' This is merely an application to the specific case of sale of the rule laid down in Art. 1138: 'l'obligation de livrer la chose .... rend le créancier propriétaire .... encore que la tradition n'en ait point été faite': Demante, Cours analytique de Code Civil, V, pp. 72 sqq.

The writer is reminded by Judge Chalmers that similarly the 'acceptance of part of the goods' under § 17 of the English Statute of Frauds may be constructive only. 'There is an acceptance of goods within the meaning of this section when the buyer does any act in relation to the goods which recognises a pre-existing contract of sale, whether there be an acceptance in performance of the contract or not': (Chalmers, Sale of Goods, p. 8). Thus in *Page* v. *Morgan*, (1885: 15 Q. B. D. 288. C. A.,) the defendant, a miller, bought of the plaintiff by verbal contract eighty quarters of wheat. The sale was by sample. The wheat was shipped by the plaintiff's agent on a barge for carriage to the defendant's mill. Upon the arrival of the barge some of the sacks were, by the direction of the defendant's foreman, drawn up into the mill and examined by him. The foreman then sent for the defendant, who came to the mill and examined the contents of the sacks already delivered, and also of some others, which he caused to be drawn up out of the barge for examination. He then rejected the wheat as not equal to sample. On trial the jury found that the wheat was equal to sample, and that the defendant had accepted it within the meaning of § 17 of the Statute of Frauds. On the Court of Appeal hearing a motion for a new trial, which was refused, Brett, M. R. said 'I rely for the purposes of my judgment in the present case on the fact that the defendant examined the goods to see if they agreed with the sample. I do not see how it is possible to come to any other conclusion with regard to that fact, than that it was a dealing with the goods involving an admission that there was a contract.' See other cases reviewed by Benjamin, pp. 137 sqq. Among other acts, the doing of which by the buyer is to be deemed a recognition of the existence of the contract, are reselling (*Chaplin* v. *Rogers*, 1 East. 192) or offering to resell (*Blenkinsop* v. *Clayton*. 7 Taunt. 597) the goods or part of them: using them (*Beaumont* v. *Brengeri*, 5 C. B. 301), and dealing with the bill of lading by which they are represented (*Currie* v. *Anderson*, 29, L. J. Q. B., 87).

NOTE B.

Inasmuch as the Common Law of Scotland seems to agree with that of Rome in imposing on the vendor no absolute obligation to give a title as owner to the purchaser, it has also adopted in substance the law as to eviction. 'The secondary obligation of the seller (the primary one being to deliver the things sold, § 113) is to warrant against eviction. Eviction is the loss of a thing, in whole or in part, to the buyer, by the judicial establishment of a right in another preferable to the seller: or by such right being admitted by the seller; or by the emerging of an unquestionable burden on the subject purchased, which the buyer is compelled to discharge. The obligation of warrandice is implied or express. Where a full price is paid, or what the parties consider as such, the warrandice is absolute. It is an engagement that the buyer shall be protected against eviction on any ground existing antecedent to the sale. To entitle the buyer to redress there must be eviction: for it is only eviction that grounds an action of warrandice. The eviction must be *ex defectu iuris*, not *ex natura rei*, nor proceeding from accident or violence. And it must be a loss, strictly speaking, not subsequent to the sale, as by a supervenient law. Partial loss must be indemnified, and burdens removed. Warrandice from fact and deed is a more limited obligation, viz., protection against eviction by reason of the seller's own act or omission, past or future. Simple warrandice protects the buyer only against the future act and deed of the seller. Express warrandice is a special bargain altering the implied engagement. The buyer is entitled to redress on eviction, provided he shall have given notice of the challenge. And although he is not bound to defend himself before eviction, he is *entitled* to defend himself: and if he choose to do so, he will be held to undertake the risk of all omissions in his defence, with the expense of the contest. The buyer, on eviction, may claim the whole loss and damage, as at the time of eviction, deducting the intermediate profits drawn. But he is entitled only to such law expense as he may have bona fide laid out in defending himself, either with the assent of the seller, or without any offer on the seller's part to give instant indemnification, or to defend against eviction': Bell's Principles of the Law of Scotland, §§ 121—126. *Scotch and English Law as to implied warranty of title on a sale of goods.*

Whether the vendor of a specific ascertained chattel, who sells in good faith, is by the law of England taken by implication to warrant that it is his to sell is 'a question to which, until tolerably recently, it was not easy to give a certain answer. So far as the older authorities go, there is, acording to Parke, B. in *Morley* v. *Attenborough* (3 Ex. 500) decided in 1849, no such implied warranty: 'from the authorities in our law, to which may be added the opinion of the late Lord Chief Justice Tindal in *Ormerod* v. *Huth*, it would seem that there is no implied warranty of title on the sale of goods, and that if there be no fraud a vendor is not liable for a bad title, unless there is an express warranty, or an equivalent to it, by declarations or conduct: and the question in each case, where there is no warranty in express terms, will be whether there are such circumstances as will be equivalent to such a warranty. Usage of trade, if proved as a matter of fact, would of course be sufficient to raise an inference of such an engagement: and without proof of such usage, the very nature of the trade may be enough to lead to the conclusion, that the person carrying it on must be understood to engage that the purchaser shall enjoy that which he buys, as against all persons. . . . . We do not suppose that there would be any doubt if the articles are bought in a shop professedly carried on for the sale of goods, that the shopkeeper must be considered as warranting that those who purchase will have a good title to keep the goods purchased. In such a case the vendor sells "as his own," and that is what is equivalent to a warranty of title.' In a case, however, decided as early as 1708 (*L'Apostre* v. *L'Plaistrier*, 1 Peere Williams, 318), it had been held that 'offering to sell generally was sufficient evidence of offering to sell as owner'; and this doctrine was followed in *Eichholz* v. *Banister*, 17 C. B. N. S. 708, where Erle, C.J., said 'in almost all ordinary transactions in modern times the vendor, in consideration of the purchaser paying the price, is understood to affirm that he is the owner of the article sold.' According to Benjamin, p. 634, the rule at present would seem to be stated more in accord with the recent decisions if put in terms like the following: 'a sale of personal chattels implies an affirmation by the vendor that the chattel is his, and therefore he warrants the title, unless it be shown by the facts and circumstances of the sale that the vendor did not intend to assert ownership, but only to transfer such interest as he might have in the chattel sold': (cf. Chalmers, Sale of Goods, p. 17, 'by a contract of sale the seller impliedly warrants his right to sell the goods, unless the circumstances of the sale or agreement to sell are such as to show that the seller is transferring only such property as he may have in the goods'). Benjamin's statement of the law was expressly confirmed in *Raphael* v. *Burt* (Cababé & Ellis, 325) by Stephen, J., who extended the application of the principle from a sale of personal chattels to all sales of personal property, so as to include bonds. The cases in which an implied warranty of title has been negatived, appear all to have arisen out of sales by sheriffs or forced sales by public auction, where the circumstances were such as to indicate that the seller was only selling such rights as he might have in the goods: Chalmers, p. 18. It seems to be still uncertain whether the purchaser can merely recover the price, if paid, as on a failure of consideration, or may sue for unliquidated damages: Benjamin (p. 634) thinks there is no reason to doubt that he may do the latter, the ratio decidendi in *Eichholz* v. *Banister* being that there was a warranty *implied as part of the contract*. There is probably also an implied warranty on the part of the seller that the goods are free from any charge or lien thereon at the time of the sale, but there appears to be no English authority on the point: Chalmers, loc. cit. By the Conveyancing and Law of Property Act, 1881 (44 & 45 Vic. c. 41), which applies to 'conveyances' of personalty, a covenant for title and quiet possession is always imported unless expressly negatived.

These are the only points upon which there is or has been any difficulty. For it is well settled that in an executory agreement the vendor warrants by implication his title in the goods which he promises to sell: 'with respect to executory contracts of purchase and sale, where the subject is unascertained, and is afterwards to be conveyed, it would probably be implied, that both parties meant that a good title to that subject should be transferred in the same manner as it would be implied, under similar circumstances, that a merchantable article was to be supplied. Unless goods which the party could enjoy as his own, and make full use of, were delivered, the contract would not be performed. The purchaser could not be bound to accept if he discovered the defect of title before delivery: and if he did, and the goods were recovered from him, he would not be bound to pay, or having paid, he would be entitled to recover back the price, as on a consideration which had failed,' per Parke, B. in *Morley* v. *Attenborough*. Again, it has always been beyond doubt that an affirmation by the vendor of a chattel that it is his, is equivalent to a warranty of title, and that this affirmation may be inferred from his conduct, as well as from his words, and may also result from the nature and circumstances of the sale: and finally that if the vendor knew that he had no title, and concealed that fact from the purchaser, he would be liable on the ground of fraud: 'if the vendor knew that he had no title, and concealed that fact, he was always held responsible to the purchaser as for a fraud, in the same way that he is if he knew of the defective quality,' per Parke, B. ubi supr.

CHAPTER X.

THE EFFECTS OF THE CONTRACT.

(c) *The Duties of the Parties. The Purchaser.*

Payment of the purchase money; the purchaser must make it the property of the vendor. By whom and to whom payment may be made. Passing of property in the goods, even when delivered, usually conditional on payment. Interest due on unpaid purchase money. Purchaser's duty to accept delivery, and to reimburse the vendor his charges. Consequences of the purchaser's mora. The Civil Law on the subject of vendor's lien, and unpaid purchase money.

Payment of the purchase money:

THE first duty of the purchaser is to pay the purchase money[1]. He is not entitled to any demand, so that if there has been no agreement for postponing payment he is bound to pay it immediately the contract is concluded, on the vendor's delivering or offering to deliver the goods[2]: and he must of course pay it in full, unless payment by instalments at stated intervals or otherwise has been provided for in the contract. The money with which he

the purchaser must make it the property of the vendor.

pays the vendor must be his own, or at any rate money of which he is entitled to dispose: for although a man can

---

[1] Dig. 19. 1. 13. 8 & 20. La principale obligation de l'acheteur est de payer le prix au jour et au lieu réglés par la vente. S'il n'a rien été réglé à cet égard lors de la vente, l'acheteur doit payer au lieu et dans le temps ou doit se faire la délivrance: Code Civil, Arts. 1650, 1651.

[2] Lorsque le contrat ne porte aucun terme, le vendeur peut former incontinent cette action *ex vendito* contre l'acheteur, aux offres qu'il doit lui faire de lui livrer la chose, si elle ne l'a déjà été: Pothier, 279: Bell's Principles of the Law of Scotland, § 127: Benjamin, pp. 678–680.

THE PURCHASER'S DUTIES. 143

validly sell property which is not his own[1], and is under no liability when the purchaser discovers this to be the case until he is actually evicted, the purchaser is bound to 'make the money the property of the vendor':

> emptor enim, nisi nummos accipientis fecerit, tenetur ex vendito[2].

Consequently, the vendor can sue him at once, if he pays him with money which belongs to some one else, and of which he has no right to dispose, even before the rightful owner has called upon him to refund it: and the equity of this is obvious, for on learning that the money does not belong to the purchaser, he will have no right to use it or pay it away, and if he does so will be liable to be proceeded against by the owner as a thief[3]. If the money with which the vendor is paid as a matter of fact belongs to him already, he is deemed not to have been paid at all[4]: if it belongs to some third person, and is paid over by the purchaser without authority, the owner can recover it by real action unless it is so mixed with other money of the vendor's as no longer to be separable or distinguishable. In that event it becomes the property of the vendor by the title of Commixtion[5], the owner's remedy being in theft against the purchaser[6], and the vendor is considered to be paid, exactly as he is if he acquires property in the money by usucapion[7].

Although the matter belongs to the general law relating to the discharge of contract rather than to that of sale in particular, it may not be amiss to point out that it is immaterial who pays the vendor, provided it is done in the name and on account of the purchaser, and with money of which the payer has the right to dispose, and of which

By whom and to whom payment may be made.

---

[1] P. 17 supr.
[2] Dig. 19. 4, 1. pr.: cf. 19. 1. 11. 2.
[3] Dig. 6. 1. 4.
[4] Cod. 4. 49. 7.
[5] Inst. ii. 1. 28.
[6] Dig. 46. 3. 78.
[7] Dig. 46. 3. 60.

he can make the vendor owner: and such payment will discharge the purchaser even though made without his knowledge and against his will:

> solvere pro ignorante et invito cuique licet, cum sit iure civili constitutum licere etiam ignorantis invitique meliorem conditionem facere [1].

But payment, by whomsoever made, must be made to the vendor himself, unless he has duly authorised an agent to receive it on his behalf [2], or unless he is disabled from giving a valid discharge, in which case it must be made to his proper representative [3].

Where property is purchased by two or more persons jointly, or where, before having paid, the purchaser dies, leaving two or more joint heirs, although the vendor cannot be compelled to deliver the property until he has been paid in full, each can be called upon to pay his share only of the purchase money [4]. In fact, the only case in which the vendor can be required to deliver before he has been paid is where he has agreed to give credit.

Passing of property in the goods, even when delivered, usually conditional on payment.

It is a peculiar rule of the Civil Law that even though the vendor be the owner of the goods which he sells, or otherwise has the right to dispose of them, and actually delivers them to the purchaser, the latter does not become their owner, and the property in them does not pass, until either the purchase money has been paid, or some security (whether by way of surety or mortgage) has been given for its payment, unless the vendor gives the purchaser credit:

[1] Dig. 46. 3. 53: cf. ib. 40: Inst. iii. 29. 1. The English rule seems to be that payment by a third person, a stranger to the debtor, without his knowledge, would not discharge the debtor: see per Willes, J. in *Cook* v. *Lister*, 13 C. B. N. S. 543: and *Baker* v. *Belshaw*, 11 C. B. 191: *Lucas* v. *Wilkinson*, 26 L. J. Ex. 13. The Code Civil, Art. 1236, and the Scotch Law (Bell's Principles of the Law of Scotland, § 557), agree with the law of Rome.

[2] Dig. 46. 3. 12. pr.   [3] Dig. 46. 3. 49: ib. 15: Cod. 8. 42. 12.
[4] Dig. 18. 1. 78. 2.

venditae vero res et traditae non aliter emptori adquiruntur, quam si is venditori pretium solverit, vel alio modo ei satisfecerit, veluti expromissore aut pignore dato ... sed si is qui vendidit fidem emptoris secutus est, dicendum est statim rem emptoris fieri [1].

It would seem that, in the absence of evidence to the contrary, the giving of credit is to be inferred from the vendor's sending the goods to the purchaser, or allowing him to take possession of them, before he has received the purchase money [2], so that in practice the rule that the property did not pass without payment had ceased to be the rule, and had become an exception [3].

[1] Inst. ii. 1. 41: cf. Dig. 14. 4. 5. 18 : 18. 1. 19 & 53. The reason, according to Pothier, 322, is 'que le vendeur qui vend au comptant est censé n'avoir volonté de transférer la propriété que sous cette condition : mais lorsque le vendeur a bien voulu faire crédit du prix à l'acheteur, la tradition qui lui est faite de la chose lui en transfère la propriété avant qu'il en ait payé le prix.' The Roman rule does not seem to be followed in Scotland; at least that appears to be the natural inference from Bell's Principles of the Law of Scotland, § 103 : 'a special condition of "ready money" suspends the passing of the property even in a question with creditors.'

[2] See the authorities cited in the preceding note, none of which require an express agreement to give credit, and cf. Dig. 21. 3. 1. 2 : in this passage an agent sells and delivers on behalf of his principal : the latter, who brings a vindicatio against the buyer to recover the goods, as being still his own, is bound to prove that in delivering them before payment the agent acted against his instructions. The contrary is maintained by Pothier, 324 : l'acheteur qui soutient que le vendeur a bien voulu lui faire crédit et suivre la foi doit le prouver : le crédit ne se présume point : au contraire dans les contrats synallagmatiques chacun est présumé ne vouloir accomplir son engagement qu'autant que l'autre partie accomplira en même temps le sien. Si la tradition seule et par elle-même faisoit présumer ce crédit, ce seroit mal-à-propos que Justinian enseigneroit comme un principe particulier au contrat de vente, que la tradition des choses vendues n'en transfère pas la propriété, si le vendeur n'a suivi la foi de l'acheteur, puisqu'il seroit toujours présumé l'avoir suivie. Mais si le vendeur, après avoir livré la chose, avoit laissé écouler un temps considérable sans en demander le prix, il est évident en ce cas qu'il a suivi la foi de l'acheteur, et par conséquent la propriété sera censée transférée par la tradition.

[3] By English law, 'if goods are sold on credit, and nothing is

Interest due on unpaid purchase money.

The purchaser must further pay interest on the unpaid purchase money from the date of delivery[1], quite apart from any demand for payment[2]; the reason of this rule being that as soon as he is put in possession of the property he is able to use and enjoy it, and that it would be inequitable that he should be able to derive advantage from both it and the money as well. Such interest is recoverable only by means of an action to enforce payment of the purchase money; if this is once paid, the interest cannot be demanded[3]: and the vendor cannot require to be paid

agreed upon as to the time of delivering the goods, the vendee is immediately entitled to the possession, and the *right of possession* and the *right of property* vest at once in him : but his *right of possession* is not absolute : it is liable to be defeated if he becomes insolvent before he *obtains* possession,' per Bayley, J., in *Bloxam* v. *Sanders*, 4 B. & C. 941. That is to say, although the buyer has thus acquired the *right of possession*, not to be questioned for any legal purpose by anyone save his vendor, the latter may refuse to part with the goods, and may exercise his lien as vendor to secure payment of the price, if the purchaser has become insolvent before obtaining *actual* possession : Benjamin, p. 679 : Chalmers, Sale of Goods, p. 46.

[1] Dig. 19. 1. 13. 20 : 22. 1. 16. 1 : ib. 18. 1 : Cod. 4. 32. 2 : 4. 49. 5. By the Code Civil, Art. 1652, 'l'acheteur doit l'intérêt du prix de la vente jusqu'au paiement du capital dans les trois cas suivans : s'il a été ainsi convenu lors de la vente : si la chose vendue et livrée produit des fruits ou autres revenus : si l'acheteur a été sommé de payer. Dans ce dernier cas, l'intérêt ne court que depuis la sommation.' These rules are based upon Pothier, 283-289, but do not seem quite in accord with the Civil Law : see the next note.

[2] From Cod. 4. 49. 13 it would seem that the purchaser's mora (which as a rule dated from such demand) was a condition of the liability to pay interest: but even assuming that this passage does not relate to an unusual case (as is supposed by Glück, Pandekten, 16. p. 135), it cannot override the numerous authorities the other way. So too in Cod. 4. 54. 5 it is said that where there is no express agreement as to payment of interest, the purchaser is bound to pay it 'ex mora duntaxat,' but the case is a peculiar one, in which the vendor had neither delivered nor tendered the property before suing for the purchase money : see Mommsen, Beiträge zum Obligationenrecht, iii. p. 237, note 5.

[3] Pretii sorte licet post moram soluta, usurae peti non possunt, cum hae non sint in obligatione, sed officio iudicis praestentur : Dig. 19. 1. 49. 1.

more than ordinary interest, even though he may be able to show that he has lost more in consequence of being deprived of his money[1]. If the purchaser is prevented from paying the price through no fault of his own—e.g. by the vendor's absence, or his refusal to accept it when tendered, or by his death followed by a dispute as to who is his heir—he can relieve himself from the obligation to pay interest by paying the money into court[2]: but if he is in possession of the property he is not exempted from paying it merely by the fact that he is entitled to withhold the purchase money, as where an action to evict him has been commenced by a third person[3]. He is of course not bound to pay either price or interest if the vendor disables himself from performing the contract, or if performance becomes impossible without any fault in the vendor, provided the latter is in mora—has failed, that is to say, to deliver the goods after being requested to do so and having the purchase money tendered to him[4].

It is also the purchaser's duty, unless otherwise agreed, to fetch and take away the property, or to accept delivery of possession of land, as soon as the vendor is able or ready to deliver it—as a rule, immediately on the conclusion of the contract[5], and to reimburse him all reasonable costs and charges which he may have been put to in connection with it, such as warehousing, repairs[6], taxes[7], keep of

<small>Purchaser's duty to accept delivery, and to reimburse the vendor his charges.</small>

---

[1] Dig. 18. 6. 20. [2] Dig. 22. 1. 7: ib. 18. 1.
[3] Dig. 19. 1. 13. 20 & 21: Pothier, 284.   [4] Pothier, 279.
[5] Si is qui lapides ex fundo emerit tollere eos nolit, ex vendito agi cum eo potest, ut eos tolleret, Dig. 19. 1. 9: Pothier, 290: Bell's Principles of the Law of Scotland, § 128. 'When the vendor has tendered delivery, if there be no stipulated place, and no special agreement that the vendor is to send the goods, the buyer must fetch them: for it is settled law that the vendor need not aver nor prove in an action against the buyer anything more than his own readiness and willingness to deliver on payment of the price': Benjamin, p. 708: Chalmers, Sale of Goods, p. 47.
[6] Dig. 19. 1. 13. 22: Pothier, 291.   [7] Cod. 4. 49. 13

Consequences of the purchaser's mora.

cattle[1], or maintenance of slaves[2]. If he fails to accept delivery of the property at the vendor's request, or if a time has been agreed upon for such delivery and he has not come to take it, the vendor is no longer bound to show any high degree of care in the charge of it, and is for the future answerable only for wilful misconduct and gross negligence[3]. Moreover, where the goods are of a perishable nature, or where to retain them in his custody would entail on him excessive inconvenience[4], he may resell[5] them, and in that case, if he has been paid he must hand over what he gets for them to the original purchaser, who has no ground for complaint if this is less than he agreed to give for them himself, provided the vendor acts in good faith and without extreme negligence, and does the best he can for him consistently with his own interests: the purchaser is equally entitled to the money, or to the surplus if he has not paid the price which he promised himself, if the second sale realises more than the first. Finally, the purchaser is bound to save the vendor harmless from any loss or detriment which his own fraud may have occasioned him: thus, if desiring to buy a certain property or lot of goods, he steals some of them, so as to induce the owner to sell the residue more readily[6].

---

[1] Cod. 4. 49. 16.
[2] Dig. 19. 1. 38. 1.
[3] Dig. 18. 6. 15. pr.: ib. 18: p. 107 supr.
[4] Dig. 18. 6. 1. 3.
[5] In the English law 'where the goods are of a perishable nature, or where the unpaid seller gives notice to the buyer of his intention to resell, and the buyer does not within a reasonable time pay or tender the price, the unpaid seller may resell the goods and recover from the original buyer damages for any loss occasioned by his breach of contract. Where the seller expressly reserves a right of resale in case the buyer should make default, and on the buyer making default, resells the goods, the original contract of sale is thereby rescinded, but without prejudice to the seller's claim for damages': Chalmers, Sale of Goods, p. 73: Benjamin, pp. 791-805. By the Code Civil, Art. 1653, the vendor can demand the rescission of the contract if the purchaser does not pay the price.
[6] Dig. 19. 1. 13. 5.

A chapter on the purchaser's duties is perhaps the most appropriate place for a discussion of certain subjects which are more commonly associated with the rights of the vendor. English lawyers will look for some examination of the question how far the doctrines of the vendor's lien for unpaid purchase money, and of stoppage in transitu, are derived from or have any counterpart in the Civil Law. *The Civil Law on the subject of vendor's lien,*

The Roman vendor has substantially the same rights as are included in the English lien, but they belong to him as a matter of course, and are not the subject of any such detailed exposition in the texts as would correspond to the mass of authority in our own books, because of fundamental differences between the two systems which have been already explained.

By the English law, as has been seen, the property usually passes by the contract. If then the purchaser demands his goods from the vendor, who still has them in his possession, before he has paid the price, we have a kind of conflict between the logical consequences of a rule of law and the conclusions which would be suggested by considerations of abstract justice. The goods are no longer the vendor's, so he ought to give them up: and yet on all grounds of equity he ought to be allowed to retain possession of them until he has received the purchase money. The English doctrine on the subject [1], which is derived by

---

[1] Stated as follows by Chalmers, Sale of Goods, p. 59. sqq. :

43.—(1) Subject to the provisions of §§ 44 & 45, the unpaid seller of goods who is in possession of them is entitled to retain possession of them until payment or tender of the price in the following cases, namely :—

    (a) When the goods have been sold without any stipulation as to credit ;

    (b) When the goods have been sold on credit, but have been permitted to remain in the seller's possession until the term of credit has expired ;

Story [1], in the case of purchases of land, from the Roman rule as to property not passing by delivery unless the price is paid, appears to be an equitable qualification of the unreasonable consequences which ensue from the rule as to the passing of the property by the contract, engrafted on that rule since its adoption about the beginning of the sixteenth century.

But by the Roman law the property did not pass by the contract: it did not necessarily pass even by delivery. The goods remained the vendor's until he had delivered them, and he was not bound to deliver them until he had been paid or at least offered the purchase money [2], unless

(c) When the buyer becomes insolvent, whether the goods have been sold on credit or not;

(2) Where the buyer is insolvent, the seller may exercise his right of lien notwithstanding that he is in possession of the goods as agent or bailee for the buyer.

44. Where an unpaid seller has made part delivery of the goods, he may exercise his right of lien on the remainder, unless such part delivery has been made under such circumstances as to show an intention of waiving the lien.

45.—(1) The unpaid seller of goods loses his lien thereon:—
(a) When he delivers the goods to a carrier or other person for the purpose of transmission to the buyer without reserving the right of disposal of the goods;
(b) When the buyer or his agent obtains possession of the goods unless there be an agreement to the contrary;
(c) by waiver thereof.

(2) The unpaid seller of goods, having a lien thereon, does not lose his lien by reason only that he has obtained judgment for the price of the goods.

[1] Equity Jurisprudence, §§ 1221, 1222.
[2] In Dig 19. 1. 13. 8 ('offerri pretium ab emptore debet, cum ex empto agitur, et ideo etsi pretii partem offerat, nondum est ex empto actio: venditor enim quasi pignus retinere potest eam rem quam vendidit') the words 'quasi pignus' are misleading, for they suggest that (as in English law) the vendor is no longer owner. If the vendor was relieved by law (e.g. by bankruptcy, or novae tabulae) from the obligation to pay, he could not enforce delivery: but if delivery was made the vendor had no remedy: bona fides non patitur, ut cum emptor alicuius legis beneficio pecuniam rei venditae debere desisset

he consented to take some security instead, or to give the purchaser credit. The answer to the question, consequently, whether under ordinary circumstances he might retain possession until paid is obvious; his right to do so is merely an incident of his continuing ownership. Similarly, if he delivered the goods without either giving credit or receiving any security for payment, no property passed, and, if not paid, he could recover possession by action *in rem*: nor apparently in such a case could the purchaser acquire a prescriptive title to the goods, for he knew all along that he was not the owner, and moreover possession was not delivered to him with the intention of passing the property. Where, however, the vendor had expressly or by implication waived his right to immediate payment, the matter stood otherwise. He was bound to deliver at once, and by such delivery the property would pass.

The English lien in fact is a right which the possessing vendor has over the goods, notwithstanding that the property therein has passed to the purchaser, because the latter has not paid the purchase money. In Roman law the case cannot arise, except perhaps under circumstances where by his own conduct the vendor has, or must be taken to have, waived all possible claim to such a privilege—where in short he has sold on credit, or received some substitute for immediate payment, and the goods have been left in his possession as bailee or agent after actual delivery to the purchaser. On the question whether, in such a case, he would have any lien if the goods remained in his possession until the term of credit had expired, there seems to be no definite authority.

The right of stoppage in transitu is a right which the

antequam res ei tradatur, venditor tradere compelletur et re sua careret: possessione autem tradita futurum est, ut rem venditor aeque amitteret, utpote cum petenti eam rem [emptor exceptionem rei venditae et traditae opponere possit nec perinde sit, quasi eam rem] petitor ei neque vendidisset neque tradidisset: Dig. 19. 1. 50.

and unpaid purchase money.

unpaid vendor, who has parted with the possession of, as well as the property in, the goods to a carrier or other bailee for conveyance to the purchaser, has, under English law, of stopping the goods in transit, on hearing that the purchaser has become insolvent, with a view to resuming possession [1]. The Roman law on the matter, as on that of

---

[1] The law is thus stated by Chalmers, Sale of Goods, pp. 63, sqq :

46. Subject to the provisions of §§ 47-49, when the buyer of goods becomes insolvent the unpaid seller who has parted with the possession of the goods has the right of stopping them in transitu, that is to say, he may resume possession of the goods as long as they are in course of transit, and may retain them until payment or tender of the price.

47.—(1) Goods are deemed to be in course of transit from the time when they are delivered to a carrier by land or water, or other bailee, for the purpose of transmission to the buyer, until the buyer, or his agent in that behalf, takes delivery of them from such carrier or other bailee.

(2) If the buyer or his agent in that behalf obtains delivery of the goods before their arrival at the appointed destination, the transit is at an end.

(3) If, after the arrival of the goods at the appointed destination, the carrier or other bailee attorns to the buyer, or his agent, and continues in possession of them as bailee for the buyer, or his agent, the transit is at an end, and it is immaterial that a further destination for the goods may have been indicated by the buyer.

(4) If the goods are rejected by the buyer, and the carrier or other bailee continues in possession of them, the transit is not deemed to be at an end, even if the seller has refused to receive them back.

(5) When goods are delivered to a ship chartered by the buyer, it is a question depending on the circumstances of the particular case, whether they are in the possession of the master as a carrier, or as agent or servant to the buyer.

(6) Where the carrier or other bailee wrongfully refuses to deliver the goods to the buyer, or his agent in that behalf, the transit is deemed to be at an end.

(7) Where part delivery of the goods has been made to the buyer, or his agent in that behalf, the remainder of the goods may be stopped in transitu unless such part delivery has been made under such circumstances as to show an agreement to give up possession of the whole of the goods.

the vendor's lien, is not to be found explicitly stated in the texts relating to the contract, but is to be inferred from general principles. It would seem that there is only one case in which there can be any difficulty. Speaking generally, the unpaid vendor is not divested of his property in the goods even by delivery to the purchaser, and therefore if in the case of the latter's insolvency he can recover possession from him, he can obviously do the same from a bailee to whom the goods have been delivered as his agent for conveyance to him. If the vendor has given credit, or received some security for payment, it is material to consider who the person is to whom he entrusts the goods for transmission. Such person may be agent either for the vendor himself, or for the purchaser. In the first case the vendor can clearly revoke the agent's authority at any moment before the commission is executed by delivery of the goods, and he will naturally do so if, before such execution, he hears that the purchaser has become insolvent. But supposing that the bailee to whom he delivers the goods is the purchaser's agent, the vendor has no right such as that of stoppage in transitu, for conveyance to the agent vests the property in the principal if it was previously in the vendor himself. The latter can

(8) The right of stoppage in transitu may be determined by waiver thereof on the part of the unpaid seller.

48.—(1) The unpaid seller may exercise his right of stoppage in transitu either by taking actual possession of the goods, or by giving notice of his claim to the carrier or other bailee in whose possession the goods are. Such notice may be given either to the person in actual possession of the goods or to his principal. In the latter case, the notice, to be effectual, must be given at such time and under such circumstances that the principal, by the exercise of reasonable diligence, may communicate it to his servant or agent in time to prevent a delivery to the buyer.

(2) When notice of stoppage in transitu is lawfully given to the carrier, or other bailee in possession of the goods, he must deliver the goods to or according to the directions of the seller.

protect himself in such cases only by a term in the contract, and this by either of two expedients, each of which goes beyond the right given in all cases, without express agreement, by the English law. By the term known as 'pactum reservati dominii' the vendor who agrees to give credit may stipulate that, notwithstanding actual delivery of the goods, no property in them shall pass to the purchaser until the whole of the purchase money has been paid, and such a term will be implied from an agreement that until such payment the purchaser shall be entitled only 'precario[1]' or as under a contract of hiring[2]: or (more simply) it may be agreed that in the event of the purchaser becoming insolvent before the price is paid the property (notwithstanding it having passed to the purchaser owing to credit having been given) shall revest in the vendor by the operation of a resolutive condition or condition subsequent[3]. By the term which we may call 'pactum reservatae hypothecae' the vendor who agrees to give credit, and from whom the property passes by delivery, may reserve a security over the goods entitling him to take possession in the event of non-payment, and to sell them with a view to satisfying his claims against the purchaser. But neither of these terms appear to have been common among the Romans, and we may perhaps conclude that the rights which the vendor had under the ordinary law were in practice found sufficient to secure him against loss of both the goods and the purchase money[4].

[1] Dig. 43. 26. 20. [2] Dig. 18. 6. 17.
[3] Glück, Pandekten, 16. p. 233.
[4] In *Gibson v. Carruthers* (1841), 8. M. & W., p. 336 sq., Lord Abinger, C.B., says that the right of stoppage in transitu seems to be general in the mercantile law of the continental nations, but he does not connect it with the Civil Law. But in *Kendal v. Marshall, Stevens & Co.* (1883), 11 Q. B. D. at p. 361, Bowen, L.J., observed 'the right of stoppage in transitu is founded upon mercantile rules, and is borrowed from the custom of merchants: from their custom it has been engrafted

upon the law of England. The doctrine was at variance with the Civil Law, which laid down that although the goods had been sold upon credit, and although the goods were in the possession of the vendee, there might be recaption by the vendor if the vendee became insolvent.' The writer has been unable to find any text upon which this statement can be supported : but it is probable that the case of which the L. J. was thinking was one in which there had been a reservation of either dominium or hypotheca until the whole of the purchase money had been paid.

CHAPTER XI.

CONDITIONAL SALES.

Conditions in general distinguished into suspensive and resolutive. Conditions distinguished from terms in the contract. Conditions affirmative and negative. Conditions attached for the benefit of the vendor. (i) Addictio in diem. What is a 'better offer'? Effects of addictio when the condition is suspensive, and resolutive. When is the condition satisfied? Sales by auction. (ii) Lex commissoria: the condition here always resolutive: when it is satisfied. Effect of a sale subject to a lex commissoria. Conditions attached for the benefit of the purchaser; (i) emptio ad gustum; (ii) pactum displicentiae. Common terms in sales; reservation by vendor of right of preemption; pactum de retrovendendo and de retroemendo.

Conditions in general distinguished into suspensive and resolutive.

WHERE the ordinary effect of a contract, whether of sale or otherwise, is either suspended until the occurrence or non-occurrence of some uncertain event, or is subjected by the agreement of the parties, express or implied, to some limitation, it is said to be made under a condition, and the theory of conditions is perhaps more fully worked out and exemplified in connection with sale than with any other disposition, whether belonging to the sphere of contract or to some other branch of law, such as inheritances and legacies. If the full effect of the contract is made to depend on such occurrence or non-occurrence (as e.g. on a purchaser's expressing himself satisfied with goods) the condition is said to be suspensive: if, while the contract produces at once its ordinary effects, it is agreed that they shall be cancelled, and that the avoidance shall relate back to the date of its conclusion, on such occurrence or non-occurrence, the condition is said to be resolutive—as,

e. g. where a sale is nullified by the vendor's subsequently accepting an offer of a higher price from a third party[1]. In the first case the sale is conditional from the outset, and there is no obligation until the condition is satisfied[2]: in the second the sale is absolute, but is liable, as an English lawyer would say, to defeasance on condition subsequent:

> quotiens fundus in diem addicitur, utrum pura emptio est, sed sub conditione resolvitur, an vero conditionalis sit magis emptio, quaestionis est. Et mihi videtur verius interesse, quid actum sit: nam si quidem hoc actum est, ut meliore allata conditione discedatur, erit pura emptio, quae sub conditione resolvitur: sin autem hoc actum est, ut perficiatur emptio nisi melior conditio offeratur, erit emptio conditionalis[3].

In many cases, as is evident from this passage, it is uncertain whether the parties to the contract intended the condition to be suspensive or resolutive: the presumption of law would seem to be in favour of the latter, if the property has been delivered, and of the former, if not. Whether the condition is one whose fulfilment or non-fulfilment depends on the will of either of the parties themselves is immaterial.

A condition has to be distinguished from a term in the contract (pactum adiectum). The latter is where either party undertakes simultaneously with and as part of his contract[4], to do some other thing or things as incidental

Conditions distinguished from terms in the contract.

---

[1] L'obligation est conditionnelle lorsqu'on la fait dépendre d'un événement futur et incertain, soit en la suspendant jusqu'à ce que l'événement arrive, soit en la résiliant, selon que l'événement arrivera ou n'arrivera pas: Code Civil, Art. 1168.

[2] Dig. 20. 1. 13. 5.

[3] Ulpian in Dig. 18. 2. 2. pr. It would appear from the opinion of Julianus, cited by Paulus in Dig. 41. 4. 2. 4, that in the earlier period there was a strong presumption in favour of the condition of an in diem addictio being held to be resolutive, and that even Paulus (loc. cit.) leant to that view.

[4] Dig. 18. 1. 72. pr.

or ancillary to its main purpose, as where, for instance, in selling land the vendor promises to give the purchaser a lease of an adjoining estate[1]. To the lay mind it might appear a matter of indifference whether I agree to take your house at an annual rental of £100, if you paper and paint it throughout, or whether I agree to take it at that rental in consideration of your undertaking to do so; but the difference is this, that whereas one can be compelled to perform a term in the contract by the ordinary action upon it, one cannot be sued for non-fulfilment of a condition, even though its fulfilment be in one's own power[2]. But pacta adiecta may, like the main contract, be themselves subjected to a condition, either suspensive or resolutive[3].

A condition may be for the benefit of, or rather the contract may be conditional for, one of the parties only, as where one attaches a condition to his assent, while the other assents unconditionally: but unless this is clear, the condition is to be deemed to affect both, and cases are conceivable in which it is quite uncertain, at the moment the contract was made, for whose benefit it will turn out to have been annexed[4]. Where it is for the benefit of one

---

[1] E.g. Dig. 18. 1. 79.

[2] Si vero sub conditione facta emptio est, non poterit agi ut conditio impleatur: Dig. 18. 1. 41. pr.

[3] Whether a condition could by subsequent agreement be annexed to a sale originally unconditional is to be regarded as questionable. As to resolutive conditions there is no doubt: and, according to Paulus (Dig. 18. 5. 7. pr.), it was equally true that a suspensive condition subsequently agreed on was void. But it is difficult to deny to such a pact, if attached to a purely executory contract, the effect (in general beyond all doubt) of giving rise to an exception: and Paulus can hardly have meant that a party who agrees to annex a condition to a sale originally unconditional could enforce it before satisfaction of the condition if the other pleaded some such defence as exceptio doli: cf. Treitschke, Kaufcontract, pp. 144-146.

[4] E.g. where goods on board ship and in transit are bought subject to their arrival by a certain day. If they arrived late, and had risen

party, it can be waived by him alone : where it is imposed for the benefit of both, whether expressly or by implication, it can be discharged only by agreement.

An affirmative or positive condition is one which is satisfied by the happening of something : a negative condition is one which is satisfied by something not happening, and it is deemed to have been satisfied as soon as it is certain that the event, on whose non-occurrence the contract depends, cannot possibly happen, or (where a limit of time has been fixed) has not happened within that limit. A negative suspensive condition is liable to confusion with a resolutive one, and a negative resolutive one with a suspensive[1] : but their effects, as has been already indicated, are totally different. A resolutive condition does not in any way impede the existence of the ordinary effects of the contract, such as the duties which it engenders, and the passing of the risk to the purchaser : whereas none of these effects ensue when the condition is suspensive until it is fulfilled. Consequently a party who has made a contract under a suspensive condition cannot be sued upon it until the condition is satisfied ; while on the other hand where the condition is resolutive there is no need to wait until it is certain that it will not occur, but the contract can be enforced at once, although on its occurrence (if affirmative), or on its becoming certain that it cannot occur (if negative) both parties, or the party in whose favour the condition was annexed, can sue for the recovery of the property or of the purchase money, as the case may be, on showing himself to be ready to surrender the benefit which he may himself have derived from the performance of the contract. Sufficient

Conditions affirmative and negative.

---

in value, the condition would be for the benefit of the vendor: in the converse case it would be for that of the purchaser.

[1] Si res ita distracta sit, ut si displicuisset inempta esset, constat non esse sub conditione distractam, sed resolvi emptionem sub conditione: Dig. 18. 1. 3.

160   CONDITIONAL SALES.

Conditions attached for the benefit of the vendor.

illustrations of these principles will be found in what follows relating to the most common sorts of conditions and terms which are met with in sales.

These may be most conveniently considered according as they are for the benefit of the vendor or for that of the purchaser. The first will be exemplified by the pacts known as addictio in diem and lex commissoria.

(i) Addictio in diem.

Addictio in diem[1] is where it is agreed between the parties that the sale shall be good (suspensive[2]) or remain good (resolutive condition) only if the vendor does not sell the property to another purchaser on better terms (melior conditio) within a fixed time[3]:

> si in diem addictio ita fit: ille fundus centum esto tibi emptus, nisi si quis intra calendas Januarias proximas meliorem conditionem fecerit, quo res a domino abeat[4].

It is commonly said that the presumption was in favour of the condition being resolutive, but there seems no reason for this view, except in cases where the vendor has delivered the property without a reservation of ownership, which is implied in the passage usually cited in support of it[5]. Any offer is deemed a better offer by which the vendor gets

What is a 'better offer'?

---

[1] Pothier, 445. The antiquity of this pact is attested by Plautus, *Captivi*, I. 2. 76: 'emptum nisi quis meliorem adferet, quae mihi atque amicis placeat conditio magis.'

[2] Such suspensive condition may be either negative, as in the passage of Plautus cited, and in Dig. 18. 2. 1: or affirmative, as in Dig. ib. 4. 3: in diem addicto fundo si melior conditio allata sit.

[3] As is clear from the name of the pact, it is essential that a time should be fixed: if there were none the pact would be void.

[4] Dig. 18. 2. 1: cf. ib. 2. pr. Whether 'dominus' means the vendor or the purchaser, or the one or the other according as the condition is suspensive or resolutive, is much debated: see Glück, Pandekten, 16. p. 240, note 3.

[5] Si in diem addictio facta sit, id est, nisi si quis meliorem conditionem attulerit, perfectam esse emptionem ... Julianus putabat: alii, et hanc sub conditione esse contractam; ille non contrahi, sed resolvi dicebat, quae sententia vera est: Dig. 41. 4. 2. 4.

more favourable terms for himself [1], whether a higher price, or earlier or more convenient payment, or payment at a more suitable place, or a more substantial purchaser, or one who is willing to buy on easier conditions to the vendor, or without sureties: or even one who, while offering a lower price, agrees to waive certain consequences of the contract, or certain express terms, which were burdensome to the vendor under the original sale, such as his liability to make compensation for eviction, or for undisclosed defects in the goods which form the subject matter of the contract [2]. On the other hand, the requirement that the offer shall be a better one is not satisfied merely because, though the second bid is identical only in amount with the first, the vendor obtains pecuniary compensation for fruits taken from the property by the original purchaser, if in possession, and which would have been his had the first sale not been disturbed; for this advantage accrues to him not from the second buyer, but in virtue of the law relating to the contract [3]: indeed otherwise any second buyer who offered no more than the first would be a buyer on better terms, provided that the value of these fruits were more than the interest on the purchase money, which the vendor must pay to the first purchaser if he had been paid and the sale falls to the ground, or which he loses if the purchase money had not been paid at all [4]. Nor, again, are the terms to be deemed better if the second purchaser, while offering a higher price, bargains for something additional from the vendor, of sufficient value to neutralise that advantage [5], or if the payment of the price,

[1] Dig. 18. 2. 5: Pothier, 447.
[2] Dig. 18. 2. 4. 6: ib. 5: ib. 15. 1.
[3] Dig. 18. 2. 14. 5.   [4] Arg. Dig. 21. 1. 29. 2.
[5] Dig. 18. 2. 15. 1. In Dig. ib. 19 this reasonable principle seems to be controverted by Javolenus, who writes as if the validity of the second sale made under these circumstances depended entirely on the vendor's good faith; but it is difficult to accept this view; see Treitschke, Kaufcontract, p. 172.

M

though higher in amount, is so postponed by agreement that the discount balances the increase [1]. Moreover, it is necessary that an actual and bona fide better offer shall be made by a third party: the vendor cannot assume the rôle of purchaser himself, except where two or more persons have jointly sold property subject to an addictio in diem, in which case one of them may offer a higher price than the original purchaser for the whole, allowance of course being made for the value of his own undivided share [2]. A better offer made by a pupillus without his guardian's authorisation, if accepted, is sufficient to deprive the first sale of all effect [3]. If the vendor made a collusive arrangement with a third person, who pretended to offer better terms, in order to cancel the first sale for his own purposes, or to force the first purchaser to offer better terms himself, the latter's contract was unaffected: and if he accepted a bona fide offer from a second purchaser who really offered no more than the first, and pretended to the latter that he had got more, he was liable on account of his fraud to both, the first being entitled to the property, and the second to damages [4]. Conversely, if the purchaser fraudulently contrived that the vendor should accept an offer from a third person who was to his own knowledge insolvent, in order to relieve himself from his contract, the second sale was valid, but the vendor could recover compensation for fruits which he had taken from the first by action ex vendito, and damages in addition for any other loss which the fraud might have occasioned him [5].

[1] Dig. 18. 2. 15. 1: Pothier, 448.
[2] Verum est autem vel unum ex venditoribus posse meliorem adferre conditionem: emere enim cum tota re etiam nostram partem possumus: Dig. 18. 2. 13. 1, and see p. 23 supr. So too if two or more persons make a joint purchase subject to an addictio in diem, one of them alone can make a better offer: quum in diem duobus sociis fundus sit addictus, uno ex his pretium adiiciente etiam pro ipsius parte a priore venditione discedi rectius existimatur: Dig. 18. 2. 18.
[3] Dig. 18. 2. 14. 3.   [4] Dig. 18. 2. 14. pr.   [5] Dig. 18. 2. 14. 1.

The effects of an addictio in diem, of course, are different according as the condition is suspensive or resolutive.

(i) If the condition is suspensive, the contract, so far as relates to the consequences which would ordinarily ensue from it, is deemed not to have been made at all, until the time has completely elapsed within which the property might have been sold to a second purchaser. Even though it is delivered, it is still at the vendor's risk [1], and the purchaser has no right to its fruits, and no capacity to acquire a title to it by usucapion [2]. If the condition is eventually fulfilled by no better offer being made and accepted within the time limited, or if the vendor dies but no heir accepts the inheritance before it has elapsed [3], the sale becomes binding by relation back to the moment at which it was first agreed upon, and its effects are as though it had been unconditional from the outset, notwithstanding the death of either party or both in the meanwhile: fruits gathered since its conclusion belong to the purchaser [4]; usucapion by him becomes possible as from that moment [5], and even though the property has in the meanwhile become less valuable the loss falls upon him, unless of course the depreciation was due to the fault of the vendor [6]. If a better offer is in fact made to the latter, he is bound to give the first purchaser notice of it [7], that he may have the opportunity of retaining the property [8]: such notice

Effects of addictio when the condition is suspensive,

---

[1] P. 78 supr.
[2] Dig. 18. 2. 4. pr.
[3] Dig. 18. 2. 15. pr.
[4] Dig. 18. 2. 6. pr.
[5] Dig. 41. 4. 2. 2.
[6] Dig. 18. 6. 8. pr.
[7] Dig. 18. 2. 8.
[8] Licet autem venditori meliore allata conditione addicere posteriori, nisi prior paratus sit plus adicere. Necesse autem habebit venditor . . . . priorem emptorem certiorem facere, ut si quid alius adicit, ipse quoque adicere possit: Dig. 18. 2. 7 & 8. By the purchaser's 'adding more' is meant adding to his original offer, i.e. offering to buy the property on the terms offered by the second bidder, as seems clear from Dig. 49. 14. 50, though Dig. 4. 4. 35 makes the acceptance of this construction rather difficult. So Pothier, 452, 519: Glück, Pandekten,

amounts to an offer to sell it to him, notwithstanding the advance made by the second purchaser, on condition of his ousting the latter, so that no acceptance by the vendor is necessary in order to finally complete the contract, nor can he choose between the offer of the second purchaser and the equally good or better offer made by the first. If, however, the second purchaser becomes the purchaser in fact, the first must reimburse the vendor for all fruits which he has gathered [1], though he is entitled to be repaid all necessary outlay which he has made on the property while in his possession [2]. The purchaser does not acquire any right to the fruits, that is to say, he is not relieved from his obligation to pay for them, by the fact that he consents to buy the property on the improved terms offered by the second purchaser [3], unless it has been otherwise agreed; for he gets the property by the later, not by the original contract.

and resolutive.

(ii) If the condition be resolutive, the sale is binding, and produces all its usual effects, from the moment of its conclusion, though it is liable to be defeated by the fulfilment of the condition. The purchaser becomes owner of the property by delivery, if the vendor had the right to dispose of it, exactly as if there had been no condition attached to the transaction at all, while if he had not, usucapion runs in his favour [4]; he has all the ordinary rights and remedies of an owner [5]: he can mortgage and create servitudes over it, and its fruits and accessions are his [6]. So too the loss falls on him if the property perishes

---

16. 246, 259: Windscheid, Lehrbuch, § 323. Others (including Bechmann, Kauf, II. § 251, and Treitschke, Kaufcontract, p. 174) held that 'plus' cannot mean 'totidem,' and that in order to get the preference the first buyer must outbid the second. But why should he be ousted if he is willing to give the vendor precisely the same advantages?

[1] Dig. 18. 2. 6. pr.
[2] Dig. 18. 2. 16.
[3] Dig. 18. 2. 6. 1 : cf. Dig. 18. 1. 37.
[4] Dig. 18. 2. 2. 1 : 41. 4. 2. 4.
[5] Dig. 18. 2. 4. 4. : 6. 1. 41. pr.
[6] Dig. 18. 2. 2. 1.

before the condition is fulfilled, for the risk is his [1], though if two things are bought for one price, one of which is accidentally destroyed, and a third person is willing to buy the one remaining for at least as much as the first purchaser gave for both, this offer may be accepted by the vendor, and such acceptance will avoid the original sale [2]. If a better offer is made and accepted within the time limited, the first sale is defeated: the property re-vests in the vendor: mortgages or servitudes created by the original purchaser, unless assented to by him [3], are avoided [4]; he must reimburse the vendor for fruits and accessions which he has taken [5], exactly as in the previous case, subject (as there) to his right to be repaid all outlay on the property which has been necessary [6]; and he can recover the purchase money if it has been paid [7]. The avoidance of the contract, however, has no general retrospective operation: for praedial servitudes acquired by the purchaser while the property was in his possession are not extinguished [8]: rights of action for damages done to it during the same time can and must be assigned by him [9], and the time during which he has possessed it 'ad usucapionem' benefits the vendor and through him the second purchaser [10].

In order, however, to produce these effects, the offer of the third person must have been accepted. As a rule, of course, the vendor is free to accept it or not at his discretion [11]: but he has not this option when what he is selling is property over which he has got a mortgage, because a refusal would be a fraud on the mortgagor, unless indeed the offer is made by a person of no substance, acting in

When is the condition satisfied?

---

[1] Dig. 18. 2. 2. 1 : ib. 3.
[2] Dig. 18. 2. 4. 2.
[3] Dig. 39. 3. 9.
[4] Dig. 18. 2. 4. 3.
[5] Dig. 18. 2. 4. 4 : ib. 14. 1.
[6] Dig. 18. 2. 6. pr.
[7] Dig. 18. 2. 16.
[8] Arg. Dig. 8. 6. 11. 1.
[9] Dig. 18. 2. 4. 4.
[10] Arg. Dig. 44. 3. 6. 1 : 41. 3. 19.
[11] Dig. 18. 2. 9 : Pothier, 449.

collusion with the latter in order to delay the sale of the property [1]. It is, however, lawful for the parties to agree that the purchaser shall be at liberty to terminate his own contract on a second better offer being made to the vendor, whether he chooses to accept it or not [2]. If two or more articles are sold together subject to an addictio in diem, but each for its own distinct price, a better offer may be made either for all together or for anyone of them individually: but if they are sold at different times or otherwise by distinct contracts, a general offer to take the whole together on improved terms will suffice to avoid those contracts only if it is clear that the vendor will be better off on each, considered by itself: otherwise those only will be avoided in respect of which this is the case, and in the event of doubt all will stand [3]. Similarly, if two or more persons jointly sell property under this kind of condition, the assent of all to the acceptance of the better offer is essential to the avoidance of the first sale [4], unless the property is divisible, and each sells his own share for a distinct and separate price, in which case a better offer for one portion can be accepted by its owner without rescinding the original sale of the residue. Of course if the original purchaser bought it expressly as a whole, and on the condition that he should not be deprived of a part only by the acceptance of a better offer by one alone of the joint owners, this cannot be done [5].

The acceptance by the vendor of a better offer subject to the condition of none better still being made within the time fixed by the agreement with the first purchaser (a second addictio in diem) does not affect the latter's contingent rights, which can be cancelled only by an absolute contract with a second purchaser, unless it was agreed at

---

[1] Dig. 18. 2. 10. [2] Dig. 18. 2. 9.
[3] Dig. 18. 2. 17. [4] Dig. 18. 2. 11. 1 & 12: Pothier, 450.
[5] Dig. 18. 2. 13: Pothier, 451.

the outset by the parties, or was clearly their intention, that those rights should be terminated by such a conditional acceptance[1].

An addictio in diem can be attached to a sale by express convention only, and there is no case in which it is implied. There are some, it is true, who apply the principles of this transaction to public sales ordered by state authority, and even to sales by auction in general[2]: but to do this consistently would lead to strange results, among others, that the auctioneer might sell the thing to one who had been outbid by a later bidder, which would be against the common sense of the matter upon any view of its true legal construction. The truth would seem to be that the law relating to auctions is not laid down in the authorities, and that consequently it has to be deduced from general principles; which no doubt explains why it has been so variously expounded by different writers on the Civil Law. In point of fact it can scarcely be doubted that no hard and fast abstract rule can be stated, and that the matter turns upon the intention of the seller or his agent, the auctioneer, as evidenced by his words or conduct. If that intention is that the highest bidder is to have the goods, without reference to the relation between the amount of his bid and their real value, then the vendor is the proposer, and the contract is concluded by the making of the last bid, each bid being an acceptance conditional on no higher bid being made[3], and the presumption is in favour of the condition having been

Sales by auction.

---

[1] Dig. 18. 2. 11. pr. The passage is otherwise explained by Treitschke, Kaufcontract, p. 172, after Westphal, who thinks that the first contract falls to the ground through such a conditional acceptance, provided the second purchaser's obligation is no less binding than was that of the first.

[2] E. g. Glück, Pandekten, 16 § 1005.

[3] Ihering, Jahrbuch, vii. pp. 167, 178, denies the possibility of an offer or proposal being made 'in incertam personam' or, as we say, to all the world. The nearest Roman analogies are the jactus missilium and legacies to incertae personae.

intended to be suspensive[1]. On the other hand, if the intention of the vendor is not necessarily to sell to any of the bidders, the putting of the goods up is an invitation of offers from those attending the sale, of which offers he is of course not bound to accept any, and there is no contract until one of them is accepted by him in fact[2]. The best authorities on the Civil Law[3] are of opinion that where there is any doubt it is to be presumed that this was what was intended, and a majority of them seem to be in favour of the view that, in the absence of evidence of a contrary intention, each bid or offer is to be deemed to be withdrawn or to lapse as

---

[1] Pothier, 518.

[2] The same distinction is drawn in English law. The putting of an article up for sale by auction is an invitation of offers : each bid is an offer, which may be withdrawn before it is accepted by the fall of the hammer: *Payne* v. *Cave*, 3 T. R. 148: and the auctioneer is not bound to accept any bid if he does not choose. But if the sale is announced to be 'without reserve,' this is an undertaking 'that the goods shall be sold to the highest bidder, whether the sum bid be equivalent to the real value or not . . . . the auctioneer contracts that it shall be so, and this contract is made with the highest *bona fide* bidder': per Martin, B. in *Warlow* v. *Harrison*, 1 E. & E. 295, 29 L. J. Q. B. 14. From this it would seem that in such a case as this the putting of the goods up is the offer: that each bid is a conditional acceptance, and that therefore such bids cannot be withdrawn: but this is discountenanced by what Lord Campbell said in *Warlow* v. *Harrison*.

The employment of puffers, i. e. of persons engaged to bid on behalf of the vendor in order to force up the price against the public, has been held fraudulent since 1776 (*Bexwell* v. *Christie*, 1 Cowp. 395): and the parties interested cannot in any case bid unless they have reserved the right to do so: *Dimmock* v. *Hallett*, 2 Ch. 21 : Chalmers, Sale of Goods, p. 89: by 30 & 31 Vic. c. 48, which however applies only to sales of land, they may apparently even in that case only make one bid. The authority for the Roman law as to puffers is Cicero: tollendum est igitur ex rebus contrahendis omne mendacium, non licitatorem venditor, nec qui contra se liceatur (reliceatur?) emptor opponat : de Off. iii. 15, cited in *Warlow* v. *Harrison*. For the Scotch law as to sales by auction see Bell, Principles of the Law of Scotland, §§ 130–132.

[3] E. g. Vangerow, § 636, Windscheid, § 308, and other writers cited by the latter in note 16.

soon as a higher bid is made, so that the vendor can accept no bid except the highest: on the analogy of addictio in diem of course he would be both bound and entitled to sell to the first bidder rather than not sell at all. It also seems to be very generally held that even where a bid is a mere offer, and not a conditional acceptance, it cannot be retracted [1], and this is explained by assuming a tacit 'pactum de emendo,' or an implied undertaking that it shall not be withdrawn.

A lex commissoria is where a sale is made on condition that the purchase money shall be paid by a day fixed, and that in default it shall be voidable at the purchaser's option [2]. No doubt it was equally allowable to make the condition in favour of the purchaser, entitling him to avoid the contract in default of the property being delivered within a prescribed period, but no instance of this form of the proviso is found in the authorities. It might also be agreed that in addition to the vendor's right of rescission the purchaser should be bound to reimburse him the loss which he sustained through selling the property, on failure

(ii) Lex commissoria:

---

[1] Glück, Pandekten, 16. p. 269: Ihering, Jahrbuch, loc. cit.: Vangerow, § 636, p. 441.

[2] By the French law of the eighteenth century a lex commissoria did not entitle the vendor to rescind ipso iure; he could only bring an action to have the contract declared void, and until judgment was given in such action the purchaser might still save it by tendering the money, notwithstanding that the time fixed for payment had elapsed: Pothier, 459. This rule is in some measure preserved by the Code Civil in respect of sales of immoveables, but in sales of moveables the Civil Law is restored: s'il a été stipulé lors de la vente d'immeubles, que, faute de paiement du prix dans le terme convenu, la vente serait résolue de plein droit, l'acquéreur peut néanmoins payer après l'expiration du délai, tant qu'il n'a pas été mis en demeure par une sommation: mais, après cette sommation, le juge ne peut pas lui accorder de délai. En matière de vente de denrées et effets mobiliers, la résolution de la vente aura lieu de plein droit et sans sommation, au profit du vendeur, après l'expiration du terme convenu pour le retirement: Arts. 1656, 1657. For the reason of the distinction see Demante, Cours analytique de Code Civil, pp. 125-127.

of the condition, at a lower price or on less favourable terms to a third person [1]. The condition is always resolutive:

the condition here always resolutive.

si fundus lege commissoria venierit, magis est ut sub conditione resolvi emptio, quam sub conditione contrahi videatur [2].

No doubt it might be agreed that the sale should not be binding unless the purchase money were paid by a certain day, in which case the condition would be suspensive: but this would not be a lex commissoria in the proper sense, because 'committere' denotes the forfeiture of an actually existing right [3].

When the condition is satisfied.

The conditions of the operation of a lex commissoria are three in number: a time must have been fixed within which the purchase money must be paid [4]: the whole of that time must have elapsed [5], and some portion of the purchase money at least must still remain unpaid at its termination. The purchaser, in order to save the contract from liability to rescission, was bound to tender the money, the vendor's rights being in no way dependent on his having demanded it [6]: indeed, demand by him before the day was premature [7],

[1] Dig. 18. 3. 4. 3.
[2] Dig. 18. 3. 1: ib. 2. 4. 5 & 8: cf. Dig. 41. 4. 2. 3: 18. 2. 2. pr.: 44. 7. 23: Cod. 4. 54. 3.
[3] This however is denied by Glück, Pandekten, 16. p. 275.
[4] Dig. 18. 3. 2: ib. 4. pr. & 5.
[5] Inst. iii. 15. 2: Dig. 45. 1. 42.
[6] Marcellus libro vicensimo dubitat, commissoria utrum tunc locum habet, si interpellatus non solvat, an vero si non optulerit, et magis arbitror offerre eum debere, si vult se legis commissoriae potestate solvere: Dig. 18. 3. 4. 4.
[7] This of course assumes that a lex commissoria implies a giving of credit during the term limited. This is denied by Bechmann, Kauf, II. § 254: 'wer sich ausbedingt, dass er nicht länger als bis zu einem gewissen Zeitpunct an den Vertrag gebunden ist, verpflichtet sich damit keineswegs ohne weiteres, bis zu diesem Zeitpunct mit der Geltendmachung seiner Ansprüche zu warten, und selbst wenn Stundung vorliegt, so ist dieselbe nach römischer Anschauung noch nicht ohne weiteres Creditirung mit der Wirkung des Eigenthumsübergangs.'

and a requisition to pay it, or acceptance of any portion of it, after the period fixed for payment, was deemed an irrevocable waiver of the benefit of the condition [1]. The failure of the purchaser to pay, however, must not be in any way attributable to the fault of the vendor—in refusing to accept the money when tendered, for instance, or in absenting himself without having left an agent duly authorised to receive it [2]—though in such cases it is advisable for a purchaser who desires to avoid all imputation of negligence to pay the money into court [3]: nor is the purchaser prejudiced if he withholds it on being served with a judicial order not to pay the vendor at the instance of a creditor of the latter [4]. Finally, it may be observed that the purchaser is under no obligation to pay the purchase money so long as the vendor fails to perform a duty undertaken by the contract, performance of which was intended to be a condition precedent to such payment: as where, for instance, it is agreed that the former shall be entitled to retain a portion of it until the latter has given him a surety for the payment of the sum due under a stipulatio duplae [5]. Even if the vendor refused the money when properly tendered, he might still avail himself of the condition in the event of the purchaser's neglecting in fact to pay it by the day fixed, unless his own object in refusing the original tender was fraudulent [6].

A sale to which a lex commissoria is attached is of course perfect from its inception, and produces all its ordinary effects, so that what has been said of an addictio in diem resolutiva [7] might be repeated here. If the condition fails through the money not being paid by the day fixed, the contract does not become ipso facto void, but the vendor has the option of rescinding it:

[1] Dig. 18. 3. 6. 2 : ib. 7 : Cod. 4. 54. 4. [2] Dig. 18. 3. 4. 4.
[3] Cod. 4. 54. 7. [4] Dig. 18. 3. 8.
[5] Dig. 18. 5. 10. 1. [6] Arg. Dig. 19. 1. 51. pr.
[7] P. 164 supr. : see Dig. 18. 3. 2 : ib. 5 : Cod. 4. 54. 1.

cum venditor fundi in lege ita caverit, 'si ad diem pecunia soluta non sit, ut fundus inemptus sit,' ita accipitur inemptus esse fundus, si venditor inemptum eum esse velit, quia id venditoris causa caveretur . . . . nam legem commissoriam, quae in venditionibus adicitur, si volet venditor exercebit, non etiam invitus [1]:

and if he determines to rescind it, the purchaser must return him the property [2], and pay the value of fruits and accessions which he has taken, as well as make good any damage or deterioration which it may have undergone while in his possession [3]: further, he forfeits any arra which he may have given [4], though in the absence of agreement to the contrary he is entitled to recover back any portion of the purchase money which he may have paid, but without interest [5]. The reason why the vendor has the option of adopting or avoiding the contract is well put by Pomponius [6]: if the contract became ipso facto void on non-payment of the purchase money it would always be in the power of the purchaser, by withholding it, to rescind the sale as from the moment of its conclusion, and so to throw

---

[1] Dig. 18. 3. 2 & 3.

[2] In the event of rescission the vendor cannot sue *in rem* for the property, unless he has reserved the dominium, whether the purchaser still has it in his possession or has alienated it to a third person, because he gave the purchaser credit, and therefore the dominium passed: Cod. 4. 54. 3. On this question see Glück, Pandekten, 16. p. 296.

[3] Dig. 18. 3. 4. pr.   [4] Dig. 18. 3. 6. pr.

[5] The right to recover purchase money is denied by many (e.g. Treitschke, Kaufcontract, p. 181: Bechmann, Kauf, § 255) on the ground of Dig. 18. 3. 4. 1, and their view is confirmed by the Basilica. But the question which Ulpian is there considering is whether on rescinding the contract the vendor can always recover the value of fruits taken by the purchaser, and he agrees with Neratius that he cannot, if part of the purchase money has been paid, and is forfeited by the purchaser, either in consequence of express agreement to that effect, or because given arrae nomine.

[6] Dig. 18. 3. 2.

on the vendor the loss which would result from accidental destruction or damage occurring after delivery. The vendor however was bound to rescind the sale, if he wished to do so, within a short interval after the conclusion of the period limited: Papinian was of opinion that he must do it 'statim,' at once [1], but this is scarcely reconcileable with passages to which reference has been already made, and which explain the modes in which he could ratify it by implication. It is obvious that if he were not under this obligation, he could do the purchaser an injury similar to that which the latter could do him if the contract were ipso facto avoided if the money were not paid by the day limited. Some writers even contend that if the purchaser tendered the money before he declared himself, the right of rescission was thereby lost, but this seems to be clearly wrong [2]. Analogy with other cases, however, would allow the purchaser to apply to a court to fix a time within which he must make his choice, under penalty of the election passing to the former.

A lex commissoria is never presumed: that is to say, unless it is agreed when the contract is made that it shall be voidable at the vendor's option unless the purchase money is paid by a day fixed, the vendor cannot treat it, on default in payment, as no longer binding: he can only sue for the money [3] and for damages [4].

The conditions most commonly attached to contracts of sale in the interest of the purchaser are those relieving him from liability if after trial and examination he shall not be satisfied with the goods: they fall under the heads of emptio ad gustum [5] and pactum displicentiae [6].

Conditions attached for the benefit of the purchaser;

---

[1] Dig. 18. 3. 4. 2.
[2] Cf. Dig. 44. 7. 23: de illo sane potest dubitari, si interpellatus ipse moram fecerit, an quamvis pecuniam postea offerat, nihilominus poena committatur: et hoc rectius dicitur: see Pothier, 459.
[3] Cod. 4. 38. 8. 9 & 12.   [4] Cod. 4. 44. 14.
[5] Dig. 18. 1. 34. 5.   [6] Dig. 18. 1. 3.

i) Emptio ad gustum.

An emptio ad gustum, which has already been considered with reference to the question at whose risk the property is, pending examination by the purchaser, may be made subject to either a suspensive or a resolutive condition. In the first case the vendor is bound to sell the goods to the purchaser at the price agreed upon if the latter should duly express his satisfaction with them: he is bound from the outset, though conditionally, in this sense that he is not at liberty to sell them to another person pending the fulfilment of the condition. On the other hand, the purchaser is not bound at all until the condition is satisfied, though whether it shall be satisfied depends on his own will alone, so that here we seem to have a very near approach to a non-synallagmatic sale [1]: when he has once expressed himself satisfied with the goods, both the vendor and himself are irrevocably bound [2], with all the usual effects incident to a contract made subject to a suspensive condition which is fulfilled [3]. In the second case, where the condition is resolutive, the contract is absolutely binding from its inception, but is liable to be avoided, with all its consequences, by the purchaser's rejecting the goods [4]: the effects of this need not be further examined after the ample illustration which they have received from the cases of addictio in diem and lex commissoria [5]. The question how long the purchaser is allowed in order to examine the goods, where no limit of time has been fixed by agreement, has been discussed in a previous chapter [6].

---

[1] See p. 2 supr.: and cf. Bechmann, Kauf, II. pp. 212-251.
[2] Inst. iii. 23. 4: Dig. 19. 5. 20. pr. & 1.
[3] P. 163 supr.   [4] Dig. 19. 5. 20. pr.: 18. 5. 6.
[5] Pp. 164, 171 supr.
[6] P. 81 supr. Similar transactions in English law are known as sales 'on trial' or 'on approval,' and 'sale or return.'

In a sale on trial or approval the condition is suspensive: 'there is no sale till the approval is given, either expressly or by implication resulting from keeping the goods beyond the time allowed for trial':

A pactum displicentiae is a resolutive condition annexed to the contract by the purchaser, to the effect that he shall be at liberty to rescind it at his option [1] by returning the goods to the vendor, and not (as in the previous case) by merely expressing himself dissatisfied with them, and to receive back his purchase money, if already paid, or otherwise be discharged from all obligation to pay it [2]. If no limit of time were agreed upon within which the purchaser must exercise his option, it was provided by the Ædilician Edict that he must do so within sixty days [3], though the time would be extended if he could prove that he was prevented from availing himself of the condition earlier by

(ii) Pactum displicentiae.

Benjamin, p. 593 (cited with approval as a correct statement of the law by Denman, J., in *Elphick* v. *Barnes*, 5 C. P. D. p. 326) : and where such a time is fixed the buyer is at liberty to change his mind during the whole term, and this right is not affected by his telling the vendor in the interval that the price does not suit him, if he still retains possession of the article (*Ellis* v. *Mortimer*, 1 B. & P. N. R. 257). The bargain called 'sale or return' is a sale in which the buyer is entitled to return the goods at his option within a reasonable time : the property passes, and an action for goods sold and delivered will lie, if the goods are not returned to the vendor, within such time : *Moss* v. *Sweet*, 16 Q. B. 493 : cf. *Head* v. *Tattersall*, L. R. 7. Ex. 7.

[1] According to Bechmann, Kauf, II. p. 544, only by bringing an action, not by simply returning the goods. This view is based on the connection which existed between the law on this subject and the Ædilician Edict (which will be examined in the next chapter) : 'der Zusammenhang ist klar : nach diesem Edict kann der Kauf rückgängig gemacht werden auf Grund hervortretender Mängel : es kann aber vertragsmässig die Ruckgängigmachung einfach in das Missfallen des Käufers verstellt werden.'

[2] Dig. 18. 1. 3 : 19. 5. 20 : 21. 1. 31. 22. The difference between this case and a resolutive condition proper has been pointed out on p. 80 supr.

[3] Si quid ita venierit ut, nisi placuerit, intra praefinitum tempus redhibeatur, ea conventio rata habetur : si autem de tempore nihil convenerit, in factum actio intra sexaginta dies utiles accommodatur emptori ad redhibendum, ultra non : Dig. 21. 1. 31. 22. Bechmann, Kauf, II. § 258, thinks that the time related not to a declaration of dissatisfaction by the purchaser, but to the institution of an action by him to get the sale rescinded.

causes beyond his own control, and Ulpian was even of opinion that the rule might be entirely excluded by agreement made at the outset, and the purchaser be allowed to return the goods at any length of time he pleased from the conclusion of the contract[1]. The principles of the actio redhibitoria were applied to this case by the Ædiles, so that (contrary to the usual rule in resolutive conditions) the goods were at the vendor's risk throughout[2].

Common terms in sales; reservation by vendor of right of pre-emption: This is perhaps the most convenient place to mention briefly certain terms which were sometimes embodied in contracts of sale. (1) The agreement that if the purchaser thought of selling the property, the vendor should have a right of pre-emption[3], either on terms arranged when the original contract was made, or on the terms offered by any third person who might be willing to buy it. When created by agreement such right, being *in personam*, availed only against the first purchaser, and not against any other person to whom notwithstanding the agreement the property might have been sold and delivered: but it might be created also by will, and was in certain cases given by law[4]. (2) The pactum de retrovendendo, agreement that the purchaser should be bound to resell the property to the vendor either in certain contingencies[5] or on demand (pactum de retrovendendo[6]). Usually of course the price at which it was to be resold was fixed at the time of the original sale: otherwise, according to some, it was understood to be the price paid to the vendor himself, while according to others it had to be determined by arbitration. Usually, too, a time was limited within which alone the vendor could demand a resale of the property[7]: in the

---

[1] Dig. loc. cit.
[2] Dig. 21. 1. 31. 24 : ib. 47. 1 & 48 : Vangerow, Pandekten, § 635.
[3] Dig. 18. 1. 75 : 19. 1. 21. 5. In both passages the agreement is to sell to no one except the vendor.
[4] E. g. in Emphyteusis, Cod. 4. 66. 3.
[5] E. g. Dig. 19. 5. 12.   [6] Cod. 4. 54. 2 : ib. 6 & 7.
[7] E. g. Cod. 4. 54. 7.

absence of such limitation his right of enforcing the pact was subject to the ordinary limitation of thirty years, though there is no agreement as to the precise time from which such limitation began to run [1]. On tender of the money within the time allowed, the purchaser was bound to reconvey the property: but if in contravention of the pact he had in the meanwhile sold and delivered it to some third person the vendor had no rights against the latter, but was confined to his action for damages against his own purchaser. Fruits gathered by the latter while the property was vested in himself were his, and had not to be accounted for [2], for the pact did not operate like a resolutive condition [3].

Occasionally it was agreed that the vendor should be under a similar obligation to buy the property back on the purchaser's requisition (pactum de retro-emendo). *and de retro-emendo.*

[1] See Treitschke, Kaufcontract, pp. 204, 205: Glück, Pandekten, 16. § 998: Pothier, 391.

[2] Pothier, 405 sqq.

[3] Pothier, 429. This right of repurchase, under the name of Droit de Réméré, seems to have been commonly annexed by agreement to sales of land in France, and is treated at great length by Pothier, 385-444. It also forms the subject of fifteen articles (1659-1673) in the Code Civil: but the authorities on the subject are so scanty that it can hardly have been much used among the Romans.

CHAPTER XII.

MODES OF DISCHARGE.

Contraria voluntas, or mutual waiver before performance by either party. Partial discharge by subsequent variation of terms. Rescission by the vendor for inadequacy of price (laesio enormis): difficulties of the texts on the subject. When the price is to be deemed inadequate. The courses open to the vendor. Effect of successful action for rescission. Cases in which the vendor may not rescind: other doubtful cases. The purchaser's right of rescission on account of undisclosed defects. Historical sketch of the vendor's liability for non-disclosure; the old Civil Law: the practice of exacting a covenant as to quality: the Aedilician Edict. Extension of its rules to all sales by juristic construction. What defects render the contract liable to rescission? Distinction between slaves and animals. The defect must exist at the date of the contract, and be unknown to the purchaser. Purchase by agents with knowledge. Defect in accessions: in one of several things purchased together: in part of an universitas. Vendor's duty to disclose defects of these kinds. The purchaser's remedies: (1) by exceptio: (2) by actio redhibitoria. Effects of this action: what must be done by the purchaser, and by the vendor. Covenants sometimes demandable by either party. Points in which the parties are differently treated under the actio redhibitoria. The period of limitation. (3) By actio quanti minoris or aestimatoria: its period of limitation and effects. Reaction of these Aedilician remedies on those of the Civil Law. Cases in which they are inapplicable. Note A. Implied warranty of quality in Scotch and English Law.

CERTAIN ways in which a contract of sale could be avoided have already been examined in the preceding chapter, and it will be unnecessary to repeat what has been there said respecting them. With one exception, it is not proposed here to enter upon a discussion of modes of discharge which are common to other contracts, or at any rate to those which along with sale are termed Consensual. The exception is that method of terminating a consensual obligation known as 'contraria voluntas[1]': the rest of this chapter will be occupied with an examination of certain grounds upon which either vendor or purchaser was allowed by law to rescind a sale which he had validly contracted.

So long as nothing has been done in fulfilment of the contract by either party (re integra) it can be discharged by their agreeing to be off their bargain[2], and this is merely an application of the principle often cited by English judges that an obligation ex contractu can be dissolved by a process corresponding to that by which it was incurred[3]. Such agreement amounts to a mutual waiver, or undertaking not to sue upon the promise of the other party, which in relation to an obligation of the bonae fidei class did not require to be inserted, in the guise of an exceptio, in the formula of the action[4]: and the equitable character of the contract required that the waiver should be mutual, so that even where one of the parties alone released the other by a formal admission of performance (acceptilatio) it operated as a discharge for both[5].

Contraria voluntas, or mutual waiver before performance by either party.

The requirement that the res must still be 'integra' means that nothing must have been done in performance of the contract. Mere delivery of possession, however, by the vendor does not suffice to prevent a mutual waiver, for the property is still in him, and the waiver will disable the purchaser from setting up the exceptio rei venditae et traditae[6], and similarly the novation of the contract is no

---

[1] Inst. iii. 29. 4.

[2] Abire, discedere ab emptione: Dig. 18. 1. 6. 2: 18. 5. 1: ib. 5.

[3] Nihil tam naturale est quam eo genere quidque dissolvere quo colligatum est: ideo verborum obligatio verbis tollitur, nudi consensus obligatio nudo consensu dissolvitur: Dig. 50. 17. 35: cf. ib. 153.

[4] Adeo autem bonae fidei iudiciis exceptiones postea factae, quae ex eodem sunt contractu, insunt, ut constet in emptione caeterisque bonae fidei iudiciis re nondum secuta posse abiri ab emptione: Dig. 2. 14. 7. 6: cf. ib. 27. 2.

[5] Dig. 46. 4. 23: cf. ib. 19: Dig. 2. 14. 27. 9: 44. 7. 47.

[6] Dig. 2. 14. 52.

obstacle to its practical dissolution by contraria voluntas [1]. But if one of the parties had performed his side of the contract, it could be agreed that, on the return of what had been given, nothing should be due from the other [2], the waiver being unilateral and subject to a condition precedent: though in order to bind the other to return what he had received a stipulation was necessary [3].

Partial discharge by subsequent variation of terms. Finally, as a contract of sale might be absolutely discharged by subsequent agreement, so it might be partially, by the elimination of some of its terms, or by their being subjected to some modification which did not constitute a material addition to the duties undertaken by the parties:

> pacta conventa, quae postea facta detrahunt aliquid emptioni, contineri contractu videntur: quae vero adiiciunt, credimus non inesse [4].

By an alteration in the amount of the purchase money the original contract was deemed to be wholly discharged, because its very essence lay in the price fixed upon at the outset [5]. A conditional sale was rescinded at once by a new agreement to the same effect, but omitting the condition [6]: while if a condition were subsequently attached to a sale originally absolute the latter was unaffected by the conditional agreement until the condition was fulfilled [7].

Rescission by the vendor for inadequacy of price (laesio enormis): The vendor has the right of rescinding a sale if the price agreed upon is less than half the true value of the thing sold (laesio enormis, seu ultra dimidium), unless the purchaser will pay so much more as will make the price a fair one. This principle seems to have been quite unknown to the earlier law, which left the parties to make their own bargain, and in the absence of fraud would assist neither

---

[1] Dig. 18. 5. 3.   [2] Dig. 2. 14. 58.
[3] Arg. Cod. 4. 45. 2.
[4] Dig. 18. 1. 72. pr.: cf. Dig. 2. 14. 7. 6: 18. 5. 2: ib. 4.
[5] Dig. 18. 1. 72. pr.   [6] Pothier, 327.
[7] Dig. 18. 5. 7. pr.

to undo an engagement into which he had voluntarily entered[1]. The first trace of it is found in two rescripts of Diocletian and Maximian in 285 and 295 A.D.[2], which do not appear to have been understood as laying down a general rule of law, but to have given extraordinary relief in a case of great hardship without being intended to be followed in subsequent similar cases, for there are constitutions of Constantine and later emperors in the Theodosian Code[3] in which it is emphatically laid down that, unless there has been fraud, no sale can be rescinded for mere inadequacy of price. These enactments however were adopted, as containing a general rule of law, in his Code by Justinian, who either omitted the inconsistent dicta of

---

[1] Idem Pomponius ait, in pretio emptionis et venditonis naturaliter licere contrahentibus se circumvenire: Dig. 4. 4. 16. 4 : quemadmodum in emendo et vendendo naturaliter concessum est quod pluris sit minoris emere, quod minoris sit pluris vendere, et ita invicem se circumscribere: Dig. 19. 2. 22. 3 : cf. ib. 23.

[2] Rem maioris pretii si tu vel pater tuus minoris pretii distraxerit, humanum est ut vel pretium te restituente emptoribus fundum venditum recipias, auctoritate iudicis intercedente, vel si emptor elegerit, quod deest iusto pretio recipias. Minus autem pretium esse videtur, si nec dimidia pars veri pretii soluta sit : Cod. 4. 44. 2.

Si voluntate tua fundum tuum filius tuus venumdedit, dolus ex calliditate atque insidia emptoris argui debet, vel metus mortis vel cruciatus corporis imminens detegi, ne habeatur rata venditio. Hoc enim solum, quod paulo minore pretio fundum venditum significas, ad rescindendam venditionem invalidum est. Quodsi videlicet contractus emptionis atque venditionis cogitasses substantiam, et quod emptor viliore comparandi venditor cariore distrahendi votum gerentes ad hunc contractum accedant, vixque post multas contentiones, paulatim venditore de eo, quod petierat, detrahente, emptore autem huic, quod obtulerat, addente, ad certum consentiant pretium, profecto perspiceres, neque bonam fidem, quae emptionis atque venditionis conventionem tuetur, pati, neque ullam rationem concedere, rescindi propter hoc consensu finitum contractum vel statim, vel post pretii quantitatis disceptationem : nisi minus dimidia iusti pretii, quod fuerat tempore venditionis, datum est, electione iam emptori praestita servanda : Cod. ib. 8.

[3] 3. 1. 1. 4 & 7.

the Emperors after Diocletian, or so altered them as no longer to conflict with the law laid down by this Emperor. They have given rise to a vast amount of controversy. Taken literally, they give the right of rescission to the vendor only, and in no case to the purchaser, and they strongly appear to relate only to sales of land. Writers on the theoretical side of the law [1] seem for the most part to incline to the view that as they are opposed to the general principles of the law of sale, as stated elsewhere in the Corpus Juris, they must be construed strictly, and not extended [2]: and this contention is supported by the reason underlying these rescripts, for people are often driven by an overwhelming necessity to sell property on the spur of the moment at a great undervalue, while one is practically never obliged to buy too high unless one chooses. In practice, on the other hand, they have been variously taken to cover sales of moveables [3] no less than of immoveables, to confer on the purchaser [4] a right equivalent to that undoubtedly given by the terms of the law to the vendor, and even to apply to transactions other than sales, but of a similar character, such as hirings and exchanges [5].

difficulties of the texts on the subject.

---

[1] See the names cited in Glück, 17 pp. 27 sqq. Among more recent writers may be mentioned Vangerow, iii. § 611, note: Windscheid, § 396, note 2: and Wächter, § 20 .

[2] In the law of France, as stated by Pothier (339) the rule applied only to sales of land and rights over land, but the purchaser had a corresponding right to that of the vendor (372 sqq). In the Code Civil (arts. 1674-1685) the right belongs to the vendor only, and only on a sale of an immovable, but a 'lesion' is newly defined as a sale at less than seven-twelfths of the true value.

[3] This may perhaps be justified by the use of the word 'rem' at the commencement of Cod. 4. 44. 2, and by general considerations of the object (equity: 'humanum est') aimed at by that enactment: see Glück, 17. pp. 51. 52.

[4] For a discussion of the alleged right of the purchaser see Pothier, 372-384, and Glück, 17. pp. 27-50. There seems to be no agreement as to what constitutes a laesio enormis on his side.

[5] This wide extension is given to the law, for instance, in the

The vendor is entitled to rescind when the purchase money is less than one-half the true value of the thing sold: but this right lapses if the purchaser is willing to pay so much in addition as will make the price 'iustum'[1]. Some writers have supposed that by iustum pretium is meant merely half the true value, and that consequently the purchaser is entitled to retain the land or goods if he will pay so much in the aggregate as would, if originally agreed upon, have excluded the vendor's right of rescission: but the prevailing view, which is uniformly followed in the tribunals where the Civil Law obtains[2], is that he must pay the true value—i.e. more than double what he has agreed to pay[3]. It is also held that it was not the intention of the legislator to impose any further liability on the purchaser for mesne profits, or to pay interest on the additional purchase money from the date of the contract: he is to pay only 'quod deest iusto pretio'[4]. *When the price is to be deemed inadequate.*

The true value is declared by the enactment to be that which the thing possessed at the time when the contract was concluded, any increase or diminution in the meanwhile being immaterial. On general principles, this is to be ascertained by the judgment of experts[5].

The vendor who has suffered a laesio enormis can assert his rights either by exception or by action. The first is the appropriate method when he has not yet delivered the property, and is sued for such delivery by an actio ex *The courses open to the vendor.*

Austrian bürgerliches Gesetzbuch, §§ 934, 935. See Holtzendorff, Rechtslexicon, II. p. 624.

[1] Cod. 4. 44. 8.   [2] Glück, 17. pp. 53, 54.

[3] By the French Code Civil the purchaser, in order to escape rescission, must pay a price equivalent to nine-tenths of the true value, with interest on the balance from the date of the contract: Arts. 1681, 1682.

[4] Pothier, 336.

[5] On this subject see Treitschke, Kaufcontract, § 104: Glück, 17. pp. 56–66.

empto: the second, when he has made conveyance, and seeks to procure the rescission of the contract with a view to the revesting of the property in himself, on condition of repaying the purchase money, if already received. In this case the defendant has the option of surrendering the property, or of retaining it on making the requisite addition to the price; a consequence of which is that if it perishes while in the defendant's possession, but without fraud on his part, before judgment, the plaintiff's action must fail. The precise character of the action has been much debated[1], but the majority of the authorities hold it to be no other than the ordinary action ex vendito, which was used for the rescission of the contract in other cases[2]. Both exception and action devolve on the vendor's heirs, and the first might be used by his surety no less than by himself. Of course the action, being personal, could be brought only against the purchaser or his heirs, so that, if he has conveyed the property to a third person, no proceedings can be taken against the latter, nor is he himself suable unless his alienation was fraudulent, or he has made money by the transaction.

Effects of successful action for rescission. If the vendor succeeds in his action, the property and the purchase money have to be respectively restored, the parties thus being replaced in statum quo ante. Whether the vendor must pay interest on the purchase money for the period during which it has been in his hands, and the purchaser in turn compensate him for the value of fruits which he has enjoyed[3], is a point upon which the text of the law throws no light, but which on general principles

---

[1] Some contend that it should be a condictio 'ex lege,' others a condictio indebiti, others a 'civil' in integrum restitutio. Pothier (331) calls it an actio utilis in rem: 'le vendeur revendique la chose, comme si elle n'avoit jamais cessé de lui appartenir': but the 'fiction de Droit' appears to be merely a 'fiction de Pothier.'

[2] E.g. Dig. 19. 1. 11. 3, 5, & 6.

[3] Pothier, 357, 361.

seems to require an answer in the affirmative[1], though it is said that a different rule is followed in practice. There is no doubt however that the purchaser must surrender accessions (such as treasure found upon land[2]), or that he can recover the amount of all necessary or beneficial outlay which he has made upon the property from the time of its conveyance to him[3]: and the weight of authority[4] inclines to the view that any charge created over it by him will bind it in the vendor's hands after rescission of the contract[5], though the latter can require him to discharge the encumbrance, and withhold the purchase money, if he has not yet repaid it, until this has been done.

The effect of the property being lost or destroyed while in the purchaser's possession, but without any fraud on his part, has been already noticed. The object of the vendor's action is to obtain restitution of the property, and as this is no longer possible the plaintiff cannot succeed[6]: he cannot even require the increase in the purchase money by paying which only the purchaser could under ordinary circumstances retain the property, for this he cannot claim as of right in any case[7]. Both parties are sufferers, and

---

[1] Cum enim verbum 'restituas' lege invenitur, etsi non specialiter de fructibus additum est, tamen etiam fructus sunt restituendi: Dig. 50. 17. 173. 1 ; usurae vicem fructuum optinent et merito non debent a fructibus separari : Dig. 22. 1. 34. Si l'acquéreur préfère rendre la chose et recevoir le prix, il rend les fruits du jour de la demande. L'intérêt du prix qu'il a payé lui est aussi compté du jour de la même demande, ou du jour du paiement, s'il n'a touché aucuns fruits: Code Civil, art. 1682.

[2] Pothier, 359.   [3] Pothier, 362–367.

[4] On the analogy of a sale rescinded by redhibitio. Pothier (371) is of the contrary opinion.

[5] See Glück, 17. p. 109.

[6] On the principles laid down in Dig. 45. 1. 23 : ib. 33 & 37.

[7] The case is like that of noxal surrender: at iudicium solius noxae deditionis nullum est, sed pecuniariam condemnationem sequitur, et ideo iudicati in decem agitur, his enim solis condemnatur: noxae deditio in solutione est, quae e lege tribuitur: Dig 42. 1. 6. 1.

'dum quaeritur de damno, et par utriusque sit, quare non potentior sit, qui teneat, quam qui persequitur[1]?' For depreciation of the property by which he has profited (e.g. for timber cut and sold), the purchaser must answer, but not apparently for any diminution of value which has not benefited him, even though due to his negligence, at any rate if he was unaware that the contract was voidable by the vendor[2].

Cases in which the vendor may not rescind: There are three cases in which a contract of sale cannot be rescinded on the ground of laesio enormis, and others in which it is questioned whether such rescission is allowable or not. There can be no rescission—

(1) If the vendor expressly waives his right to rescind when making the contract[3]; though many authorities[4] confine this rule to those cases in which the vendor was not aware of the true value of the property. A waiver is implied from a declaration by the vendor that he is selling cheap out of regard for the purchaser.

(2) If the purchase is an emptio spei, and it turns out that the purchaser's gain is more than double the price agreed upon: for the 'true value' is to be determined by reference to the date of the contract, and at that time the chance purchased had no clear and ascertainable value[5]: hence in the absence of fraud it is impossible to rebut the presumption that the vendor got what he thought the chance was worth at that time[6].

---

[1] Dig. 45. 1. 91. 3.

[2] Pothier, 360 : Demante, Cours analytique de Code Civil, vii. p. 173.

[3] Si enim ipso edicto praetoris pacta conventa, quae neque contra leges nec dolo malo inita sunt, omnimodo observanda sunt, quare et in hac causa pacta non valent, cum alia regula est iuris antiqui omnes licentiam habere his quae pro se introducta sunt renuntiare ? Cod. 2. 3. 29. 1.

[4] E. g. Treitschke, Kaufcontract, § 107.

[5] Dig. 18. 1. 8. 1 : 19. 1. 12.

[6] By the German Handelsgesetzbuch, art. 286, rescission for laesio enormis is not permitted in mercantile transactions (Handelsgeschäfte).

(3) Where the vendor, in selling the property at an undervalue, was merely obeying a direction imposed on him by a deceased person whose heir he is, or by whose decease he has taken a benefit[1]. In both cases the true value of the property is immaterial, because the obligation to carry out the deceased's direction is attached to the inheritance or other benefit, unless (in the case of a legatee) its execution entails a burden greater than the benefit itself[2].

The case in which the possibility of rescission is most disputed is where the vendor knew at the time of the sale that the true value of what he was selling was more than double the price which he had consented to take. On the one hand it is argued that if a man knowingly sells an article for less than half its real value, the transaction in respect of the residue is to be deemed a gift[3]: *qua* sale, it is unimpeachable. But the text of the law, it is objected, contains no word implying that ignorance of the true value is a condition precedent of the right of rescission: and it is clear, in view of the object of the law, which was to protect persons who are driven by temporary and overwhelming necessity to sell property at a great undervalue, that it would be unreasonable to refuse rescission on this account, for the very case which the law was designed to meet is one in which the vendor is usually fully aware that he is

other doubtful cases.

Possibly the reason of this is that dealings on a large scale between merchants are always entered into with a view to profit, and thus partake of a wagering nature. The purchase of a policy of life insurance is held not to be an emptio spei, because it has an ascertainable surrender value: cf. Dig. 35. 2. 68. For the French law, which substantially agrees with that stated above, see Demante, Cours analytique de Code Civil, vii. p. 160.

[1] Dig. 30. 49. 9: 31. 70. 1.
[2] Gaius ii. 261 : Inst. ii. 24. 1.
[3] Donari videtur, quod nullo iure cogente conceditur: Dig. 39. 5. 29. pr.: 50. 17. 82.

making an overwhelming sacrifice¹. Hence some of those who consider that knowledge is a bar to rescission exclude those cases in which the sale was made under pressing necessity: in all others they hold that a gift is to be presumed, and rescission denied. But that the necessity of the case should make no difference is a reasonable inference from another rescript of the two Emperors from whose legislation the whole law on this subject has been developed².

There are also many writers who hold that a purchase at a public auction cannot be avoided merely because the property has been knocked down at less than half its real value. The argument that an auction is a more certain means of determining the real value of a thing than even the judgment of experts is one that breaks down in particular cases³, and the supporters of this exception appeal to the known unwillingness of the Roman law to reopen on any ground, except fraud, a purchase made at a public auction⁴. The opinion, however, that sales at auction are in this respect in no way differently treated from other sales is now generally accepted and acted upon in the Courts⁵.

The purchaser's right of rescission on account of undisclosed defects.
Turning to the purchaser's right of rescission, the rule is that he is entitled to avoid the contract if the goods sold are found defective in quality, or (more correctly) if defects are discovered in them subsequently to the sale which could not have been detected on examination at the time.

---

¹ See Treitschke, Kaufcontract, § 106, p. 382.

² Non idcirco minus venditio fundi, quod hunc ad munus sumptibus necessariis urgentibus [non] vilioris pretii vel urgente debito te distraxisse contendis, rata manere debet: Cod 4. 44. 12.

³ By Vangerow (§ 611) it is derided as ludicrous (lächerlich).

⁴ Cod. 10. 3. 5 : 4. 46. 3.

⁵ See Glück, 17. pp. 87-97. In Saxony and Austria a sale at auction made by the order or with the sanction of a Court is excepted : Treitschke, Kaufcontract, p. 389.

It is thus a principle of the Roman law that a warranty of quality is implied in every sale: the more exact determination of the limits of this principle is for the moment reserved until we have traced the steps by which it was established. As Pothier [1] observes, the vendor is bound by the nature of the contract of sale to warrant the purchaser that the goods sold are free from certain defects calculated to render them entirely or nearly useless, or sometimes even injurious, for the purposes for which they are ordinarily employed. This obligation is a consequence of that contracted by the vendor, 'to cause the purchaser to have the goods': for this latter obligation, according to the intention of the parties, is not fulfilled unless he has them for effective use.

At the risk of some repetition of what has been said in a previous chapter [2] it will be convenient, and perhaps even necessary, to examine the law relating to the vendor's liability for non-disclosure from the historical point of view. The Civil, as distinct from the edictal, Law held him liable for defective quality only in two cases: firstly, where his conduct had been fraudulent; and secondly, where he either expressly represented (dicta) that the goods possessed certain desired qualities or were free from certain specific defects, or gave a warranty (promissa) to that effect. *Historical sketch of the vendor's liability for non-disclosure:*

Of fraud it is unnecessary to say more, except to remind the reader that if the vendor knew, at the time of the contract, of defects in the goods which would impair their utility for the purpose for which they were intended, and deliberately abstained from giving such information to the purchaser, his conduct was fraudulent [3]; and (as in cases of direct and wilful fraud) the purchaser could rescind the *the old Civil Law:*

---

[1] 202.   [2] Pp. 58-62 supr.
[3] Dolum malum a se abesse praestare venditor debet, qui non tantum in eo est qui fallendi causa obscure loquitur, sed etiam qui insidiose obscure dissimulat: Dig. 18. 1. 43. 2.

contract by actio de dolo, and probably also by an actio ex empto [1], by which he could also recover damages for such loss as he had sustained, whether he desired to maintain the contract or to avoid it [2].

A warranty or a representation that the article sold possesses certain qualities had, by the Civil Law, the same consequences [3], and the rule was the same if it were not of the quality or material which the purchaser might, under the circumstances, reasonably expect, for here the warranty was implied [4]. Between dicta and promissa—between, that is to say, representations inducing the purchaser to buy, and express warranties—no distinction appears to have been drawn [5]: but mere general commendation of his goods

---

[1] Whether he could rescind on this ground by actio ex empto is disputed, but apparently without good reason. Vangerow (§ 609, note 2, III) asserts the negative, but elsewhere (§ 605, note 1, II), apropos to Dig. 19. 1. 11. 5, he says that if the purchaser would never have made the contract, had he been aware of the facts known to the vendor, he can avoid it by this action, and in the passage previously referred to he admits that an avoidance of the contract might possibly be granted on an actio ex empto claiming 'id quod actoris interest' if the whole transaction is quite useless to the purchaser on account of the vendor's non-disclosure, so that his 'interest' can be fully secured only by a judicial rescission. See Dig. 19. 1. 11. 3, and compare Windscheid, Lehrbuch, § 393, note 1.

[2] Dig. 19. 1. 13. pr. & 1 : 18. 1. 35. 8.

[3] Dig. 19. 1. 6. 4: ib. 13. 3 & 4: 18. 6. 6. In English law 'where there is a contract for the sale of goods by description, there is an implied condition that the goods shall correspond with the description' (*Josling* v. *Kingsford*, 32. L. J. C. P. 94 : *Mody* v. *Gregson*, L. R. 4 Ex. p. 56), Chalmers, Sale of Goods, § 16 : Benjamin, pp. 597-602.

[4] Dig. 19. 1. 21. 2.

[5] See Dig. 19. 1. 13. 3 & 4, ib. 6. 4 : In English law 'antecedent representations made by the vendor as an *inducement* to the buyer, but not forming part of the contract when concluded, are not warranties' [and consequently, unless fraudulent, give no right of action, either for rescission of the contract, or for damages] ; Benjamin, p. 607. Upon this distinction between statements which are within and statements which are outside the contract there appears to be no definite authority in the Civil Law. But the English Courts seem to be tending

imposed no liability on a vendor[1], nor did even a more specific description if its truth or falsehood could be ascertained at once by the purchaser[2]. The purchaser has the same rights if the article is either warranted or represented to be free from certain defects, which are subsequently found to be present[3].

As in the cases of fraud and non-disclosure of defects known to the vendor at the date of the contract, the actio ex empto lay under these circumstances for damages, and even for rescission of the whole agreement if the purchaser could satisfy the court that he would not have entered into it at all had he known that the representation or warranty would turn out to be unfounded[4]. But apart from these cases which have been considered, the Civil Law gave the purchaser no remedy for defects of quality in the goods sold, unless he took care to guard himself against the contingency: its maxim, in effect, was 'caveat emptor'[5].

in the direction of granting rescission on the ground of any misrepresentation, fraudulent or not, which is a material inducement to a party to enter into a contract: see the chapter on Misrepresentation in Anson on Contract, especially in relation to the cases of *Redgrave* v. *Hurd* and *Newbigging* v. *Adam*, at p. 150 (5th ed.).

[1] Ea autem sola dicta sive promissa admittenda sunt, quaecumque sic dicuntur, ut praestentur, non ut jactentur: Dig 21. 1. 19. 3 : cf. ib. pr.—2 : Dig. 4. 3. 37. So in English law the maxim is 'simplex commendatio non obligat': Benjamin, pp. 404, 610 sq.

[2] Ea quae commendandi causa in venditionibus dicuntur, si palam appareant, venditorem non obligant, veluti si dicat servum speciosum, domum bene aedificatam : at si dixerit hominem litteratum, vel artificem, praestare debet; nam hoc ipso pluris vendit : Dig. 18. 1. 43. pr.: 4. 3. 37.

[3] Dig, 19. 1. 6. 4 : ib. 13. 3 : 21. 2. 75 : 18. 1. 59 : ib. 66.

[4] Dig. 19. 1. 11. 3.

[5] Dig. 19. 1. 13. pr. & 1 might seem to contradict this, and on the strength of it Neustetel (Römisch-rechtliche Untersuchungen, ix. pp. 160 sqq) argues that a reduction of the purchase money could always be obtained by actio ex empto. But the fact is, as will be seen below, that by the construction of the lawyers of the empire, the redress obtainable through the edictal remedies came also to be obtainable through the Civil Law actions on the contract: ea enim, quae sunt

the practice of exacting a covenant as to quality:

The mode in which purchasers protected themselves against possible loss through defects for which the Civil Law of sale would neither rescind the contract nor compensate them in damages was stipulation. This appears to have been very general in purchases of slaves and certain animals, which so frequently suffer from forms of disease or unsoundness which it is impossible to detect till some time has elapsed, and numerous formulae of such stipulations are formed in Varro[1]. Such a precautionary system, however, was ponderous and inconvenient in relation to the numberless small dealings which must have taken place every day in the open market places of Rome. Even as early as Plautus the supervision of these belonged to the Curule Ædiles, who in the interest of the purchasing public could exclude and perhaps order the destruction of bad wares offered for sale therein[2]: a very beneficent and necessary jurisdiction, when we remember how compact and united are the interests of market tradespeople, and how largely they appear even among the Romans to have subordinated commercial honesty to the desire for profit[3]. But even this protection was of little practical utility in sales of slaves or animals, defects in which of the kinds already referred to were no more immediately discoverable by a magistrate than by a purchaser: and at a later date the Ædiles regulated these by Edict, under which further aid was given to purchasers of such wares in open market. The Ædilician Edict at first almost certainly related to

the Ædilician Edict.

moris et consuetudinis, in bonae fidei iudiciis debent venire: Dig. 21. 1. 31. 20; cf. Vangerow, § 609, note 2, II.

[1] Slaves, de re rust. II. 10. 5: sheep, ib. 2. 5: goats, ib. 3: pigs. ib. 1: oxen, ib. 5: asses, ib. 6: dogs, ib. 9.

[2] ... quamvis fastidiosus Aedilis est, si quae improbae sunt merces, iactat omnis. *Rudens* II. 379: cf. *Miles Glor.* III. 727: *Captivi* IV. 823.

[3] Nam id genus hominum ad lucrum potius ... vel turpiter faciendum pronius est: Paulus in Dig. 21. 1. 44. 1.

such sales of slaves, and in this form it was known to Cicero[1], though in his day it was perhaps only of recent introduction[2]. Its import is clear: the vendor, whether he is aware of them or not, is bound without demand to notify the purchaser of certain flaws (if present) in any slave he sells in open market. The form of the Edict given in the Digest[3] suggests that from the outset it promised the purchaser an action for rescission in the event of such defects being subsequently discovered within a reasonable time: but there can be little or no doubt that this was a later innovation, and that at first the Ædiles went no further than to compel the vendor, at any time not exceeding two months from the date of the contract, to enter into a stipulation at the purchaser's demand that the slave's utility was marred by none of the defects in question[4],

---

[1] De Off. III. 17. § 71.

[2] It is preserved in Dig. 21. 1. 1. 1 : qui mancipia vendunt, certiores faciant emptores quid morbi vitiique cuique sit, quis fugitivus errove sit noxave solutus non sit : eademque omnia, cum ea mancipia venibunt, palam recte pronuntianto. From a comparison with Aulus Gellius, Noct. Att. iv. 2. 1, it may be conjectured that the second of these two sentences was the important one.

[3] Emptori omnibusque ad quos ea res pertinet iudicium dabimus, ut id mancipium redhibeatur: Dig. loc. cit.

[4] Si venditor de his quae edicto continentur non caveat, pollicentur adversus eum ad redhibendum iudicium intra duos menses: Dig. 21.1.28: cf. Dig. 21. 2. 31 & 32. There is abundant evidence in the Corpus Iuris that even under the law of Justinian the purchaser of a slave might require from the vendor a stipulatio duplae (the *duplum* is denied by Windscheid, Lehrbuch, § 394, note 17) suable on in the event of the discovery of such defects as were specified in the Edict (quia adsidua est duplae stipulatio, idcirco placuit etiam ex empto agi posse, si duplam venditor mancipii non caveat: Dig. 21. 1. 31. 20 : cf. Cod. 4. 49. 14 : Dig. 21.2. 31 & 32 : ib. 37. 1 : and Theophilus, paraphr. ad Inst. iii. 182: δεῖ γὰρ τὸν πράτην ἐπερωτᾶσθαι τῷ ἀγοραστῇ, ὡς εἰ πάθος εὑρεθῇ κρυπτὸν ἐν τῷ πιπρασκαμένῳ οἰκέτῃ, παρέξει τὸ διπλάσιον): and from Dig. 19. 1. 11. 4 it is clear that a similar stipulation could be exacted on the sale of iumenta, though there is no evidence of its extension to sales of wares of other kinds. Bechmann (Kauf, I. pp. 402, 406, note 2) appears to think that these passages were admitted

and in case of refusal to grant the purchaser an action for the recovery of the purchase money on returning the slave. Later, but probably before the extension of the Edict to beasts of burden (iumenta) it was further proclaimed that the purchaser might rescind the sale by actio redhibitoria on discovery of such defects within six months from the date of the contract. The later clause relating to sales of iumenta in market lays a heavier burden on the vendor: he is bound to disclose all[1] and not merely certain specified defects, under penalty of having the contract rescinded (redhibitio) within six months, and the purchaser is given the further right of suing at any time within twelve months for a return of his purchase money proportionate to the defects discovered (actio quanti minoris). By subsequent Edictal changes this new remedy was granted to purchasers of slaves as well as of cattle or horses, and both actions were finally made applicable by the Ædiles to sales of beasts of all kinds included in the term 'pecus'[2]. By juristic construction under the Empire this process of extension was carried even further, for even as early as Labeo the aedilician remedies were held to lie on sales of all things whatsoever[3], moveable or immoveable[4], so that an implied warranty of freedom from defects impairing reasonable use had come to be inherent in every sale of any

Extension of its rules to all sales by juristic construction.

into the Corpus Iuris by oversight, and that the system of compulsory stipulation was obsolete: 'passt die ganze Stelle überhaupt nicht in das justinianische System, das den Stipulationszwang ausgemerzt hat.'

[1] Qui iumenta vendunt, palam recte dicunto quid in quoque eorum morbi vitiique sit: Dig. 21. 1. 38. pr.

[2] Idcirco elogium huic edicto subiectum est, cuius verba haec sunt: quae de iumentorum sanitate diximus, de caetero quoque pecore omni venditores faciunto: Dig. 21. 1. 38. 5.

[3] Labeo scribit edictum aedilium curulium de venditionibus rerum esse, tam earum, quae soli sint, quam earum, quae mobiles aut se moventes: Dig. 21. 1. 1. pr.: cf. ib. 63.

[4] E. g. fundus pestilens (Dig. 21. 1. 49) or pestibilis (Cod. 4. 58. 4), vas non integrum (Dig. 19. 1. 6. 4), tignum vitiosum (Dig. ib. 13. pr.).

magnitude, wherever entered into, on the general ground that a statutory provision is to be extended to all cases requiring like remedy[1]. The rule was even engrafted upon two other transactions closely analogous to sale, viz. exchange[2] and datio in solutum[3].

Turning now to a more precise and systematic statement of the law, the first subject for examination is the definition of what may for convenience be termed redhibitory defects[4]. Speaking generally, they are those defects which either destroy or impair the usefulness of the thing sold for the purpose for which things of that kind are ordinarily intended to be used[5]. In relation to slaves and animals, which are almost exclusively used in illustration, Labeo[6] uses the words morbus and vitium, but Ulpian points out, in commenting on his definition of their meaning, that the terms are practically synonymous: ego puto aediles tollendae dubitationis gratia bis κατὰ τοῦ αὐτοῦ idem dixisse,

What defects render the contract liable to rescission?

---

[1] Nam, ut ait Pedius, quotiens lege aliquid, unum vel alterum, introductum est, bona occasio est caetera, quae tendunt ad eandem utilitatem, vel interpretatione vel certe iurisdictione suppleri: Dig. 1. 3. 13.

[2] Sed si quis permutaverit, dicendum est, utrumque emptoris et venditoris loco haberi, et utrumque posse ex hoc edicto experiri: Dig. 21. 1. 19. 5.

[3] Cod. 8. 44. 4.

[4] Pothier, 205, 206.

[5] Proinde si quid tale fuerit vitii sive morbi, quod usum ministeriumque hominis impediat, id dabit redhibitioni locum: Dig. 21. 1. 1. 8: cf. ib. 10. 2: ib. 12. 1: ib. 38. 9: 19. 1. 6. 4. Le vendeur est tenu de la garantie à raison des défauts cachés de la chose vendue qui la rendent impropre à l'usage auquel on la destine, ou qui diminuent tellement cet usage, que l'acheteur ne l'aurait pas acquise, ou n'en aurait donné qu'un moindre prix, s'il les avait connus: Code Civil, Art. 1641. For illustrations see Pothier, 214.

[6] Sed sciendum est morbum apud Sabinum sic definitum esse habitum cuiusque corporis contra naturam, qui usum eius ad id facit deteriorem, cuius causa natura nobis eius corporis sanitatem dedit ... vitiumque a morbo multum differre, ut puta si quis balbus sit, nam hunc vitiosum magis esse quam morbosum: Dig. 21. 1. 1. 7.

ne qua dubitatio superesset. Temporary or transient ailments are ground for rescission no less than those which are permanent[1], provided they are not so trivial that one would usually pay no attention to them[2]. In construing the Edict, however, it was held that in slaves mental disease or deficiency, and moral faults of temper or character, unless their absence was expressly guaranteed, were in general no ground for the application of the aedilician remedies[3]. Still, there were exceptions to this rule: for if a slave were 'fugitivus'[4] or an 'erro'[5] the fault was deemed moral, not corporal[6], and yet these are expressly mentioned as redhibitory defects in the Edict: and the right of rescission similarly existed in the case of slaves who had committed a capital offence[7], or attempted suicide[8], or procured themselves to be used for fighting with wild beasts, and where the mental affliction was a direct consequence of bodily disease[9]. A civil action ex empto for damages would lie for mental and moral no less than for physical defects if the conditions previously laid down were satisfied[10].

Distinction between slaves

---

[1] Pomponius recte ait, non tantum ad perpetuos morbos, verum ad temporarios quoque hoc edictum pertinere: Dig. 21. 1. 6. pr.

[2] Dummodo meminerimus non utique quodlibet quam levissimum efficere ut morbosus vitiosusve habeatur. Proinde levis febricula aut vetus quartana, quae tamen iam sperni potest ... contemni enim haec potuerunt: Dig. 21. 1. 1. 8.

[3] Dig. 21. 1. 1. 9–11: ib. 4. 2–4.

[4] For a full description of the meaning of this term, see Dig. 21. 1. 17: ib. 43. 1–3.

[5] Proprie erronem sic definimus: qui non quidem fugit, sed frequenter sine causa vagatur et temporibus in res nugatorias consumptis serius domum redit: Dig. 21. 1. 17. 14.

[6] Dig. 21. 1. 43.   [7] Dig. 21. 1. 23. 2.   [8] Dig. 21. 1. 23. 3.

[9] Sed si vitium corporis usque ad animum penetrat, forte si propter febrem loquantur aliena, vel qui per vicos more insanorum deridenda loquantur, in quos id animi vitium ex corporis vitio accidit, redhiberi posse: Dig. 21. 1. 4. 1: cf. ib. 1. 9.

[10] Dig. 21. 1. 1. 9 & 10: ib. 4. pr. & 4.

In respect of animals, on the other hand, this distinction between corporal and moral or mental faults was not drawn. It is not considered a corporal defect for an ox to be given to tossing, a horse to jibbing, shying, or kicking, or for any such beast to be restive or nervous, and yet these defects are redhibitory[1]. But Pomponius decides that though a mule which will stand no collar but that of the vendor is not 'sana'[2], the purchaser is not entitled to return one which will stand being harnessed on only one side or the other of the carriage, because that is a common failing in such animals[3].

and animals.

It is of course essential that the defect, whatever it be, should have been in existence at the time when the contract was made[4]: those which arise afterwards are misfortunes which the purchaser must be content to bear: and from this it follows that a fault which has existed, but which has been permanently cured or removed when the contract is made, is no ground for rescission[5]. The defect again must be unknown to the purchaser, for otherwise he cannot say that he has been deceived[6], and he is presumed to be aware of it from circumstances from which it could not fail to be inferred by a reasonable man[7], and there is some authority for saying that in such a case the vendor will not be bound even by an express warranty[8]. Further, the

The defect must exist at the date of the contract, and be unknown to the purchaser.

---

[1] Dig. 21. 1. 43.
[2] Dig. 21. 1. 38. 9.   [3] Dig. 21. 1. 38. 8.
[4] Dig. 21. 1. 54: Cod. 4. 58. 3. pr.: Pothier, 211.
[5] Dig. 21. 1. 16: ib. 17. 17.
[6] Cicero de Off. iii. c. 16: Dig. 21. 1. 48. 4.
[7] Ei qui servum vinctum vendiderit, aedilicium edictum remitti aequum est: multo enim amplius est, id facere, quam pronuntiare, in vinculis fuisse: Dig. 21. 1. 48. 3.
[8] Quaedam enim pollicitationes venditorem non obligant, si ita in promptu res sit, ut eam emptor non ignoraverit, veluti si quis hominem luminibus effossis emat, et de sanitate stipuletur: nam de cetera parte corporis potius stipulatus videtur, quam de eo, in quo se ipse decipiebat: Dig. 18. 1. 43. 1. On the other hand it is said (in Dig. 44. 4. 4.

defect must be invisible, or such that were it not pointed out to the purchaser, he could not have perceived it, although it might have been detected by an expert: if it is so obvious that he could not have failed to observe it had he kept his eyes open (as e.g. where a slave is blind, or has a dangerous wound on a conspicuous part of his body) he cannot avail himself of the aedilician remedies [1]. If he is himself an expert, and so could easily detect defects which a non-expert could not, it would seem that he cannot proceed against the vendor for non-disclosure: but upon this point there seems to be no express textual authority [2].

Purchase by agents with knowledge.
Where the purchase is made by an agent who is in the purchaser's power, and who was aware of or could easily have discovered the defects at the time of the contract, the superior is affected by such knowledge or carelessness, and has no remedy: if the agent in such case was unaware of them through no fault of his own, the superior can rescind unless they were known to him personally [3]. If, on the other hand, the agent is not in the purchaser's power, his knowledge or negligence is again the knowledge or negligence of his principal [4]; while if he is ignorant of the defects, which however are known to his principal, the

---

5) si quis fugitivum esse sciens emerit servum, et si stipulatus fuerit fugitivum non esse, deinde agat ex stipulatu, non esse cum exceptione repellendum, quoniam hoc convenit ... sed si non convenisset, exceptione repelletur. Pothier (209) thinks the latter passage contains the rule, and that the former is true only if the vendor was ignorant of the defect, so that the purchaser's exaction of the warranty is fraudulent. But this interpretation of Dig. 18. 1. 43. 1 is impossible.

[1] Ignorantia emptori prodest quae non in supinum hominem cadit: Dig. 18. 1. 15. 1 : cf. 21. 1. 1. 6: ib. 14. 10. Le vendeur n'est pas tenu des vices apparens et dont l'acheteur a pu se convaincre lui-même : Code Civil, Art. 1642: cf. Pothier, 207. For the application of these principles to mercantile transactions conducted on the modern scale, see Treitschke, Kaufcontract, § 94.

[2] See Treitschke, Kaufcontract, p. 340.

[3] Dig. 21. 1. 51. 1 : cf. 18. 1. 12 & 13.

[4] Dig. 21. 1. 51. 1 : cf. Dig. 14. 4. 5. pr.

latter cannot rescind the contract, while the agent can, but only provided he is acting in his own interest and on his own behalf, through being unable to recover from his principal[1].

When a thing is sold along with certain accessories, discovery of a redhibitory defect in one of the accessories, entitles the purchaser to rescind the sale of such accessory, provided it is sold expressly as a separate thing—tanquam res singula—not as part of an ideal whole. Thus if an estate is sold with all the slaves upon it, the rules of the Edict apply to the latter[2]: but they do not apply to one slave who forms part of another slave's peculium, when the latter is sold 'with his peculium'[3]. If the principal thing is returned on account of redhibitory defects, the purchaser is bound to take back accessories also, even though they are perfectly sound[4]. On the sale of a number of things together in one lot and for one price, the answer to the question whether a defect in one of them entitled the purchaser to rescind the contract in respect of all depends partly on whether the things are related to each other as principal and accessory. It will be clear from what has been already said that if this is so, and the defect is in the principal thing, the whole contract can be rescinded, while if the defect is in one of the accessories only, it is only in respect of that accessory that rescission is allowable[5]. But if the things are not so related, then it depends whether they were bought as a whole, so that the purchaser would not have bought one without the other or

Defect in accessions; in one of several things purchased together;

---

[1] Dig. 21. 1. 51. 1.   [2] Dig. 21. 1. 32 : 19. 1. 27.
[3] Dig. 21. 1. 33. pr.: Pothier, 204. The trappings (ornamenta) in which a horse, mule, or other beast was sold were declared accessories of the iumentum by the Edict (Dig. 21. 1. 38. pr. & 11), which provided that unless they were delivered with the animal, the purchaser might within sixty days either sue for them, or rescind the whole transaction by actio redhibitoria.
[4] Dig. 21. 1. 33. 1.   [5] Pothier, 226.

rest, for in this case he can rescind the whole contract for a redhibitory defect in one only: otherwise he is entitled to return only the defective article[1]. That a separate price is agreed upon for each of two or more things purchased simultaneously raises a strong presumption that they are bought independently of one another, though this may be rebutted by considerations of their utility, nature, or connexion with one another; in the case of rebuttal, all must be returned or none[2]. Similar principles govern the sale of an universitas. If it is an ideal whole, such as an inheritance or a peculium, whose name gives no clue to the separate articles which it comprises, the vendor (in the absence of express warranty) incurs no liability if it is sound or serviceable as a whole, because no 'certum corpus'[3] has been bought. But if the universitas is an aggregate of single things, such as a company of slave actors or singers or a menagerie, the rescission of the whole contract may be obtained on account of defects discovered in one individual, but only if the purchaser would not have bought any unless he could buy all[4].

in part of an universitas.

Of these redhibitory defects, if present, it is the duty of the vendor to advise the purchaser, under penalty of having the contract rescinded against him if they should be subsequently discovered. It is entirely immaterial that he fails to point them out simply because he is ignorant of their existence[5], though he is in worse case if he knew of them,

Vendor's duty to disclose defects of these kinds.

---

[1] Dig. 21.1. 34: ib. 38. 14: ib. 64.

[2] Interdum etsi in singula capita pretium constitutum sit, tamen una emptio est, ut propter unius vitium omnes redhiberi possint vel debeant, scilicet cum manifestum erit non nisi omnes quem empturum vel venditurum fuisse, ut plerumque circa comoedos vel quadrigas vel mulas pares accidere solet, ut neutri non nisi omnes habere expediat: Dig. 21. 1. 34. 1.

[3] Dig. 21. 1. 33. pr.

[4] Dig. 21. 1. 34 & 35: ib. 38. 12 & 14: ib. 39 & 40: ib. 64. 1.

[5] Dummodo sciamus venditorem, etiamsi ignoravit ea quae aediles praestari iubent, tamen teneri debere. nec est hoc iniquum: potuit

and dishonestly withheld his knowledge from the purchaser, for then he is liable, by action ex empto, to make good to the latter all loss whatsoever which he may have sustained through making the contract[1]. Even an express agreement that he shall not be liable for defects will not protect him from liability in respect of those of which he was aware at the time of the making of the contract[2]: for those which were at that time unknown to him he can protect himself in this manner[3].

It is necessary now to examine in detail the remedies or possible courses which under the Edict were open to a purchaser who after the conclusion of a contract of sale discovered some redhibitory defect in its subject matter.

The purchaser's remedies:

If he has not yet paid the purchase money, and is sued for it by the vendor, he can meet the latter's action by an exceptio or counteractive plea, for the purpose either of cancelling the contract (corresponding to the actio redhibitoria) or of procuring a reduction in the amount of the purchase money proportionate to the defects discovered (corresponding to the actio quanti minoris)[4]. If the purchase money has been paid, he can bring an actio redhibitoria[5] for the rescission of the contract and to recover it back, while if the vendor has taken the goods back voluntarily[6], but refuses to repay the purchase money, the latter can be

(1) by exceptio:

(2) by actio redhibitoria.

enim ea nota habere venditor: neque enim interest emptoris, cur fallatur, ignorantia venditoris an calliditate: Dig. 21. 1. 1. 2.

[1] Dig. 19. 1. 13. pr. The same distinction is drawn in the Code Civil, Art. 1645.

[2] Dig. 19. 1. 6. 9.

[3] Dig. 21. 1. 19. 4: Pothier, 210. Il est tenu des vices cachés, quand même il ne les aurait pas connus, à moins que, dans ce cas, il n'ait stipulé qu'il ne sera obligé à aucune garantie: Code Civil, Art. 1643.

[4] Dig. 21. 1. 59. pr. & 1.

[5] So named from the return of the goods: redhibere est facere, ut rursus habeat venditor quod habuerit, et quia reddendo id fiebat, idcirco redhibitio est appellata quasi redditio: Dig. 21. 1. 21 pr.

[6] Dig. 21. 1. 31. 18.

reclaimed by actio in factum, whether defects have been discovered or not, and even though the short period of limitation fixed for the actio redhibitoria may have expired [1].

Effects of this action; Speaking generally, the effect of the actio redhibitoria is that, on proof by the vendor of defective quality, the parties will be restored in statum quo ante, with the consequence that neither will be allowed either to derive advantage or to suffer detriment from the contract [2]. The acts which are *what must be done by the purchaser,* incumbent on the purchaser may first be examined. He is bound (1) to restore to the vendor the thing which he bought, along with its accessions, including those which have accrued since the making of the contract [3]. (2) To indemnify the vendor for the value of all fruits or profits which he has derived from the property, or which he might have derived from it but for his own negligence [4], even though the vendor himself could not have appropriated them had he never sold it [5]: but he is under no obligation to surrender any sum which he may have recovered as damages in an actio injuriarum on account of an assault or libel aimed at himself through the slave [6]. (3) To give up the property to the vendor uninjured, and in as good a condition as when received by himself. Hence he is responsible for any damage or deterioration which it has suffered since delivery at the hands or through the fault of himself or those for whom he is bound to answer (including a free agent [7]), and which would not have befallen it had the sale not taken

---

[1] Dig. 21. 1. 31. 17.

[2] Facta redhibitione, omnia in integrum restituuntur, perinde ac si neque emptio neque venditio intercessit: Dig. 21. 1. 60: iudicium redhibitoriae actionis utrumque, id est venditorem et emptorem, quodammodo in integrum restituere debere: Dig. ib. 23. 7 : ib. 21. pr.

[3] Dig 21. 1. 1. 1 : ib. 23. 1 : ib. 31. 19. Illustrations: child born of ancilla, Dig. ib. 31. 2 : usufruct which has accrued to the nuda proprietas, ib. 31. 3 : peculium acquired by slave otherwise than ex re emptoris, ib. 31. 4.

[4] Dig 21. 1. 1. 1 : ib. 23. 9 : Pothier, 219.   [5] Dig. 21. 1. 23. 9.
[6] Dig. 21. 1. 43. 5.   [7] Dig. 21. 1. 25. 3.

FOR UNDISCLOSED DEFECTS. 203

place [1]; and here moral deterioration is put on the same footing as corporal injury [2]. However slight might be the negligence of the purchaser or his subordinates, he must answer for it, if it resulted in the property being diminished in value [3]: he is bound to take the same care of property which he may become entitled to return as the vendor is bound to show in the custody of it before delivery [4]. For mere accidental injury of course the purchaser will not be held responsible, nor for any liability which may attach to the owner of the property by reason of circumstances beyond his control, so that (for instance) if a slave commits a theft, the penalty recoverable from the vendor after redhibition cannot be demanded by him from the purchaser, unless the theft was committed by his instructions or default, or by those of his alienee [5]. What has been said of the purchaser and his subordinates is equally true of his heir and of persons for whom such heir is answerable [6]. Finally, if the purchaser has created any charge or encumbrance, such as a mortgage or servitude, over the property after conveyance to him, such charge or encumbrance is not avoided by its return to the vendor, and accordingly the latter is entitled on redhibition either to have it released at the purchaser's cost, or, if the encumbrancer (being entitled so to do) will not consent to its extinction, to receive proportionate compensation [7]: and he can require the purchaser to give security for compensation in respect of such charges as may be unknown [8].

On the part of the vendor, it is necessary *and by the vendor.*

[1] Dig. 21. 1. 23. pr: ib. 25. pr.—7.
[2] Dig. 21. 1. 25. 6. The defendant's form of pleading in respect of damages done before joinder of issue was different from that in respect of those occasioned pendente lite: the former must be expressly mentioned in iure, and the claim for compensation inserted in the formula; the latter need not: Dig. 21. 1. 25. 8.
[3] Dig. 21. 1. 31. 11–15.
[4] P. 106 sq. supr.
[5] Dig. 21. 1. 46.
[6] Dig. 21. 1. 31. 9.
[7] Dig. 21. 1. 43. 8.
[8] Dig. 21. 1. 21. 1.

(1) That he shall return the purchase money, along with interest, and with any other sum which the purchaser may have paid to him in pursuance of the contract, or which he might otherwise have been compelled to pay[1]: and where two or more things are sold together for a single price, and the sale is rescinded by the purchaser in respect of one of them only, the price of that one has to be apportioned by the court[2]. The vendor is responsible

(2) for any necessary costs which the purchaser may have incurred in connection with the property, but not for the expenses of maintenance, such as the food and lodging of a slave or a horse, at any rate if the purchaser has been able to make use of it, for such use will be deemed to be set off against them[3]. These costs however cannot be recovered by action: the purchaser can assert his right to them only by withholding the property until they are paid[4], which he may do irrespective of his right to recover the purchase money[5]; and the vendor may conceivably find it to his

---

[1] Debet autem recipere pecuniam, quam dedit pro eo homine, vel si quid accessionis nomine. Dari autem non solum id accipiemus, quod numeratur venditori, ut puta pretium, et usuras eius, sed et si quid emptionis causa erogatum est : hoc autem ita demum deducitur, si ex voluntate venditoris datur : ceterum si quod sua sponte datum esse proponatur, non imputabitur : neque enim debet quod quis suo arbitrio dedit a venditore exigere. Quid ergo si forte vectigalis nomine datum est, quod emptorem forte sequeretur? dicemus hoc quoque restituendum : indemnis enim emptor debet discedere : Dig. 21. 1. 27 : cf. ib. 29. 2. So too Pothier says (217) : 'l'acheteur a droit aussi de demander que le vendeur soit condamné à le rembourser de tous les frais du marché, et de tous ceux qu'il a été obligé de faire par rapport à la chose vendue, tels que sont les frais de voiture, de barrage, de douane, &c. : non ceux qu'il auroit pu se dispenser de faire.

[2] Dig. 21. 1. 36 : ib. 64. Illustrations in Glück, 20. pp. 82-84.

[3] Dig. 21. 1. 30. 1.

[4] Si quid tamen damni sensit vel si quid pro servo impendit consequetur arbitrio iudicis, sic tamen, non ut ei horum nomine venditor condemnetur, ut ait Iulianus, sed ne alias compellatur hominem venditori restituere, quam si eum indemnem praestet : Dig. 21. 1. 29. 3.

[5] Dig. 21. 1. 31. pr.

own interest to abandon the property rather than to pay them in addition to other sums which he will have to pay in any case.

(3) The vendor must make good to the purchaser any loss which he has sustained through the article purchased, as for instance by thefts committed on his property by a slave [1], or in the form of damages paid by him to other persons for such slave's delicts. Here again the right is enforceable by retention only, and the vendor can evade the obligation by allowing the purchaser to keep the slave or other article in question [2], unless he had been aware of the defect, or had warranted its absence either expressly or by implication [3]; in which case of course the purchaser could recover damages by actio ex empto for all loss he had sustained [4]. Lastly

(4) The vendor must release the purchaser from all liabilities which he has been obliged to undertake in connection with the contract or the property to which it relates [5].

---

[1] Dig. 21. 1. 23. 8.   [2] Dig. 21. 1. 31. pr : ib. 58. pr. & 1.

[3] To adopt the language in which the English law is stated by Judge Chalmers (Sale of Goods, § 17. (2)) 'where the buyer, relying on the seller's skill or judgment, orders goods for a particular purpose known to the seller, and the goods are of a description which it is in the course of the seller's business to supply (whether he be the manufacturer or not) there is an implied warranty that the goods shall be reasonably fit for such purpose.' Il y a un cas auquel le vendeur, quand même il auroit ignoré absolument le vice de la chose vendue, est néanmoins tenu de la réparation du tort que ce vice a causé à l'acheteur dans ses autres biens : c'est le cas auquel le vendeur est un ouvrier, ou un marchand qui vend des ouvrages de son art, ou de commerce dont il fait profession : cet ouvrier ou ce marchand est tenu de la réparation de tout le dommage que l'acheteur a souffert par le vice de la chose vendue, en s'en servant à l'usage auquel elle est destinée, quand même cet ouvrier ou ce marchand prétendroit avoir ignoré ce vice ... La raison est qu'un ouvrier, par la profession de son art, *spondet peritiam artis* : Pothier, 213.

[4] Dig. 18. 1. 45 : 19. 1. 13. pr : Cod 4. 58. 1. : Pothier, 212–216.

[5] Dig. 21. 1. 29. 1.

The vendor is not relieved from the performance of these duties by the fact that the purchaser is no longer able to return the property to him, provided his inability is not due to any fault of his own or his subordinates [1]. If it is through such fault that the property has ceased to exist, so that he is prevented from returning it, the purchaser can still bring the actio redhibitoria, subject to a deduction from the sum payable to him by the vendor of whatever it would have been worth at the time, were it still in existence [2]. But if his inability to return it is due to its alienation by him, he can rescind only on its reconveyance to himself [3]; if (in the case of a slave) to manumission by himself, all remedies which he might have had are extinguished, as by an implied waiver of his rights [4].

Covenants sometimes demandable by either party. It is further to be observed that both parties could under certain circumstances require one another to enter into stipulations in the nature of security or guarantee. One of these cases has been already mentioned [5]. A second is where litigation had arisen in respect of the property between the purchaser and a third party. Here the former, if plaintiff, could be compelled to bind himself with sureties to surrender to the vendor, in the event of redhibition, any damages which he might recover, or but for his own fault might have recovered in the action; while if he were

---

[1] E.g. si la chose n'existe plus : si c'est sans sa faute qu'elle a cessé d'exister, comme si le cheval que j'ai acheté est mort de la maladie pour laquelle j'ai formé l'action redhibitoire, il me suffira de rendre ce qui en reste, comme la peau : Pothier, 220. See Dig. 21. 1. 31. 11 & 12 : ib. 47. 1 : ib. 48. pr. The Code Civil has here departed from the Civil Law : si la chose qui avait des vices a péri par suite de sa mauvaise qualité, la perte est pour le vendeur . . . . mais la perte arrivée par cas fortuit sera pour le compte de l'acheteur : Art. 1647 : the departure is defended and justified by Demante, Cours analytique de Code Civil, vii. p. 109.

[2] Dig. 21. 1. 31. 6 & 11–15 : ib. 38. 3 : ib. 44. 2 : ib. 47. 1. & 48 : Pothier, 221.

[3] Dig. 21. 1. 43. 8.   [4] Dig. 21. 1. 47. pr.

[5] P. 203 supr.

defendant he could compel the vendor to give him security for payment of the damages which might be assessed against him [1]. Thirdly, if one sold a slave knowing him to be 'fugitivus,' and concealed that knowledge from the purchaser, the latter on the slave's flight could bring the actio redhibitoria for the recovery of the purchase money, notwithstanding his inability to restore him, on giving security that he would do all he could to recover and redeliver him to the vendor [2].

It was laid down by the aedilician edict that the purchaser must perform his own duties under the actio redhibitoria before he could demand restitution of the purchase money and payment of any other sums which might be due from the vendor [3]. The only exception allowed to this rule was where there was reason to suspect that the vendor would be unable to make such restitution, in which case it was sufficient for the purchaser to give security that he would redeliver the property on repayment of the purchase money within a fixed time [4].

Although the general principle of the law as to redhibition is to treat both parties in precisely the same manner, there are one or two points in which for special reasons they were treated differently.

Points in which the parties are differently treated under the actio redhibitoria.

Firstly, if a slave or a filius familias sold some article which belonged to his peculium, and in which a defect was subsequently discovered, the master or father was liable under an actio redhibitoria only to the extent of that peculium, provided that it still belonged to the actual vendor, and had not been revoked or resumed by the master or father, and including in it the purchase money actually paid for the article, but deducting any thing which might be due to the master or father himself [5]. If on the

---

[1] Dig. 21. 1. 21. 2 : ib. 30. pr.
[2] Dig. 21. 1. 21. 3 : ib. 22 : Cod. 4. 58. 5.
[3] Dig. 21. 1. 25. 10.
[4] Dig. 21. 1. 26.   [5] Dig. 21. 1. 23. 4 : ib. 57. 1.

other hand, a slave or filius familias bought a defective article, the master or father could bring the actio redhibitoria; but as he thereby adopted the contract as his own, he could do so only on the condition of doing everything which he would have had to do had he made the contract personally, irrespective of the amount of the peculium, so that he must pay or give security for the payment of the whole of the purchase money before he is entitled to rescind it [1].

Secondly, the vendor can be compelled, nolens volens, to return the purchase money: the purchaser cannot be compelled to return the goods, unless he chooses to do so as the condition of getting his money back [2]: and, moreover, if after return or tender of the goods the vendor refuses to repay the purchase money or to discharge the security given by the purchaser for its payment, he could be condemned 'in duplum.' [3]

Thirdly, difficulties might arise from the fact of the defective article having been either bought or sold by two or more persons jointly, or through the vendor or purchaser leaving two or more co-heirs [4].' Where there were joint purchasers, or co-heirs of a single purchaser, no redhibition could take place unless it were assented to by all, such assent being followed by the joint appointment of a common attorney for the purpose of the suit, for otherwise the

---

[1] Dig. 21. 1. 57. pr.

[2] Illud sciendum est, si emptor venditori haec non praestet, quae desiderantur in hac actione, non posse ei venditorem condemnari: si autem emptori venditor ista non praestet, condemnabitur ei: Dig. 21. 1. 29. pr.: Pothier, 225.

[3] Nam si neque pretium neque accessionem solvat, neque eum qui eo nomine obligatus erit liberet, dupli pretii et accessionis condemnari iubetur: Dig. 21. 1. 45.

[4] But if two or more bought distinct shares in a thing from its owner, there were deemed to be as many separate contracts as there were shares sold: si plures singuli partes ab uno emant, tunc pro parte quisque eorum experietur: Dig. 21. 1. 31. 10.

vendor might be unreasonably prejudiced[1]. But after restoration of the property, or if it had ceased to exist through no fault of any of the joint purchasers, each might sue separately for his share of what he could have claimed in its entirety had he been the sole purchaser, and each must separately make good his proportion of accessions fruits and profits, or of damages done to the goods since delivery, unless such damages are indivisible[2], or unless the damage has been caused by one of them only[3]. Where there were joint vendors who sold a thing as a whole to a single purchaser, the actio redhibitoria could be brought 'in solidum' against the owner of any but the smallest share[4], lest the innocent purchaser should be driven to a multiplicity of actions[5]: but the joint heirs of a single vendor could be sued only in the ratio in which they succeeded to the inheritance[6].

The actio redhibitoria could be brought only within six months of the date of the contract[7]: the time was tempus utile—i.e. only those days were reckoned on which the action could have been brought[8]; and the passages in which this rule is laid down are too numerous and explicit to allow us to believe that Justinian's enactment[9] substituting a period of four ordinary years for an annus utilis in all cases of in integrum restitutio could have been intended to apply to this remedy[10]. It is contended by some authori-

The period of limitation.

---

[1] Dig. 21. 1. 31. 5: Pothier, 223.   [2] Dig. 21. 1. 31. 5-7.
[3] Dig. 21. 1. 31. 9.   [4] Dig. 21. 1. 44. 1.
[5] Ne cogeretur emptor cum multis litigare: Dig. loc. cit.
[6] Dig. 21. 1. 31. 10: Pothier, 223.   [7] See next note.
[8] Dig. 21. 1. 19. 6: ib. 38. pr.: ib. 55. The last passage shows that the time began to run against the purchaser only from the discovery of the defect, if it were of such a kind (e.g. servus fugitivus) that he could not have been aware of it earlier: but the presumption of negligence could apparently not be lightly rebutted.
[9] Cod. 2. 52. 7.
[10] Cum proponas servum, quem pridie comparasti, post anni tempus fugisse, qua ratione eo nomine cum venditore eiusdem congredi

ties that the exceptio redhibitoria[1] was governed by the same period of limitation: but there appears to be no reason for excepting this case from the principle 'quae ad agendum sunt temporalia ad excipiendum sunt perpetua,' and the analogy of the actio and exceptio doli[2] strongly supports the contrary opinion[3].

(3) By actio quanti minoris or aestimatoria:

It has however been already pointed out that the purchaser was not left by the Aediles entirely without redress, if he allowed the time within which he could bring the actio redhibitoria to elapse without availing himself of its protection. He had the option[4], during the first six months, of either rescinding the contract, or suing the vendor by actio quanti minoris, also called aestimatoria, for a return of part of his purchase money proportionate to the defects which had appeared[5]: an action which he could bring

quaeras, non possum animadvertere: etenim redhibitoriam actionem sex mensum temporibus vel quanto minoris anno concludi manifesti iuris est: Cod. 4. 58. 2.

[1] P. 201 supr.

[2] Non sicut de dolo actio certo tempore finitur ita etiam exceptio eodem tempore danda est: Dig 44. 4. 5. 6.

[3] The Code Civil enacts (Art. 1648) 'L'action résultant des vices redhibitoires doit être intentée par l'acquéreur dans un bref délai, suivant la nature des vices redhibitoires, et l'usage du lieu où la vente a été faite.' For the law of the province of Orleans on the subject in the last century see Pothier, 231: for that of Austria and some of the German States Treitschke, Kaufcontract, p. 365. As a rule the times are shorter than under the Civil Law.

[4] Dig. 21. 1. 48. 1.

[5] Pothier, 232. L'acheteur a le choix de rendre la chose et de se faire restituer le prix, ou de garder la chose et de se faire rendre une partie du prix: Code Civil, Art. 1644. Glück (20, p. 116) points out the utility of the actio quanti minoris to the purchaser of an estate over which a servitude is found existing which was unknown to him when the price was fixed: the case is dealt with in Dig. 21. 1. 61: cf. Dig. 21. 2. 15. According to English law, if there be a breach of warranty of quality, the purchaser may keep the goods, and plead the breach in diminution of the price (*Mondel* v. *Steel*, 8 M. & W. 858), so that the principle of the actio quanti minoris is recognised. In the Scotch law, on the other hand, the Roman rule has disappeared: 'there

a second or third time, and so on, according as new and distinct defects were brought to light[1]. This latter remedy also lay during another six months; that is to say, it could be brought at any time within twelve months (tempus utile) from the making of the contract[2]. Sometimes, indeed, the judge who tried an actio quanti minoris had power to deal with the matter as if the action had been redhibitoria, apparently even after the lapse of time by which the latter would have been barred; this being the case where the property was so entirely valueless that a mere reduction in the amount of the purchase money would have been quite out of the question[3]. The proportion of the purchase money which had to be returned was determined by ascertaining, on the purchaser's oath[4], how much less he would have given for the article had he known of the defects when he first bought it[5]: and where one of two or more things which had been purchased together for one price, and which could not conveniently be separated, was found to be defective, the depreciation of the others was taken into consideration[6].

There has been some controversy on the question whether even during the first six months the purchaser could always

its period of limitation and effects.

is no right to retain the goods and claim an abatement of the price as in the actio quanti minoris of the Roman law, unless where there is fraud, or a special bargain or usage': Bell, Principles of the Law of Scotland, § 99.

[1] Dig. 21. 1. 31. 16: 21. 2. 32. 1.
[2] Cod. 4. 58. 2, cited on the previous page: Dig. 21. 1. 48. 2.
[3] Aliquando etiam redhiberi mancipium debebit, licet aestimatoria, id est, quanto minoris, agamus: nam si adeo nullius sit pretii, ut ne expediat quidem tale mancipium domino habere, veluti si furiosum aut lunaticum sit, licet aestimatoria actum fuerit, officio tamen iudicis continebitur, ut reddito mancipio pretium recipiatur: Dig. 21. 1. 43. 6.
[4] Under the Code Civil by the evidence of experts: the same is the modern practice in Germany: Treitschke, Kaufcontract, p. 358.
[5] Dig. 21. 1. 61: 21. 2. 32. 1: 19. 1. 13. pr.
[6] Dig. 21. 1. 38. 13.

rescind the contract, or whether he was not sometimes restricted to the actio quanti minoris. Some authorities are of opinion that he could rescind only if the defect were such as to render the article quite useless, and that if it merely diminished its usefulness he could only sue for a return of part of his purchase money. But this distinction is quite unknown to the authorities [1], and it is clear that if the defect is not quite trivial [2], and the actio redhibitoria is not yet barred by lapse of time, the purchaser can choose between the two remedies, subject to the rule that after bringing one he cannot bring the other action as well [3], and to the possibility, already noticed, of an actio quanti minoris actually resulting in an order for redhibition.

The effect of the introduction of these Aedilician remedies upon the Civil Law relating to defects of quality (which has been already considered [4]) requires a brief examination.

Reaction of these Aedilician remedies on those of the Civil Law.
The actiones redhibitoria and quanti minoris may be used in any case of fraud (including wilful non-disclosure), warranty, or representation in which the purchaser could previously have resorted to the actio ex empto [5], and by this innovation he secures two advantages. Firstly, it enabled him to rescind many contracts to which the Civil Law would have held him, subject to his claim for damages, for, as has been already observed, rescission could not be obtained on these grounds by actio ex empto proper unless

---

[1] See Glück, 20, pp. 121–125.
[2] P. 196 supr.   [3] Dig. 44. 2. 25. 1.   [4] P. 189 supr.
[5] Nam et qui ex empto potest conveniri, idem etiam redhibitoriis actionibus conveniri potest: Dig. 21. 1. 19. 2. For fraud or wilful nondisclosure see further the words of the Edict in Dig. ib. 1. 1: hoc amplius si quis adversus ea sciens dolo malo vendidisse dicetur, iudicium dabimus: for warranties or representations Dig. ib. 18. pr. & 1: ib. 19. 2. It may perhaps be doubted whether this rule can be held to apply to a wilful nondisclosure of a mental or moral defect in a slave, for such vitia in general, as has been observed, were not within the scope of the Aedilician remedies. Of course there would be an action ex empto in such a case: Dig. 21. 1. 1. 9 & 10: ib. 4. pr. & 4.

the purchaser could satisfy the court that he would not have entered into the contract at all had it not been for the fraud practised upon him, or had he known that the representation or warranty would turn out to be unfounded: and secondly, if after rescission and return of the goods the vendor refused to repay the purchase money, he might be condemned in duplum [1].

That the converse proposition is true, and that the vendor could be sued by actio ex empto in lieu of redhibitoria or quanti minoris wherever either of these remedies would have lain, though affirmed by some authorities [2], is not so free from doubt. Assuming it to be true, the ordinary action on the contract could be brought in two important cases where it would not lie before: against a vendor who was ignorant of the defects in the article sold: and where the purchaser could not show that he had sustained any actual damage by reason of its defective quality. The text of Ulpian upon which the proposition is usually founded [3] certainly does not mean that a purchaser could always demand rescission by actio ex empto wherever he could have demanded it by actio redhibitoria: it means merely that rescission might possibly be the result of such an action, in the sense already explained, exactly as Julian says [4] that an actio quanti minoris also might possibly end in redhibition [5]. It is, however, certain that a purchaser could sue ex empto, and thereby recover a proportion of his purchase money, where the defect was unknown to the vendor [6]—a case properly remediable by actio quanti minoris: and it is possible that under similar circumstances he might also claim rescission by the ordinary action on the contract

[1] P. 208 supr.
[2] E. g. Glück, 20. p. 136.
[3] Redhibitionem quoque contineri empti iudicio et Labeo et Sabinus putant et nos probamus: Dig. 19. 1. 11. 3.
[4] Dig. 44. 2. 25. 1.   [6] Cf. p. 211 supr.
[5] Dig. 19. 1. 13. pr.

instead of by actio redhibitòria[1]. It is noticeable, however, that whenever the civil action was used in a case in which it would not have lain before the extension to it of the Aedilician principles, it was strictly regulated by those principles, in respect both of limitation[2] and of the sum or sums recoverable from the vendor[3].

Cases in which they are inapplicable. It has already been pointed out[4] that the purchaser had no right to use the Aedilician actions if either he was aware of the defects at the time when he made the contract, or they were so obvious that he must have observed them but for his own negligence. There are in addition four other cases in which these remedies (or one of them) are inapplicable, viz. :

(1) Where the sale is made subject to a suspensive condition or condition precedent, unless and until the condition has been fulfilled[5], for the restitution involved in a redhibition implies a complete and absolute contract.

(2) No redhibition was allowed of what are called 'simplariae venditiones,' the small transactions of every-day life[6]: but they appear to have been subject to the actio quanti minoris.

(3) Sales by the State could not be impeached by either action[7], but if there had been fraud or warranty they could be made the subject of the ordinary action on the contract. Municipal and other corporations were not similarly privileged[8].

[1] See Windscheid, Lehrbuch II. § 393, notes 1 & 9.
[2] Vangerow, § 609, note 2. II : Windscheid, § 393, note 12.
[3] Dig. 19. 1. 13. pr. & 1 : 18. 1. 45.
[4] Pp. 197 supr.   [5] Dig. 21. 1. 43. 9.
[6] Simplariarum venditionum causa ne sit redhibitio in usu est: Dig. 21. 1. 48. 8 : cf. Dig. 18. 1. 54.
  Illud sciendum est hoc edictum non pertinere ad venditiones fiscales : Dig. 21. 1. 1. 3. By the Code Civil the action resulting from redhibitory defects 'n'a pas lieu dans les ventes faites par autorité de justice': Art. 1649.
[7] Dig. 21. 1. 1. 4.

(4) Where the benefit of the law had been renounced by the purchaser, whether at the time the contract was made, or subsequently[1]. The most usual form of this was the vendor's bargaining that he should not be liable, either for any defects at all, or for certain specified defects[2]. If, however, notwithstanding such a compact, the purchaser were able to show that the vendor actually knew at the time of making the contract that the defect existed, and had not merely a suspicion about it, the agreement was inoperative, for the exceptio pacti pleaded to the purchaser's action would be destroyed by the replicatio doli[3]. Certain defects in slaves are expressly mentioned in the authorities as insufficient to entitle the purchaser to employ the Aedilician actions: it is perhaps sufficient to give the references to the passages in question[4].

There are many writers on the Civil Law[5] who contend that these remedies are inapplicable to purchasers of things determined generically[6]. They argue that it is an implied term in every such contract that the goods actually delivered by the vendor shall be of good quality, and that if they are defective the contract simply has not been performed, so that the purchaser can demand others, and damages for any loss which he may have suffered through the consequent delay, or may even under circumstances refuse to accept any at all. Others[7] are unable to discover any reason

---

[1] Pacisci contra edictum aedilium omnimodo licet, sive in ipso negotio venditionis gerendo convenisset sive postea: Dig. 2. 14. 31.

[2] Si venditor nominatim exceperit de aliquo morbo et de cetero sanum esse dixerit aut promiserit, standum est eo quod convenit, remittentibus enim actiones suas non est regressus dandus: Dig. 21. 1. 14. 9: cf. Dig. 19. 1. 39.

[3] Dig. 21. 1. 14. 9: Pothier, 210, 229, 230.

[4] Dig. 21. 1. 6. 2: ib. 7: ib. 10. 5: ib. 11: ib. 12. 1. 2 & 4: ib. 14. 3 & 7.

[5] E.g. Windscheid, Lehrbuch, § 394, note 19.   [6] P. 28 supr.

[7] E.g. Thöl, Handelsrecht, I. § 83: Vangerow, § 609, note 1.

The French law has been materially altered by an enactment of

in the peculiar nature of the contract for excluding the application of these actions. The point, however, is one upon which there is no Roman authority.

August 2, 1884, relating to 'les vices redhibitoires dans les ventes et échanges d'animaux domestiques': which

(1) defines precisely what are to be deemed 'vices redhibitoires' in horses, mules, asses, sheep and pigs:

(2) excludes the actions resulting from such defects wherever the price of the animal does not exceed 100 francs:

(3) entitles the vendor, when sued by an action corresponding to the Roman quanti minoris, to have the animal back on repaying the purchase money and the costs of the contract:

(4) fixes the period of limitation (subject to two exceptions) at nine days, with certain exceptions when the animal is sent to a distant purchaser, or removed out of the vendor's 'domicil.' See Demante, Cours analytique de Code Civil. vii. pp. 111-117.

NOTE A.

Implied warranty of quality in Scotch and English Law. By the Common law of Scotland, which corresponded in general with the Civil Law, there was an implied warranty against latent faults, even though the buyer should see the commodity (1 Stair, 10, § 15: Bell's Principles of the Law of Scotland, I. § 97): the goods might, on discovery of the fault, be rejected, and if the article perished by such latent fault the buyer was relieved from payment, or entitled to have back the price. But the law was assimilated to that of England by 19 & 20 Vic. c. 60. § 5, which enacted that 'where goods shall, after the passing of this Act, be sold, the seller, if at the time of the sale he was without knowledge that the same were defective or of bad quality, shall not be held to have warranted their quality or sufficiency: but the goods, with all faults, shall be at the risk of the purchaser, unless the seller shall have given an express warranty of the quality or sufficiency of such goods, or unless the goods have been expressly sold for a specified and particular purpose, in which case the seller shall be considered, without such warranty, to warrant that the same are fit for such purpose.'

The English law on the subject differs fundamentally from the Roman: speaking generally, in the absence of fraud or of express warranty its maxim is *caveat emptor*. 'In the bargain and sale of an existing chattel, by which the property passes, the law does not (in the absence of fraud) imply any warranty of the good quality or condition of the chattel so sold': per Parke, B. in *Barr* v. *Gibson*, 3 M. & W. 390: and see the other cases referred to by Chalmers, Sale of Goods, p. 20, note 2. The last named writer observes that the English rule probably owes its origin to the fact that in early times nearly all sales of goods took place in market overt: but the judgment of Parke, B. (in *Morley* v. *Attenborough*), to which he refers in support of this suggestion, had reference to the question of implied warranty of *title* in the vendor, not of *quality* in the goods. There seems however to be no doubt as to the truth of his further remark that 'the distinct tendency of modern cases is to limit its scope.'

The following observations will serve to indicate generally the limitations to which the rule is subject:—

I. At the outset a distinction must be drawn between the sale of a specific ascertained chattel, already existing, which the buyer has inspected, and an order given for the making or supplying of an article. In sales of the first kind there is never any implied warranty of quality. 'Where goods are *in esse* and may be inspected by the buyer, and there is no fraud on the part of the seller, the maxim *caveat emptor* applies, even though the defect which exists in them is latent, and not discoverable on examination, at least where the seller is neither the grower nor manufacturer': per Mellor, J., in *Jones* v. *Just*, L. R. 3 Q. B. 197 : *Parkinson* v. *Lee*, 2 East, 314: *Emmerton* v. *Matthews*, 7 H. & N. 586: *Chanter* v. *Hopkins*, 4 M. & W. 64. It must, however, be remembered that if the chattel is sold by description, and does not correspond with that description, the vendor has simply not performed his contract: Benjamin, pp. 598, 638 : *Josling* v. *Kingsford*, 13 C. B. N. S. 447. [So too 'it was and still is the law in Scotland, that specific goods sold by description may be rejected even when the buyer has seen and examined them, if they turn out to be different in kind from those described, provided that the difference was not apparent on inspection, e. g. where one sells flax yarn, and delivers yarn partly consisting of jute. In such a case the vendor does not fulfil the terms of his contract': Bell, I. § 97.]

But where an order is given for the making or supplying of an article, there is an implied warranty 'that it is reasonably fit for the purpose for which it is ordinarily used, or that it is fit for the purpose intended by the buyer, if that purpose be communicated to the vendor when the order is given' (Benjamin, p. 638). Separated from this by only a fine line of distinction is the rule that

II. Where goods are sold by description, or supplied in compliance with an order by description, by a seller who deals in goods of that kind (whether he be the manufacturer or not), and they have not been inspected by the buyer, there is

(*a*) a condition precedent that the goods shall answer to the description: otherwise the contract has not been performed. 'If a man offers to buy peas of another, and he sends him beans, he does not perform his contract: but that is not a warranty: there is no *warranty* that he should sell him peas, the contract is to sell peas, and if he sell him anything else in their stead, it is a non-performance of it': per Lord Abinger in *Chanter* v. *Hopkins*, 4 M. & W. 399: cf. *Shand* v. *Bowes*, 2 App. Cas. 455: and Chalmers, Sale of Goods, p. 19.

(*b*) An implied warranty, amounting to a condition (for on breach of it the buyer is entitled to reject the goods: see per Lord Esher, M. R., in *Randall* v. *Newson*, 2 Q. B. D. at p. 109, cited in Chalmers, p. 22) that they shall be 'saleable or merchantable' (Benjamin, p. 653) or 'of merchantable quality and condition' (Chalmers, p. 21). In *Gardiner* v. *Gray* (4 Camp. 144) Lord Ellenborough said 'where there is no opportunity to inspect the commodity, the maxim of *caveat emptor* does not apply: and in *Jones* v. *Just* (L. R. 3 Q. B. 197) the Court observed 'we are aware of no case in which the maxim *caveat emptor* has been applied where there has been no opportunity of inspection, or where that opportunity has not been waived.' But if the goods are to be supplied to a purchaser at a distant place, the warranty does not extend to deterioration which is the necessary and inevitable result of the transit (*Bull* v. *Robinson*, 10 Ex. 342), and if deterioration results from exceptional or accidental causes during the transit (such as a railway accident) the loss must be borne by the owner, who may be either the vendor or the purchaser according to circumstances (Benjamin, p. 657). So too in the Scotch law: 'When the goods are afterwards to be furnished or sent to the buyer, they may be rejected on implied warranty, where they are not merchantable according to the denomination of the commodity': Bell, § 98.

III. An implied warranty of quality, fitness, or condition may be annexed by the usage of trade. Thus in *Weall* v. *King* (12 East, 452) it was held that where sheep were sold as stock, there was an implied warranty that they were sound, proof having been given that such was the custom of the trade: and in *Jones* v. *Bowden* (4 Taunt. 847) it was shown that in auction sales of certain drugs, as pimento, it was usual to state in the catalogue whether they were sea-damaged or not, and in the absence of a statement that they were sea-damaged they would be assumed to be free from that defect: cf. *Syers* v. *Jonas*, 2 Ex. 111: Indian Contract Act, 1872, § 110.

IV. Where an article is bought for a particular purpose made known to the seller at the time of the contract, and the purchaser relies upon the skill and judgment of the seller to supply what is wanted, it being an article of a description which it is in the course of the latter's business to supply, there is an implied warranty that the article supplied shall be reasonably fit for such purpose: and it is immaterial that the defect is latent, and was unknown to and even undiscovered by the seller: *Randall* v. *Newson*, 2·Q. B. D. 102. C. A.: and see the other cases referred to by Chalmers, Sale of Goods, p. 20, n. 4. The Scotch law is the same: Bell, § 98.

V. The Court of Appeal, in 1881, held, in *Johnson* v. *Raylton*, 7 Q. B. D. 438, that where there is a contract for the sale of goods by a manufacturer, as such, there is, in the absence of any trade usage to the contrary, an implied warranty that the goods are of the seller's own manufacture. Upon this matter the Scotch law is different: *West Stockton Iron Co.* v. *Nielson*, 17 Sc. L. R. 719: *Johnson* v. *Nicoll*, 18 Sc. L. R. 268: but this point is not exactly relevant to the subject under discussion.

VI. In a contract of sale by sample, there is (a) an implied warranty that the bulk shall correspond with the sample in quality and condition: *Parker* v. *Palmer*, 4 B. & Ald. 387: *Parkinson* v. *Lee*, 2 East, 314: (b) an implied condition that the buyer shall have a reasonable opportunity of comparing the bulk with the sample: *Lorymer* v. *Smith*, 1 B. & C. 1: and, further, if a manufacturer agrees to furnish goods according to sample, the sample is to be considered as if free from any secret defect of manufacture not discoverable on inspection, and unknown to both parties: *Drummond* v. *Van Ingen*, 12 App. Ca. 284: *Heilbutt* v. *Hickson*, L. R. 7 C. P. 438: Benjamin, p. 643 sq.: Chalmers, p. 24. As a rule, there is no implied warranty as to the merchantable quality of goods sold by sample: but 'the facts and circumstances of the case may justify the inference that this implied warranty is superadded to the contract': *Mody* v. *Gregson*, L. R. 4 Ex. 49: Benjamin, p. 664: 'when a purchaser states generally the nature of the article he requires, and asks the manufacturer to supply specimens of the mode in which he proposes to carry out the order, he trusts to the skill of the manufacturer just as much as if he asked for no such specimens: and I think he has a right to rely on the samples supplied representing a manufactured article which will be fit for the purposes for which such an article is ordinarily used, just as much as he has a right to rely on manufactured goods supplied on an order without samples complying with such a warranty': per Lord Herschell, in *Drummond* v. *Van Ingen*, 12 App. Ca. at p. 293.

VII. Certain warranties, though not exactly of quality, are implied by statute: e.g. the Merchandise Marks Act, 1887, 50 & 51 Vic. c. 28: the Chain Cables and Anchors Act, 1874, 37 & 38 Vic. c. 51. s. 4: and the Sale of Food and Drugs Act, 1875, 38 & 39 Vic. c. 63.

These implied warranties (except the last) are excluded if there is an express warranty, either by words or acts, which is inconsistent with them (Chalmers, Sale of Goods, p. 13): *Bigge* v. *Parkinson*, 31 L. J. Ex. 301 : *Dickson* v. *Zizania*, 10 C. B. 602 : and as a rule the warranty resulting from a sale by sample cannot be supplemented by a further implied warranty that the goods are merchantable, though this must be taken subject to the limitation stated above on the authority of *Mody* v. *Gregson* and *Drummond* v. *Van Ingen*.

Dig. XVIII. 1.

DE CONTRAHENDA EMPTIONE ET DE PACTIS INTER EMPTOREM ET VENDITOREM COMPOSITIS ET QUAE RES VENIRE NON POSSUNT.

[The references in the margin are to the preceding pages.]

1. PAULUS *libro trigensimo tertio ad edictum* Origo emendi vendendique a permutationibus coepit. olim enim non ita erat nummus neque aliud merx, aliud pretium vocabatur, sed unusquisque secundum necessitatem temporum ac rerum utilibus inutilia permutabat, quando plerumque evenit, ut quod alteri superest alteri desit. sed quia non semper nec facile concurrebat, ut, cum tu haberes quod ego desiderarem, invicem haberem quod tu accipere velles, electa materia est, cuius publica ac perpetua aestimatio difficultatibus permutationum aequalitate quantitatis subveniret. eaque materia forma publica percussa usum dominiumque non tam ex substantia praebet quam ex quantitate, nec ultra merx utrumque, sed alterum pretium vocatur. Sed an sine nummis venditio dici hodieque 1 possit, dubitatur, veluti si ego togam dedi, ut tunicam acciperem. 66 Sabinus et Cassius esse emptionem et venditionem putant: Nerva et Proculus permutationem, non emptionem hoc esse. Sabinus Homero teste utitur, qui exercitum Graecorum aere ferro hominibusque vinum emere refert, illis versibus:

> ἔνθεν ἄρ' οἰνίζοντο καρηκομόωντες Ἀχαιοί
> ἄλλοι μὲν χαλκῷ, ἄλλοι δ' αἴθωνι σιδήρῳ,
> ἄλλοι δὲ ῥινοῖς, ἄλλοι δ' αὐτῇσι βόεσσι,
> ἄλλοι δ' ἀνδραπόδεσσιν.

sed hi versus permutationem significare videntur, non emptionem, sicut illi:

ἔνθ' αὖτε Γλαύκῳ Κρονίδης φρένας ἐξέλετο Ζεύς,
ὃς πρὸς Τυδείδην Διομήδεα τεύχε' ἄμειβεν.

magis autem pro hac sententia illud diceretur, quod alias idem poeta dicit:

πρίατο κτεάτεσσιν ἑοῖσιν.

sed verior est Nervae et Proculi sententia: nam ut aliud est vendere, aliud emere, alius emptor, alius venditor, sic aliud est pretium, aliud merx: quod in permutatione discerni non potest, 2 uter emptor, uter venditor sit. Est autem emptio iuris gentium, et ideo consensu peragitur et inter absentes contrahi potest et per nuntium et per litteras.

2. *ULPIANUS libro primo ad Sabinum* Inter patrem et filium contrahi emptio non potest, sed de rebus castrensibus potest. 1 Sine pretio nulla venditio est: non autem pretii numeratio, sed conventio perficit sine scriptis habitam emptionem.

3. *IDEM libro vicensimo octavo ad Sabinum* Si res ita distracta sit, ut si displicuisset inempta esset, constat non esse sub condicione distractam, sed resolvi emptionem sub condicione.

4. *POMPONIUS libro nono ad Sabinum* Et liberi hominis et loci sacri et religiosi, qui haberi non potest, emptio intellegitur, si ab ignorante emitur,

5. *PAULUS libro quinto ad Sabinum* quia difficile dinosci potest liber homo a servo.

6. *POMPONIUS libro nono ad Sabinum* Sed Celsus filius ait hominem liberum scientem te emere non posse nec cuiuscumque rei si scias alienationem esse: ut sacra et religiosa loca aut quorum commercium non sit, ut publica, quae non in pecunia populi, 1 sed in publico usu habeantur, ut est campus Martius. Si fundus annua bima trima die ea lege venisset, ut, si in diem statutum pecunia soluta non esset, fundus inemptus foret et ut, si interim emptor fundum coluerit fructusque ex eo perceperit, inempto eo facto restituerentur et ut, quanti minoris postea alii venisset, ut id emptor venditori praestaret: ad diem pecunia non soluta placet venditori ex vendito eo nomine actionem esse. nec conturbari debemus, quod inempto fundo facto dicatur actionem ex vendito futuram esse: in emptis enim et venditis potius id quod actum, quam id quod dictum sit sequendum est, et cum lege id dictum sit, apparet hoc dumtaxat actum esse, ne venditor

emptori pecunia ad diem non soluta obligatus esset, non ut omnis obligatio empti et venditi utrique solveretur. Condicio, quae initio contractus dicta est, postea alia pactione immutari potest, sicuti etiam abiri a tota emptione potest, si nondum impleta sunt, quae utrimque praestari debuerunt.

7. *ULPIANUS libro vicensimo octavo ad Sabinum* Haec venditio servi 'si rationes domini computasset arbitrio' condicionalis est: condicionales autem venditiones tunc perficiuntur, cum impleta fuerit condicio. sed utrum haec est venditionis condicio, si ipse dominus putasset suo arbitrio, an vero si arbitrio viri boni? nam si arbitrium domini accipiamus, venditio nulla est, quemadmodum si quis ita vendiderit, si voluerit, vel stipulanti sic spondeat 'si voluero, decem dabo': neque enim debet in arbitrium rei conferri, an sit obstrictus. placuit itaque veteribus magis in viri boni arbitrium id collatum videri quam in domini. si igitur rationes potuit accipere nec accepit, vel accepit, fingit autem se non accepisse, impleta condicio emptionis est et ex empto venditor conveniri potest. Huiusmodi emptio 'quanti tu cum emisti,' 'quantum pretii in arca habeo,' valet: nec enim incertum est pretium tam evidenti venditione: magis enim ignoratur, quanti emptus sit, quam in rei veritate incertum est. Si quis ita emerit: 'est mihi fundus emptus centum et quanto pluris eum vendidero,' valet venditio et statim impletur: habet enim certum pretium centum, augebitur autem pretium, si pluris emptor fundum vendiderit.

8. *POMPONIUS libro nono ad Sabinum* Nec emptio nec venditio sine re quae veneat potest intellegi. et tamen fructus et partus futuri recte ementur, ut, cum editus esset partus, iam tunc, cum contractum esset negotium, venditio facta intellegatur: sed si id egerit venditor, ne nascatur aut fiant, ex empto agi posse. Aliquando tamen et sine re venditio intellegitur, veluti cum quasi alea emitur, quod fit, cum captum piscium vel avium vel missilium emitur: emptio enim contrahitur etiam si nihil inciderit, quia spei emptio est: et quod missilium nomine eo casu captum est si evictum fuerit, nulla eo nomine ex empto obligatio contrahitur, quia id actum intellegitur.

9. *ULPIANUS libro vicensimo octavo ad Sabinum* In venditionibus et emptionibus consensum debere intercedere palam est: ceterum sive in ipsa emptione dissentient sive in pretio sive in

quo alio, emptio imperfecta est. si igitur ego me fundum emere putarem Cornelianum, tu mihi te vendere Sempronianum putasti, quia in corpore dissensimus, emptio nulla est. idem est, si ego me Stichum, tu Pamphilum absentem vendere putasti: nam cum in corpore dissentiatur, apparet nullam esse emptionem. Plane si in nomine dissentiamus, verum de corpore constet, nulla dubitatio est, quin valeat emptio et venditio: nihil enim facit error nominis, cum de corpore constat. Inde quaeritur, si in ipso corpore non erratur, sed in substantia error sit, ut puta si acetum pro vino veneat, aes pro auro vel plumbum pro argento vel quid aliud argento simile, an emptio et venditio sit. Marcellus scripsit libro sexto digestorum emptionem esse et venditionem, quia in corpus consensum est, etsi in materia sit erratum. ego in vino quidem consentio, quia eadem prope οὐσία est, si modo vinum acuit: ceterum si vinum non acuit, sed ab initio acetum fuit, ut embamma, aliud pro alio venisse videtur. in ceteris autem nullam esse venditionem puto, quotiens in materia erratur.

10. *PAULUS libro quinto ad Sabinum* Aliter atque si aurum quidem fuerit, deterius autem quam emptor existimaret: tunc enim emptio valet.

11. *ULPIANUS libro vicensimo octavo ad Sabinum* Alioquin quid dicemus, si caecus emptor fuit vel si in materia erratur vel in minus perito discernendarum materiarum? in corpus eos consensisse dicemus? et quemadmodum consensit, qui non vidit? 1 Quod si ego me virginem emere putarem, cum esset iam mulier, emptio valebit: in sexu enim non est erratum. ceterum si ego mulierem venderem, tu puerum emere existimasti, quia in sexu error est, nulla emptio, nulla venditio est.

12. *POMPONIUS libro trigensimo primo ad Quintum Mucium* In huiusmodi autem quaestionibus personae ementium et vendentium spectari debent, non eorum, quibus adquiritur ex eo contractu actio: nam si servus meus vel filius qui in mea potestate est me praesente suo nomine emat, non est quaerendum, quid ego existimem, sed quid ille qui contrahit.

13. *IDEM. libro nono ad Sabinum* Sed si servo meo vel ei cui mandavero vendas sciens fugitivum illo ignorante, me sciente, non teneri te ex empto verum est.

14. *ULPIANUS libro vicensimo octavo ad Sabinum* Quid tamen

dicemus, si in materia et qualitate ambo errarent? ut puta si et ego me vendere aurum putarem et tu emere, cum aes esset? ut puta coheredes viriolam, quae aurea dicebatur, pretio exquisito uni heredi vendidissent eaque inventa esset magna ex parte aenea? venditionem esse constat ideo, quia auri aliquid habuit. nam si inauratum aliquid sit, licet ego aureum putem, valet venditio: si autem aes pro auro veneat, non valet.

15. *PAULUS libro quinto ad Sabinum* Et si consensum fuerit in corpus, id tamen in rerum natura ante venditionem esse desierit, nulla emptio est. Ignorantia emptori prodest, quae non in supinum hominem cadit. Si rem meam mihi ignoranti vendideris et iussu meo alii tradideris, non putat Pomponius dominium meum transire, quoniam non hoc mihi propositum fuit, sed quasi tuum dominium ad eum transire: et ideo etiam si donaturus mihi rem meam iussu meo alii tradas, idem dicendum erit.

16. *POMPONIUS libro nono ad Sabinum* Suae rei emptio non valet, sive sciens sive ignorans emi: sed si ignorans emi, quod solvero repetere potero, quia nulla obligatio fuit. Nec tamen emptioni obstat, si in ea re usus fructus dumtaxat ementis sit:

17. *PAULUS libro trigensimo tertio ad edictum* officio tamen iudicis pretium minuetur.

18. *POMPONIUS libro nono ad Sabinum* Sed si communis ea res emptori cum alio sit, dici debet scisso pretio pro portione pro parte emptionem valere, pro parte non valere. Si servus domini iussu in demonstrandis finibus agri venditi vel errore vel dolo plus demonstraverit, id tamen demonstratum accipi oportet, quod dominus senserit: et idem Alfenus scripsit de vacua possessione per servum tradita.

19. *IDEM libro trigensimo primo ad Quintum Mucium* Quod vendidi non aliter fit accipientis, quam si aut pretium nobis solutum sit aut satis eo nomine factum vel etiam fidem habuerimus emptori sine ulla satisfactione.

20. *IDEM libro nono ad Sabinum* Sabinus respondit, si quam rem nobis fieri velimus etiam, veluti statuam vel vas aliquod seu vestem, ut nihil aliud quam pecuniam daremus, emptionem videri, nec posse ullam locationem esse, ubi corpus ipsum non detur ab eo cui id fieret: aliter atque si arcam darem, ubi insulam aedificares, quoniam tunc a me substantia proficiscitur.

21. *PAULUS libro quinto ad Sabinum* Labeo scripsit obscuritatem pacti nocere potius debere venditori qui id dixerit quam emptori, quia potuit re integra apertius dicere.

22. *ULPIANUS libro vicensimo octavo ad Sabinum* Hanc legem venditionis 'si quid sacri vel religiosi est, eius venit nihil' supervacuam non esse, sed ad modica loca pertinere. ceterum si omne religiosum vel sacrum vel publicum venierit, nullam esse emptionem,

23. *PAULUS libro quinto ad Sabinum* (et quod solverit eo nomine, emptor condicere potest)

24. *ULPIANUS libro vicensimo octavo ad Sabinum* in modicis autem ex empto esse actionem, quia non specialiter locus sacer vel religiosus venit, sed emptioni maioris partis accessit.

25. *IDEM libro trigensimo quarto ad Sabinum* Si ita distrahatur 'illa aut illa res,' utram eliget venditor, haec erit empta. Qui vendidit necesse non habet fundum emptoris facere, ut cogitur qui fundum stipulanti spopondit.

26. *POMPONIUS libro septimo decimo ad Sabinum* Si sciens emam ab eo cui bonis interdictum sit vel cui tempus ad deliberandum de hereditate ita datum sit, ut ei deminuendi potestas non sit, dominus non ero: dissimiliter atque si a debitore sciens creditorem fraudari emero.

27. *PAULUS libro octavo ad Sabinum* Qui a quolibet rem emit, quam putat ipsius esse, bona fide emit: at qui sine tutoris auctoritate a pupillo emit, vel falso tutore auctore, quem scit tutorem non esse, non videtur bona fide emere, ut et Sabinus scripsit.

28. *ULPIANUS libro quadragensimo primo ad Sabinum* Rem alienam distrahere quem posse nulla dubitatio est: nam emptio est et venditio: sed res emptori auferri potest.

29. *IDEM libro quadragensimo tertio ad Sabinum* Quotiens servus venit, non cum peculio distrahitur: et ideo sive non sit exceptum, sive exceptum sit, ne cum peculio veneat, non cum peculio distractus videtur. unde si qua res fuerit peculiaris a servo subrepta, condici potest videlicet quasi furtiva: hoc ita, si res ad emptorem pervenit.

30. *IDEM libro trigensimo secundo ad edictum* Sed ad exhibendum agi posse nihilo minus et ex vendito puto.

31. *POMPONIUS libro vicensimo secundo ad Sabinum* Sed et si quid postea accessit peculio, reddendum est venditori, veluti partus et quod ex operis vicarii perceptum est.

32. *ULPIANUS libro quadragensimo quarto ad Sabinum* Qui tabernas argentarias vel ceteras quae in solo publico sunt vendit, non solum, sed ius vendit, cum istae tabernae publicae sunt, quarum usus ad privatos pertinet.

33. *POMPONIUS libro trigensimo tertio ad Sabinum* Cum in lege venditionis ita sit scriptum: 'flumina stillicidia uti nunc sunt, ut ita sint,' nec additur, quae flumina vel stillicidia primum spectari oportet, quid acti sit: si non id appareat, tunc id accipitur quod venditori nocet: ambigua enim oratio est.

34. *PAULUS libro trigensimo tertio ad edictum* Si in emptione fundi dictum sit accedere Stichum servum neque intellegatur, quis ex pluribus accesserit, cum de alio emptor, de alio venditor senserit, nihilo minus fundi venditionem valere constat: sed Labeo ait eum Stichum deberi quem venditor intellexerit. nec refert, quanti sit accessio, sive plus in ea sit quam in ipsa re cui accedat an minus: plerasque enim res aliquando propter accessiones emimus, sicuti cum domus propter marmora et statuas et tabulas pictas ematur. Omnium rerum, quas quis habere vel possidere vel persequi potest, venditio recte fit: quas vero natura vel gentium ius vel mores civitatis commercio exuerunt, earum nulla venditio est. Liberum hominem scientes emere non possumus. sed nec talis emptio aut stipulatio admittenda est: 'cum servus erit,' quamvis dixerimus futuras res emi posse: nec enim fas est eiusmodi casus exspectare. Item si et emptor et venditor scit furtivum esse quod venit, a neutra parte obligatio contrahitur: si emptor solus scit, non obligabitur venditor nec tamen ex vendito quicquam consequitur, nisi ultro quod convenerit praestet: quod si venditor scit, emptor ignoravit, utrinque obligatio contrahitur, et ita Pomponius quoque scribit. Rei suae emptio tunc valet, cum ab initio agatur, ut possessionem emat, quam forte venditor habuit, et in iudicio possessionis potior esset. Alia causa est degustandi, alia metiendi: gustus enim ad hoc proficit, ut improbare liceat, mensura vero non eo proficit, ut aut plus aut minus veneat, sed ut appareat, quantum ematur. Si emptio ita facta fuerit: 'est mihi emptus Stichus aut Pamphilus,' in potestate est venditoris,

quem velit dare, sicut in stipulationibus, sed uno mortuo qui superest dandus est: et ideo prioris periculum ad venditorem, posterioris ad emptorem respicit. sed et si pariter decesserunt, pretium debebitur: unus enim utique periculo emptoris vixit. idem dicendum est etiam, si emptoris fuit arbitrium quem vellet habere, si modo hoc solum arbitrio eius commissum sit, ut quem voluisset emptum haberet, non et illud, an emptum haberet.

7 Tutor rem pupilli emere non potest: idemque porrigendum est ad similia, id est ad curatores procuratores et qui negotia aliena gerunt.

35. *GAIUS libro decimo ad edictum provinciale* Quod saepe arrae nomine pro emptione datur, non eo pertinet, quasi sine arra conventio nihil proficiat, sed ut evidentius probari possit 1 convenisse de pretio. Illud constat imperfectum esse negotium, cum emere volenti sic venditor dicit: 'quanti velis, quanti aequum putaveris, quanti aestimaveris, habebis emptum.' 2 Veneni mali quidam putant non contrahi emptionem, quia nec societas aut mandatum flagitiosae rei ullas vires habet: quae sententia potest sane vera videri de his quae nullo modo adiectione alterius materiae usu nobis esse possunt: de his vero quae mixta aliis materiis adeo nocendi naturam deponunt, ut ex his antidoti et alia quaedam salubria medicamenta conficiantur, 3 aliud dici potest. Si quis amico peregre eunti mandaverit, ut fugitivum suum quaerat et si invenerit vendat, nec ipse contra senatus consultum committit, quia non vendidit, neque amicus eius, quia praesentem vendit: emptor quoque, qui praesentem 4 emit, recte negotium gerere intellegitur. Si res vendita per furtum perierit, prius animadvertendum erit, quid inter eos de custodia rei convenerat: si nihil appareat convenisse, talis custodia desideranda est a venditore, qualem bonus pater familias suis rebus adhibet: quam si praestiterit et tamen rem perdidit, securus esse debet, ut tamen scilicet vindicationem rei et condictionem exhibeat emptori. unde videbimus in personam eius, qui alienam rem vendiderit: cum is nullam vindicationem aut condictionem habere possit, ob id ipsum damnandus est, quia, si suam rem vendidisset, potuisset eas actiones ad emp-5 torem transferre. In his quae pondere numero mensurave constant, veluti frumento vino oleo argento, modo ea servantur quae in ceteris, ut simul atque de pretio convenerit, videatur

perfecta venditio, modo ut, etiamsi de pretio convenerit, non tamen aliter videatur perfecta venditio, quam si admensa adpensa adnumeratave sint. nam si omne vinum vel oleum vel frumentum vel argentum quantumcumque esset uno pretio venierit, idem iuris est quod in ceteris rebus. quod si vinum ita venierit, ut in singulas amphoras, item oleum, ut in singulas metretas, item frumentum, ut in singulos modios, item argentum, ut in singulas libras certum pretium diceretur, quaeritur, quando videatur emptio perfici. quod similiter scilicet quaeritur et de his quae numero constant, si pro numero corporum pretium fuerit statutum. Sabinus et Cassius tunc perfici emptionem existimant, cum adnumerata admensa adpensave sint, quia venditio quasi sub hac condicione videtur fieri, ut in singulas metretas aut in singulos modios quos quasve admensus eris, aut in singulas libras quas adpenderis, aut in singula corpora quae adnumeraveris. Ergo et si grex venierit, si quidem universa- 6 liter uno pretio, perfecta videtur, postquam de pretio convenerit : si vero in singula corpora certo pretio, eadem erunt, quae proxime tractavimus. Sed et si ex doliario pars vini venierit, 7 veluti metretae centum, verissimum est (quod et constare videtur) antequam admetiatur, omne periculum ad venditorem pertinere : nec interest, unum pretium omnium centum metretarum in semel dictum sit an in singulas eas. Si quis in vendendo 8 praedio confinem celaverit, quem emptor si audisset, empturus non esset, teneri venditorem.

36. *ULPIANUS libro quadragensimo tertio ad edictum* Cum in venditione quis pretium rei ponit donationis causa non exac- turus, non videtur vendere.

37. *IDEM libro tertio disputationum* Si quis fundum iure hereditario sibi delatum ita vendidisset : 'erit tibi emptus tanti, quanti a testatore emptus est,' mox inveniatur non emptus, sed donatus testatori, videtur quasi sine pretio facta venditio, ideoque similis erit sub condicione factae venditioni, quae nulla est, si condicio defecerit.

38. *IDEM libro septimo disputationum* Si quis donationis causa minoris vendat, venditio valet : totiens enim dicimus in totum venditionem non valere, quotiens universa venditio donationis causa facta est : quotiens vero viliore pretio res donationis causa distrahitur, dubium non est venditionem valere. hoc

inter ceteros: inter virum vero et uxorem donationis causa venditio facta pretio viliore nullius momenti est.

39. *IULIANUS libro quinto decimo digestorum* Si debitor rem pigneratam a creditore redemerit, quasi suae rei emptor actione ex vendito non tenetur et omnia in integro sunt creditori. 1 Verisimile est cum, qui fructum olivae pendentis vendidisset et stipulatus est decem pondo olei quod natum esset, pretium constituisse ex eo quod natum esset usque ad decem pondo olei: idcirco solis quinque collectis non amplius emptor petere potest quam quinque pondo olei, quae collecta essent, a plerisque responsum est.

40. *PAULUS libro quarto epitomarum Alfeni digestorum* Qui fundum vendebat, in lege ita dixerat, ut emptor in diebus triginta proximis fundum metiretur et de modo renuntiaret, et si ante eam diem non renuntiasset, ut venditoris fides soluta esset: emptor intra diem mensurae quo minorem modum esse credidit renuntiavit et pecuniam pro eo accepit: postea eum fundum vendidit et cum ipse emptori suo admetiretur, multo minorem modum agri quam putaverat invenit: quaerebat, an id quod minor is esset consequi a suo venditore posset. respondit interesse, quemadmodum lex diceretur: nam si ita dictum esset, ut emptor diebus triginta proximis fundum metiatur et domino renuntiet, quanto modus agri minor sit, quo post diem trigensimum renuntiasset, nihil ei profuturum: sed si ita pactum esset, ut emptor in diebus proximis fundum metiatur et de modo agri renuntiet, etsi in diebus triginta renuntiasset minorem modum agri esse, quamvis multis post 1 annis posse eum quo minor is modus agri fuisset repetere. In lege fundi aquam accessuram dixit: quaerebatur, an etiam iter aquae accessisset. respondit sibi videri id actum esse, et ideo 2 iter quoque venditorem tradere oportere. Qui agrum vendebat, dixit fundi iugera decem et octo esse, et quod eius admensum erit, ad singula iugera certum pretium stipulatus erat: viginti 3 inventa sunt: pro viginti deberi pecuniam respondit. Fundi venditor frumenta manu sata receperat: in eo fundo ex stipula seges erat enata: quaesitum est, an pacto contineretur. respondit maxime referre, quid est actum: ceterum secundum verba non esse actum, quod ex stipula nasceretur, non magis quam si quid ex sacco saccarii cecidisset aut ex eo quod avibus

ex aere cecidisset natum esset. Cum fundum quis vendiderat 4
et omnem fructum receperat, et arundinem caeduam et silvam
in fructu esse respondit. Dolia, quae in fundo domini essent, 5
accessura dixit: etiam ea, quae servus qui fundum coluerat
emisset peculiaria, emptori cessura respondit. Rota quoque, 6
per quam aqua traheretur, nihilo minus aedificii est quam
situla.

41. *IULIANUS libro tertio ad Urseium Ferocem* Cum ab eo,
qui fundum alii obligatum habebat, quidam sic emptum rogasset, ut esset is sibi emptus, si eum liberasset, dummodo ante
kalendas Iulias liberaret, quaesitum est, an utiliter agere
possit ex empto in hoc, ut venditor eum liberaret. respondit:
videamus, quid inter ementem et vendentem actum sit. nam
si id actum est, ut omni modo intra kalendas Iulias venditor
fundum liberaret, ex empto erit actio, ut liberet, nec sub condicione emptio facta intellegetur, veluti si hoc modo emptor
interrogaverit: 'erit mihi fundus emptus ita, ut eum intra
kalendas Iulias liberes,' vel 'ita, ut eum intra kalendas a Titio
redimas.' si vero sub condicione facta emptio est, non poterit
agi, ut condicio impleatur. Mensam argento coopertam mihi 1
ignoranti pro solida vendidisti imprudens: nulla est emptio
pecuniaque eo nomine data condicetur.

42. *MARCIANUS libro primo institutionum* Domini neque
per se neque per procuratores suos possunt saltem criminosos
servos vendere, ut cum bestiis pugnarent. et ita divi fratres
rescripserunt.

43. *FLORENTINUS libro octavo institutionum* Ea quae commendandi causa in venditionibus dicuntur, si palam appareant,
venditorem non obligant, veluti si dicat servum speciosum,
domum bene aedificatam: at si dixerit hominem litteratum vel
artificem, praestare debet: nam hoc ipso pluris vendit. Quae- 1
dam etiam pollicitationes venditorem non obligant, si ita in
promptu res sit, ut eam emptor non ignoraverit, veluti si quis
hominem luminibus effossis emat et de sanitate stipuletur:
nam de cetera parte corporis potius stipulatus videtur quam de
eo, in quo se ipse decipiebat. Dolum malum a se abesse prae- 2
stare venditor debet, qui non tantum in eo est, qui fallendi
causa obscure loquitur, sed etiam qui insidiose obscure dissimulat.

44. *MARCIANUS libro tertio regularum* Si duos quis servos emerit pariter uno pretio, quorum alter ante venditionem mortuus est, neque in vivo constat emptio.

45. *IDEM libro quarto regularum* Labeo libro posteriorum scribit, si vestimenta interpola quis pro novis emerit, Trebatio placere ita emptori praestandum quod interest, si ignorans interpola emerit. quam sententiam et Pomponius probat, in qua et Iulianus est, qui ait, si quidem ignorabat venditor, ipsius rei nomine teneri, si sciebat, etiam damni quod ex eo contingit: quemadmodum si vas aurichalcum pro auro vendidisset ignorans, tenetur, ut aurum quod vendidit praestet.

46. *IDEM libro singulari de delatoribus* Non licet ex officio, quod administrat quis, emere quid vel per se vel per aliam personam: alioquin non tantum rem amittit, sed et in quadruplum convenitur secundum constitutionem Severi et Antonini: et hoc ad procuratorem quoque Caesaris pertinet. sed hoc ita se habet, nisi specialiter quibusdam hoc concessum est.

47. *ULPIANUS libro vicensimo nono ad Sabinum* Si aquae ductus debeatur praedio, et ius aquae transit ad emptorem, etiamsi nihil dictum sit, sicut et ipsae fistulae, per quas aqua ducitur,

48. *PAULUS libro quinto ad Sabinum* licet extra aedes sint:

49. *ULPIANUS libro vicensimo nono ad Sabinum* et quamquam ius aquae non sequatur, quod amissum est, attamen fistulae et canales dum sibi sequuntur, quasi pars aedium ad emptorem perveniunt. et ita Pomponius libro decimo putat.

50. *IDEM libro undecimo ad edictum* Labeo scribit, si mihi bibliothecam ita vendideris, si decuriones Campani locum mihi vendidissent, in quo eam ponerem, et per me stet, quo minus id a Campanis impetrem, non esse dubitandum, quin praescriptis verbis agi possit. ego etiam ex vendito agi posse puto quasi impleta condicione, cum per emptorem stet, quo minus impleatur.

51. *PAULUS libro vicensimo primo ad edictum* Litora, quae fundo vendito coniuncta sunt, in modum non computantur, quia nullius sunt, sed iure gentium omnibus vacant: nec viae publicae aut loca religiosa vel sacra. itaque ut proficiant venditori, caveri solet, ut viae, item litora et loca publica in modum cedant.

52. *IDEM libro quinquagensimo quarto ad edictum* Senatus censuit, ne quis domum villamve dirueret, quo plus sibi adquireretur neve quis negotiandi causa eorum quid emeret venderetve: poena in eum, qui adversus senatus consultum fecisset, constituta est, ut duplum eius quanti emisset in aerarium inferre cogeretur, in eum vero, qui vendidisset, ut irrita fieret venditio. plane si mihi pretium solveris, cum tu duplum aerario debeas, repetes a me: quod a mea parte irrita facta est venditio. nec solum huic senatus consulto locus erit, si quis suam villam vel domum, sed et si alienam vendiderit.

53. *GAIUS libro ricensimo octavo ad edictum provinciale* Ut res emptoris fiat, nihil interest, utrum solutum sit pretium an eo nomine fideiussor datus sit. quod autem de fideiussore diximus, plenius acceptum est, qualibet ratione si venditori de pretio satisfactum est, veluti expromissore aut pignore dato, proinde sit, ac si pretium solutum esset.

54. *PAULUS libro primo ad edictum aedilium curulium* Res bona fide vendita propter minimam causam inempta fieri non debet.

55. *IDEM libro secundo ad edictum aedilium curulium* Nuda et imaginaria venditio pro non facta est et ideo nec alienatio eius rei intellegitur.

56. *IDEM libro quinquagensimo ad edictum* Si quis sub hoc pacto vendiderit ancillam, ne prostituatur et, si contra factum esset, uti liceret ei abducere, etsi per plures emptores mancipium cucurrerit, ei qui primo vendit abducendi potestas fit.

57. *PAULUS libro quinto ad Plautium* Domum emi, cum eam et ego et venditor combustam ignoraremus. Nerva Sabinus Cassius nihil venisse, quamvis area maneat, pecuniamque solutam condici posse aiunt. sed si pars domus maneret, Neratius ait hac quaestione multum interesse, quanta pars domus incendio consumpta permaneat, ut, si quidem amplior domus pars exusta est, non compellatur emptor perficere emptionem, sed etiam quod forte solutum ab eo est repetet: sin vero vel dimidia pars vel minor quam dimidia exusta fuerit, tunc coartandus est emptor venditionem adimplere aestimatione viri boni arbitratu habita, ut, quod ex pretio propter incendium decrescere fuerit inventum, ab huius praestatione liberetur.

1 Sin autem venditor quidem sciebat domum esse exustam, emptor autem ignorabat, nullam venditionem stare, si tota domus ante venditionem exusta sit: si vero quantacumque pars aedificii remaneat, et stare venditionem et venditorem 2 emptori quod interest restituere. Simili quoque modo ex diverso tractari oportet, ubi emptor quidem sciebat, venditor autem ignorabat: et hic enim oportet et venditionem stare et omne pretium ab emptore venditori, si non depensum est, solvi 3 vel si solutum sit, non repeti. Quod si uterque sciebat et emptor et venditor domum esse exustam totam vel ex parte, nihil actum fuisse dolo inter utramque partem compensando et iudicio, quod ex bona fide descendit, dolo ex utraque parte veniente stare non concedente.

58. *PAPINIANUS libro decimo quaestionum* Arboribus quoque vento deiectis vel absumptis igne dictum est emptionem fundi non videri esse contractam, si contemplatione illarum arborum, veluti oliveti, fundus comparabatur, sive sciente sive ignorante venditore: sive autem emptor sciebat vel ignorabat vel uterque eorum, haec optinent, quae in superioribus casibus pro aedibus dicta sunt.

59. *CELSUS libro octavo digestorum* Cum venderes fundum, non dixisti 'ita ut optimus maximusque': verum est, quod Quinto Mucio placebat, non liberum, sed qualis esset, fundum praestari oportere. idem et in urbanis praediis dicendum est.

60. *MARCELLUS libro sexto digestorum* Comprehensum erat lege venditionis dolia sexaginta emptori accessura: cum essent centum, in venditoris fore potestate responsum est quae vellet dare.

61. *IDEM libro vicensimo digestorum* Existimo posse me id quod meum est sub condicione emere, quia forte speratur meum esse desinere.

62. *MODESTINUS libro quinto regularum* Qui officii causa in provincia agit vel militat, praedia comparare in eadem provincia non potest, praeterquam si paterna eius a fisco distrahantur. 1 Qui nesciens loca sacra vel religiosa vel publica pro privatis comparavit, licet emptio non teneat, ex empto tamen adversus venditorem experietur, ut consequatur quod interfuit eius, ne 2 deciperetur. Res in aversione empta, si non dolo venditoris

factum sit, ad periculum emptoris pertinebit, etiamsi res adsignata non sit.

' 63. *IAVOLENUS libro septimo ex Cassio* Cum servo dominus rem vendere certae personae iusserit, si alii vendidisset, quam cui iussus erat, venditio non valet: idem iuris in libera persona est: cum perfici venditio non potuit in eius persona, cui dominus venire eam noluit. Demonstratione fundi facta fines nominari supervacuum est: si nominentur, etiam ipsum venditorem nominare oportet, si forte alium agrum confinem possidet.

64. *IDEM libro secundo epistularum* Fundus ille est mihi et Titio emptus: quaero, utrum in partem an in totum venditio consistat an nihil actum sit. respondi personam Titii supervacuo accipiendam puto ideoque totius fundi emptionem ad me pertinere.

65. *IDEM libro undecimo epistularum* Convenit mihi tecum, ut certum numerum tegularum mihi dares certo pretio quod ut faceres: utrum emptio sit an locatio? respondit, si ex meo fundo tegulas tibi factas ut darem convenit, emptionem puto esse, non conductionem: totiens enim conductio alicuius rei est, quotiens materia, in qua aliquid praestatur, in eodem statu eiusdem manet: quotiens vero et immutatur et alienatur, emptio magis quam locatio intellegi debet.

66. *POMPONIUS libro trigensimo primo ad Quintum Mucium* In vendendo fundo quaedam etiam si non dicantur, praestanda sunt, veluti ne fundus evincatur aut usus fructus eius, quaedam ita demum, si dicta sint, veluti viam iter actum aquae ductum praestatu iri: idem et in servitutibus urbanorum praediorum. Si cum servitus venditis praediis deberetur nec commemoraverit venditor, sed sciens esse reticuerit et ob id per ignorantiam rei emptor non utendo per statutum tempus eam servitutem amiserit, quidam recte putant venditorem teneri ex empto ob dolum. Quintus Mucius scribit, qui scripsit 'ruta caesa quaeque aedium fundive non sunt,' bis idem scriptum: nam ruta caesa ea sunt quae neque aedium neque fundi sunt.

67. *IDEM libro trigensimo nono ad Quintum Mucium* Alienatio cum fit, cum sua causa dominium ad alium transferimus, quae esset futura, si apud nos ea res mansisset, idque toto iure civili ita se habet, praeterquam si aliquid nominatim sit constitutum.

68. *PROCULUS libro sexto epistularum* Si, cum fundum venderes, in lege dixisses, quod mercedis nomine a conductore exegisses, id emptori accessurum esse, existimo te in exigendo non solum bonam fidem, sed etiam diligentiam praestare debere, id 1 est non solum ut a te dolus malus absit, sed etiam ut culpa. Fere aliqui solent haec verba adicere: 'dolus malus a venditore 2 aberit,' qui etiam si adiectum non est, abesse debet. Nec videtur abesse, si per eum factum est aut fiet, quo minus fundum emptor possideat. erit ergo ex empto actio, non ut venditor vacuam possessionem tradat, cum multis modis accidere poterit, ne tradere possit, sed ut, si quid dolo malo fecit aut facit, dolus malus eius aestimaretur.

69. *IDEM libro undecimo epistularum* Rutilia Polla emit lacum Sabatenem Angularium et circa eum lacum pedes decem: quaero, numquid et decem pedes, qui tunc accesserunt, sub aqua sint, quia lacus crevit, an proximi pedes decem ab aqua Rutiliae Pollae iuris sint. Proculus respondit: ego existimo eatenus lacum, quem emit Rutilia Polla, venisse, quatenus tunc fuit, et circa eum decem pedes qui tunc fuerunt, nec ob eam rem, quod lacus postea crevit, latius eum possidere debet quam emit.

70. *LICINNIUS RUFINUS libro octavo regularum* Liberi hominis emptionem contrahi posse plerique existimaverunt, si modo inter ignorantes id fiat. quod idem placet etiam, si venditor sciat, emptor autem ignoret. quod si emptor sciens liberum esse emerit, nulla emptio contrahitur.

71. *PAPIRIUS IUSTUS libro primo constitutionum* Imperatores Antoninus et Verus Augusti Sextio Vero in haec verba rescripserunt: 'quibus mensuris aut pretiis negotiatores vina comparent, in contrahentium potestate esse: neque enim quisquam cogitur vendere, si aut pretium aut mensura displiceat, praesertim si nihil contra consuetudinem regionis fiat.'

72. *PAPINIANUS libro decimo quaestionum* Pacta conventa, quae postea facta detrahunt aliquid emptioni, contineri contractui videntur: quae vero adiciunt, credimus non inesse. quod locum habet in his, quae adminicula sunt emptionis, veluti ne cautio duplae praestetur aut ut cum fideiussore cautio duplae praestetur. sed quo casu agente emptore non valet pactum,

idem vires habebit iure exceptionis agente venditore. an idem dici possit aucto postea vel dominuto pretio, non immerito quaesitum est, quoniam emptionis substantia constitit ex pretio. *PAULUS notat*: si omnibus integris manentibus de augendo vel deminuendo pretio rursum convenit, recessum a priore contractu et nova emptio intercessisse videtur. *PAPINIANUS*: Lege venditionis illa facta 'si quid sacri aut religiosi aut publici est, eius nihil venit,' si res non in usu publico, sed in patrimonio fisci erit, venditio eius valebit, nec venditori proderit exceptio, quae non habuit locum.

73. *IDEM libro tertio responsorum* Aede sacra terrae motu diruta locus aedificii non est profanus et ideo venire non potest. Intra maceriam sepulchrorum hortis vel ceteris culturis loca pura servata, si nihil venditor nominatim excepit, ad emptorem pertinent.

74. *IDEM libro primo definitionum* Clavibus traditis ita mercium in horreis conditarum possessio tradita videtur, si claves apud horrea traditae sint: quo facto confestim emptor dominium et possessionem adipiscitur, etsi non aperuerit horrea: quod si venditoris merces non fuerunt, usucapio confestim inchoabitur.

75. *HERMOGENIANUS libro secundo iuris epitomarum* Qui fundum vendidit, ut eum certa mercede conductum ipse habeat vel, si vendat, non alii, sed sibi distrahat vel simile aliquid paciscatur: ad complendum id, quod pepigerunt, ex vendito agere poterit.

76. *PAULUS libro sexto responsorum* Dolia in horreis defossa si non sint nominatim in venditione excepta, horreorum venditioni cessisse videri. Eum, qui in locum emptoris successit, isdem defensionibus uti posse, quibus venditor eius uti potuisset, sed et longae possessionis praescriptione, si utriusque possessio impleat tempora constitutionibus statuta.

77. *IAVOLENUS libro quarto ex posterioribus Labeonis* In lege fundi vendundi lapidicinae in eo fundo ubique essent exceptae erant, et post multum temporis in eo fundo repertae erant lapidicinae. eas quoque venditoris esse Tubero respondit: Labeo referre quid actum sit: si non appareat, non videri eas lapidicinas esse exceptas: neminem enim nec vendere nec excipere quod non sit, et lapidicinas nullas esse, nisi quae

apparent et caedantur: aliter interpretantibus totum fundum lapidicinarum fore, si forte toto eo sub terra esset lapis. hoc probo.

78. *LABEO libro quarto posteriorum a Iavoleno epitomatorum* Fistulas emptori accessuras in lege dictum erat: quaerebatur, an castellum, ex quo fistulis aqua duceretur, accederet. respondi apparere id actum esse, ut id quoque accederet, licet scriptura 1 non continetur. Fundum ab eo emisti, cuius filii postea tutelam administras, nec vacuam accepisti possessionem. dixi tradere te tibi possessionem hoc modo posse, ut pupillus et familia eius decedat de fundo, tunc demum tu ingrediaris possessionem. 2 Qui fundum ea lege emerat, ut soluta pecunia traderetur ei possessio, duobus heredibus relictis decessit. si unus omnem pecuniam solverit, partem familiae herciscundae iudicio servabit: nec, si partem solvat, ex empto cum venditore aget, 3 quoniam ita contractum aes alienum dividi non potuit. Frumenta quae in herbis erant cum vendidisses, dixisti te, si quid vi aut tempestate factum esset, praestaturum: ea frumenta nives corruperunt: si immoderatae fuerunt et contra consuetudinem tempestatis, agi tecum ex empto poterit.

79. *IAVOLENUS libro quinto ex posterioribus Labeonis* Fundi partem dimidiam ea lege vendidisti, ut emptor alteram partem, quam retinebas, annis decem certa pecunia in annos singulos conductam habeat. Labeo et Trebatius negant posse ex vendito agi, ut id quod convenerit fiat. ego contra puto, si modo ideo vilius fundum vendidisti, ut haec tibi conductio praestaretur: nam hoc ipsum pretium fundi videretur, quod eo pacto venditus fuerat: eoque iure utimur.

80. *LABEO libro quinto posteriorum a Iavoleno epitomatorum* Cum manu sata in venditione fundi excipiuntur, non quae in perpetuo sata sunt excipi viderentur, sed quae singulis annis seri solent, ita ut fructus eorum tollatur: nam aliter interpretantibus vites et arbores omnes exceptae viderentur. Huius rei emptionem posse fieri dixi: 'quae ex meis aedibus in tuas aedes proiecta sunt, ut ea mihi ita habere liceat,' deque ea re ex 2 empto agi. Silva caedua in quinquennium venierat: quaerebatur, cum glans decidisset utrius esset. scio Servium respondisse, primum sequendum esse quod appareret actum esse: quod si in obscuro esset, quaecumque glans ex his arboribus

quae caesae non essent cecidisset, venditoris esse, eam autem, quae in arboribus fuisset eo tempore cum haec caederentur, emptoris. Nemo potest videri eam rem vendidisse, de cuius dominio id agitur, ne ad emptorem transeat, sed hoc aut locatio est aut aliud genus contractus.

81. *SCAEVOLA libro septimo digestorum* Titius cum mutuos acciperet tot aureos sub usuris, dedit pignori sive hypothecae praedia et fideiussorem Lucium, cui promisit intra triennium proximum se eum liberaturum: quod si id non fecerit die supra scripta et solverit debitum fideiussor creditori, iussit praedia empta esse, quae creditoribus obligaverat. quaero, cum non sit liberatus Lucius fideiussor a Titio, an, si solverit creditori, empta haberet supra scripta praedia. respondit, si non ut in causam obligationis, sed ut empta habent, sub condicione emptio facta est et contractam esse obligationem. Lucius Titius promisit de fundo suo centum milia modiorum frumenti annua praestare praediis Gaii Seii: postea Lucius Titius vendidit fundum additis verbis his: 'quo iure quaque condicione ea praedia Lucii Titii hodie sunt, ita veneunt itaque habebuntur:' quaero, an emptor Gaio Seio ad praestationem frumenti sit obnoxius. respondit emptorem Gaio Seio secundum ea quae proponerentur obligatum non esse.

DIG. XIX. 1.

DE ACTIONIBUS EMPTI VENDITI.

1. *ULPIANUS libro vicensimo octavo ad Sabinum* Si res vendita non tradatur, in id quod interest agitur, hoc est quod rem habere interest emptoris: hoc autem interdum pretium egreditur, si pluris interest, quam res valet vel empta est. Venditor si, cum sciret deberi, servitutem celavit, non evadet ex empto actionem, si modo eam rem emptor ignoravit: omnia enim quae contra bonam fidem fiunt veniunt in empti actionem. sed scire venditorem et celare sic accipimus, non solum si non admonuit, sed et si negavit servitutem istam deberi, cum esset ab eo quaesitum. sed et si proponas eum ita dixisse: 'nulla quidem servitus debetur, verum ne emergat inopinata servitus,

non teneor,' puto cum ex empto teneri, quia servitus debebatur
et scisset. sed si id egit, ne cognosceret emptor aliquam
servitutem deberi, opinor eum ex empto teneri. et generaliter
dixerim, si improbato more versatus sit in celanda servitute,
debere eum teneri, non si securitati suae prospectum voluit.
haec ita vera sunt, si emptor ignoravit servitutes, quia non
videtur esse celatus qui scit neque certiorari debuit qui non
ignoravit.

2. *PAULUS libro quinto ad Sabinum* Si in emptione modus
dictus est et non praestatur, ex empto est actio. Vacua possessio
emptori tradita non intellegitur, si alius in ea legatorum fideive
commissorum servandorum causa in possessione est aut creditores
bona possideant. idem dicendum est, si venter in possessione
sit: nam et ad hoc pertinet vacui appellatio.

3. *POMPONIUS libro nono ad Sabinum* Ratio possessionis,
quae a venditore fieri debeat, talis est, ut, si quis eam possessio-
1 nem iure avocaverit, tradita possessio non intellegatur. Si emptor
vacuam possessionem tradi stipulatus sit et ex stipulatu agat,
fructus non venient in eam actionem, quia et qui fundum dari
stipularetur, vacuam quoque possessionem tradi oportere stipulari intellegitur nec tamen fructuum praestatio ea stipulatione
continetur, neque rursus plus debet esse in stipulatione. sed
2 ex empto superesse ad fructuum praestationem. Si iter actum
viam aquae ductum per tuum fundum emero, vacuae possessionis
traditio nulla est: itaque cavere debes per te non fieri quo minus
3 utar. Si per venditorem vini mora fuerit, quo minus traderet,
condemnari eum oportet, utro tempore pluris vinum fuit, vel
quo venit vel quo lis in condemnationem deducitur, item quo
4 loco pluris fuit, vel quo venit vel ubi agatur. Quod si per
emptorem mora fuisset, aestimari oportet pretium quod sit cum
agatur, et quo loco minoris sit. mora autem videtur esse, si
nulla difficultas venditorem impediat, quo minus traderet,
praesertim si omni tempore paratus fuit tradere. item non
oportet eius loci pretia spectari, in quo agatur, sed eius, ubi
vina tradi oportet: nam quod a Brundisio vinum venit, etsi
venditio alibi facta sit, Brundisi tradi oportet.

4. *PAULUS libro quinto ad Sabinum* Si servum mihi ignoranti, sciens furem vel noxium esse, vendideris, quamvis duplam
promiseris, teneris mihi ex empto, quanti mea intererit scisse,

quia ex stipulatu eo nomine agere tecum non possum antequam mihi quid abesset. Si modus agri minor inveniatur, pro numero iugerum auctor obligatus est, quia, ubi modus minor invenitur, non potest aestimari bonitas loci qui non exstat. sed non solum si modus agri totius minor est, agi cum venditore potest, sed etiam de partibus eius, ut puta si dictum est vineae iugera tot esse vel oliveti et minus inveniatur: ideoque his casibus pro bonitate loci fiet aestimatio.

5. IDEM *libro tertio ad Sabinum* Si heres testamento quid vendere damnatus sit et vendiderit, de reliquis, quae per consequentias emptionis propria sunt, vel ex empto vel ex testamento agi cum eo poterit. Sed si falso existimans se damnatum vendere vendiderit, dicendum est agi cum eo ex empto non posse, quoniam doli mali exceptione actor summoveri potest, quemadmodum, si falso existimans se damnatum dare promisisset, agentem doli mali exceptione summoveret. Pomponius etiam incerti condicere cum posse ait, ut liberetur.

6. POMPONIUS *libro nono ad Sabinum* Tenetur ex empto venditor, etiamsi ignoraverit minorem fundi modum esse. Si vendidi tibi insulam certa pecunia et ut aliam insulam meam reficeres, agam ex vendito, ut reficias: si autem hoc solum, ut reficeres eam, convenisset, non intellegitur emptio et venditio facta, ut et Neratius scripsit. Sed si aream tibi vendidi certo pretio et tradidi, ita ut insula aedificata partem dimidiam mihi retradas, verum est et ut aedifices agere me posse ex vendito et ut aedificatam mihi retradas: quamdiu enim aliquid ex re vendita apud te superesset, ex vendito me habere actionem constat. Si locum sepulchri emeris et propius eum locum, antequam mortuus ibi inferatur, aedificatum a venditore fuerit, poteris ad eum reverti. Si vas aliquod mihi vendideris et dixeris certam mensuram capere vel certum pondus habere, ex empto tecum agam, si minus praestes. sed si vas mihi vendideris ita, ut adfirmares integrum, si id integrum non sit, etiam id, quod eo nomine perdiderim, praestabis mihi: si vero non id actum sit, ut integrum praestes, dolum malum dumtaxat praestare te debere. Labeo contra putat et illud solum observandum, ut, nisi in contrarium id actum sit, omnimodo integrum praestari debeat: et est verum. quod et in locatis doliis praestandum Sabinum respondisse Minicius refert. Si tibi iter vendidero,

ita demum auctorem me laudare poteris, si tuus fuerit fundus, cui adquirere servitutem volueris: iniquum est enim me teneri, si propter hoc adquirere servitutem non potueris, quia dominus vicini fundi non fueris. Sed si fundum tibi vendidero et ei fundo iter accessurum dixero, omnimodo tenebor itineris nomine, quia utriusque rei quasi unus venditor obligatus sum. 7 Si filius familias rem vendiderit mihi et tradiderit, sic ut pater 8 familias tenebitur. Si dolo malo aliquid fecit venditor in re vendita, ex empto eo nomine actio emptori competit: nam et dolum malum eo iudicio aestimari oportet, ut id, quod praestaturum se esse pollicitus sit venditor emptori, praestari oporteat. 9 Si venditor sciens obligatum aut alienum vendidisset et adiectum sit 'neve eo nomine quid praestaret,' aestimari oportet dolum malum eius, quem semper abesse oportet in iudicio empti, quod bonae fidei sit.

7. *IDEM libro decimo ad Sabinum* Fundum mihi cum venderes deducto usu fructu, dixisti eum usum fructum Titii esse, cum is apud te remansurus esset. si coeperis eum usum fructum vindicare, reverti adversus te non potero, donec Titius vivat nec in ea causa esse coeperit, ut, etiamsi eius usus fructus esset, amissurus eum fuerit: nam tunc, id est si capite deminutus vel mortuus fuerit Titius, reverti potero ad te venditorem. idemque iuris est, si dicas eum usum fructum Titii esse, cum sit Sei.

8. *PAULUS libro quinto ad Sabinum* Si tibi liberum praedium tradidero, cum serviens tradere deberem, etiam condictio incerti competit mihi, ut patiaris eam servitutem, quam debuit, imponi. 1 Quod si servum praedium in traditione fecero, quod liberum tibi tradere debui, tu ex empto habebis actionem remittendae eius servitutis gratia, quam pati non debeas.

9. *POMPONIUS libro vicesimo ad Sabinum* Si is, qui lapides ex fundo emerit, tollere eos nolit, ex vendito agi cum eo potest, ut eos tollat.

10. *ULPIANUS libro quadragesimo sexto ad Sabinum* Non est novum, ut duae obligationes in eiusdem persona de eadem re concurrant: cum enim is qui venditorem obligatum habebat ei qui eundem venditorem obligatum habebat heres exstiterit, constat duas esse actiones in eiusdem persona concurrentes, propriam et hereditariam, et debere heredem institutum, si velit

separatim duarum actionum commodo uti, ante aditam hereditatem proprium venditorem convenire, deinde adita hereditate hereditarium : quod si prius adierit hereditatem, unam quidem actionem movere potest, sed ita, ut per eam utriusque contractus sentiat commodum. ex contrario quoque si venditor venditori heres exstiterit, palam est duas evictiones eum praestare debere.

11. IDEM *libro trigesimo secundo ad edictum* Ex empto actione is qui emit utitur. Et in primis sciendum est in hoc iudicio id 1 demum deduci, quod praestari convenit: cum enim sit bonae fidei iudicium, nihil magis bonae fidei congruit quam id prae- 98 stari, quod inter contrahentes actum est. quod si nihil convenit, tunc ea praestabuntur, quae naturaliter insunt huius iudicii potestate. Et in primis ipsam rem praestare venditorem oportet, 2 id est tradere : quae res, si quidem dominus fuit venditor, facit 98, 100, et emptorem dominum, si non fuit, tantum evictionis nomine 102, 103. venditorem obligat, si modo pretium est numeratum aut eo 143 nomine satisfactum. emptor autem nummos venditoris facere cogitur. Redhibitionem quoque contineri empti iudicio et 3 184, 190, Labeo et Sabinus putant et nos probamus. Animalium quoque 4 191, 213 venditor cavere debet ea sana praestari, et qui iumenta vendidit 193 solet ita promittere 'esse bibere, ut oportet.' Si quis virginem 5 se emere putasset, cum mulier venisset, et sciens errare eum venditor passus sit, redhibitionem quidem ex hac causa non 59, 184, esse, verum tamen ex empto competere actionem ad resolvendam 190 emptionem, et pretio restituto mulier reddatur. Is qui vina 6 emit arrae nomine certam summam dedit: postea convenerat, ut emptio irrita fieret. Iulianus ex empto agi posse ait, ut arra restituatur, utilemque esse actionem ex empto etiam ad 48, 49, distrahendam, inquit, emptionem. ego illud quaero: si anulus 184 datus sit arrae nomine et secuta emptione pretioque numerato et tradita re anulus non reddatur, qua actione agendum est, utrum condicatur, quasi ob causam datus sit et causa finita sit, an vero ex empto agendum sit. et Iulianus diceret ex empto agi posse : certe etiam condici poterit, quia iam sine causa apud venditorem est anulus. Venditorem, etiamsi ignorans vendi- 7 derit, fugitivum non esse praestare emptori oportere Neratius 19 ait. Idem Neratius, etiamsi alienum servum vendideris, furtis 8 noxisque solutum praestare te debere ab omnibus receptum ait 19 et ex empto actionem esse, ut habere licere emptori caveatur, sed et ut tradatur ei possessio. Idem ait non tradentem quanti 9

intersit condemnari : satis autem non dantem, quanti plurimum
10 auctorem periclitari oportet. Idem Neratius ait propter omnia
haec satis esse quod plurimum est praestari, id est ut sequentibus
11 actionibus deducto eo quod praestitum est lis aestimetur. Idem
recte ait, si quid horum non praestetur, cum cetera facta sint,
12 nullo deducto condemnationem faciendam. Idem libro secundo
responsorum ait emptorem noxali iudicio condemnatum ex
116, 117, empto actione id tantum consequi, quanti minimo defungi
121 potuit : idemque putat et si ex stipulatu aget : et sive defendat
noxali iudicio, sive non, quia manifestum fuit noxium servum
fuisse, nihilo minus vel ex stipulatu vel ex empto agere posse.
13 Idem Neratius ait venditorem in re tradenda debere praestare
emptori, ut in lite de possessione potior sit : sed Iulianus libro
101, 117 quinto decimo digestorum probat nec videri traditum, si superior
in possessione emptor futurus non sit : erit igitur ex empto
14 actio, nisi hoc praestetur. Cassius ait eum, qui ex duplae
stipulatione litis aestimationem consecutus est, aliarum rerum
nomine, de quibus in venditionibus caveri solet, nihil consequi
posse. Iulianus deficiente dupla ex empto agendum putavit.
15 Denique libro decimo apud Minicium ait, si quis servum ea
condicione vendiderit, ut intra triginta dies duplam promitteret,
postea ne quid praestaretur, et emptor hoc fieri intra diem non
desideraverit, ita demum non teneri venditorem, si ignorans
alienum vendidit : tunc enim in hoc fieri, ut per ipsum et per
heredem eius emptorem habere liceret : qui autem alienum
sciens vendidit, dolo, inquit, non caret et ideo empti iudicio
16 tenebitur. Sententiam Iuliani verissimam esse arbitror in
pignoribus quoque : nam si iure creditoris vendiderit, deinde
haec fuerint evicta, non tenetur nec ad pretium restituendum
ex empto actione creditor : hoc enim multis constitutionibus
effectum est. dolum plane venditor praestabit, denique etiam
repromittit de dolo : sed et si non repromiserit, sciens tamen
sibi non obligatam vel non esse eius qui sibi obligavit vendiderit,
tenebitur ex empto, quia dolum eum praestare debere ostendi-
17 mus. Si quis rem vendiderit et ei accessurum quid dixerit,
omnia quidem, quae diximus in re distracta, in hoc quoque
110 sequenda sint, ut tamen evictionis nomine non in duplum
teneatur, sed in hoc tantum obligetur, ut emptori habere liceat,
18 et non solum per se, sed per omnes. Qui autem habere licere
31,123,124 vendidit, videamus quid debeat praestare. et multum interesse

arbitror, utrum hoc polliceatur per se venientesque a se personas non fieri, quo minus habere liceat, an vero per omnes. nam si per se, non videtur id praestare, ne alius evincat: proinde si evicta res erit, sive stipulatio interposita est, ex stipulatu non tenebitur, sive non est interposita, ex empto non tenebitur. sed Iulianus libro quinto decimo digestorum scribit, etiamsi aperte venditor pronuntiet per se heredemque suum non fieri, quo minus habere liceat, posse defendi ex empto eum in hoc quidem non teneri, quod emptoris interest, verum tamen ut pretium reddat teneri. ibidem ait idem esse dicendum et si aperte in venditione comprehendatur nihil evictionis nomine praestatum iri: pretium quidem deberi re evicta, utilitatem non deberi: neque enim bonae fidei contractus hac patitur conventione, ut emptor rem amitteret et pretium venditor retineret. nisi forte, inquit, sic quis omnes istas supra scriptas conventiones recipiet, quemadmodum recipitur, ut venditor nummos accipiat, quamvis merx ad emptorem non pertineat, veluti cum futurum iactum retis a piscatore emimus aut indaginem plagis positis a venatore vel pantheram ab aucupe: nam etiamsi nihil capit, nihilo minus emptor pretium praestare necesse habebit: sed in supra scriptis conventionibus contra erit dicendum. nisi forte sciens alienum vendit: tunc enim secundum supra a nobis relatam Iuliani sententiam dicendum est ex empto eum teneri, quia dolo facit.

12. *CELSUS libro vicesimo septimo digestorum* Si iactum retis emero et iactare retem piscator noluit, incertum eius rei aestimandum est: si quod extraxit piscium reddere mihi noluit, id aestimari debet quod extraxit.

13. *ULPIANUS libro trigesimo secundo ad edictum* Iulianus libro quinto decimo inter eum, qui sciens quid aut ignorans vendidit, differentiam facit in condemnatione ex empto: ait enim, qui pecus morbosum aut tignum vitiosum vendidit, si quidem ignorans fecit, id tantum ex empto actione praestaturum, quanto minoris essem empturus, si id ita esse scissem: si vero sciens reticuit et emptorem decepit, omnia detrimenta, quae ex ea emptione emptor traxerit, praestaturum ei: sive igitur aedes vitio tigni corruerunt, aedium aestimationem, sive pecora contagione morbosi pecoris perierunt, quod interfuit idonea venisse erit praestandum. Item qui furem vendidit aut fugitivum, si quidem sciens, praestare debebit, quanti

emptoris interfuit non decipi : si vero ignorans vendiderit, circa fugitivum quidem tenetur, quanti minoris empturus esset, si eum esse fugitivum scisset, circa furem non tenetur : differentiae ratio est, quod fugitivum quidem habere non licet et quasi evictionis nomine tenetur venditor, furem autem habere 2 possumus. Quod autem diximus 'quanti emptoris interfuit non decipi,' multa continet, et si alios secum sollicitavit ut 3 fugerent, vel res quasdam abstulit. Quid tamen si ignoravit quidem furem esse, adseveravit autem bonae frugi et fidum et caro vendidit? videamus, an ex empto teneatur. et putem teneri. atqui ignoravit : sed non debuit facile quae ignorabat adseverare. inter hunc igitur et qui scit[1] praemonere debuit furem esse, hic non debuit facilis esse ad temerariam indica-4 tionem. Si venditor dolo fecerit, ut rem pluris venderet, puta de artificio mentitus est aut de peculio, empti eum iudicio teneri, ut praestaret emptori, quanto pluris servum emisset, si 5 ita peculiatus esset vel eo artificio instructus. Per contrarium quoque idem Iulianus scribit, cum Terentius Victor decessisset relicto herede fratre suo et res quasdam ex hereditate et instrumenta et mancipia Bellicus quidam subtraxisset, quibus subtractis facile, quasi minimo valeret hereditas, ut sibi ea venderetur persuasit : an venditi iudicio teneri possit? et ait Iulianus competere actionem ex vendito in tantum, quanto pluris hereditas valeret, si hae res subtractae non fuissent. 6 Idem Iulianus dolum solere a venditore praestari etiam in huiusmodi specie ostendit : si, cum venditor sciret fundum pluribus municipiis legata debere, in tabula quidem conscripserit uni municipio deberi, verum postea legem consignaverit, si qua tributorum aut vectigalis indictionisve quid nomine aut ad viae collationem praestare oportet, id emptorem dare facere praestareque oportere, ex empto eum teneri, quasi decepisset 7 emptorem : quae sententia vera est. Sed cum in facto proponeretur tutores hoc idem fecisse, qui rem pupillarem vendebant, quaestionis esse ait, an tutorum dolum pupillus praestare debeat. et si quidem ipsi tutores vendiderunt, ex empto eos teneri nequaquam dubium est : sed si pupillus auctoribus eis vendidit, in tantum tenetur, in quantum locupletior ex eo factus est, tutoribus in residuum perpetuo condemnandis, quia nec transfertur in pupillum post pubertatem hoc, quod dolo tutorum

---

[1] *Talia fere exciderunt*: et tacuit non multum interest : nam qui scit . . . .

factum est. Offerri pretium ab emptore debet, cum ex empto 8
agitur, et ideo etsi protii partem offerat, nondum est ex empto
actio: venditor enim quasi pignus retinere potest eam rem quam
vendidit. Unde quaeritur, si pars sit pretii soluta et res tradita 9
postea evicta sit, utrum eius rei consequetur pretium integrum
ex empto agens an vero quod numeravit? et puto magis id
quod numeravit propter doli exceptionem. Si fructibus iam 10
maturis ager distractus sit, etiam fructus emptori cedere, nisi
aliud convenit, exploratum est. Si in locatis ager fuit, pen- 11
siones utique ei cedent qui locaverat: idem et in praediis
urbanis, nisi si quid nominatim convenisse proponatur. Sed 12
et si quid praeterea rei venditae nocitum est, actio emptori
praestanda est, damni forte infecti vel aquae pluviae arcendae
vel Aquiliae vel interdicti quod vi aut clam. Item si quid ex 13
operis servorum vel vecturis iumentorum vel navium quaesitum
est, emptori praestabitur, et si quid peculio eorum accessit, non
tamen si quid ex re venditoris. Si Titius fundum, in quo 14
nonaginta iugera erant, vendiderit et in lege emptionis dictum
est in fundo centum esse iugera et antequam modus mani-
festetur, decem iugera alluvione adcreverint, placet mihi Neratii
sententia existimantis, ut, si quidem sciens vendidit, ex empto
actio competat adversus eum, quamvis decem iugera adcreverint, quia dolo fecit nec dolus purgatur: si vero ignorans
vendidit, ex empto actionem non competere. Si fundum mihi 15
alienum vendideris et hic ex causa lucrativa meus factus sit,
nihilo minus ex empto mihi adversus te actio competit. In his 16
autem, quae cum re empta praestari solent, non solum dolum,
sed et culpam praestandam arbitror: nam et Celsus libro octavo
digestorum scripsit, cum convenit, ut venditor praeteritam
mercedem exigat et emptori praestet, non solum dolum, sed
et culpam eum praestare debere. Idem Celsus libro eodem 17
scribit: fundi, quem cum Titio communem habebas, partem
tuam vendidisti et antequam traderes, coactus es communi
dividundo iudicium accipere. si socio fundus sit adiudicatus,
quantum ob eam rem a Titio consecutus es, id tantum emptori
praestabis. quod si tibi fundus totus adiudicatus est, totum,
inquit, eum emptori trades, sed ita, ut ille solvat, quod ob eam
rem Titio condemnatus es. sed ob eam quidem partem, quam
vendidisti, pro evictione cavere debes, ob alteram autem tantum
de dolo malo repromittere: aequum est enim eandem esse con-

dicionem emptoris, quae futura esset, si cum ipso actum esset communi dividundo. sed si certis regionibus fundum inter te et Titium iudex divisit, sine dubio partem, quae adiudicata est, 18 emptori tradere debes. Si quid servo distracto venditor donavit ante traditionem, hoc quoque restitui debet: hereditates quoque 94, 99 per servum adquisitae et legata omnia, nec distinguendum, cuius respectu ista sint relicta. item quod ex operis servus praestitit venditori, emptori restituendum est, nisi ideo dies traditionis ex pacto prorogatus est, ut ad venditorem operae 19 pertinerent. Ex vendito actio venditori competit ad ea conse- 20 quenda, quae ei ab emptore praestari oportet. Veniunt autem in hoc iudicium infra scripta. in primis pretium, quanti res 142, 146, venit. item usurae pretii post diem traditionis: nam cum re 147 emptor fruatur, aequissimum est eum usuras pretii pendere. 21 Possessionem autem traditam accipere debemus et si precaria 147 sit possessio: hoc enim solum spectare debemus, an habeat 22 facultatem fructus percipiendi. Praeterea ex vendito agendo consequetur etiam sumptus, qui facti sunt in re distracta, ut puta si quid in aedificia distracta erogatum est: scribit enim 147 Labeo et Trebatius esse ex vendito hoc nomine actionem. idem et si in aegri servi curationem impensum est ante traditionem aut si quid in disciplinas, quas verisimile erat etiam emptorem velle impendi. hoc amplius Labeo ait et si quid in funus mortui servi impensum sit, ex vendito consequi oportere, si 23 modo sine culpa venditoris mortem obierit. Item si convenerit, cum res veniret, ut locuples ab emptore reus detur, 24 ex vendito agi posse, ut id fiat. Si inter emptorem praediorum et venditorem convenisset, ut, si ea praedia emptor heresve eius pluris vendidisset, eius partem dimidiam venditori praestaret et heres emptoris pluris ea praedia vendidisset, venditorem ex vendito agendo partem eius, quo pluris vendidisset, con- 25 secuturum. Si procurator vendiderit et caverit emptori, quaeritur, an domino vel adversus dominum actio dari debeat. et Papinianus libro tertio responsorum putat cum domino ex empto agi posse utili actione ad exemplum institoriae actionis, si modo rem vendendam mandavit: ergo et per contrarium dicendum est utilem ex empto actionem domino competere. 26 Ibidem Papinianus respondisse se refert, si convenerit, ut ad diem pretio non soluto venditori duplum praestaretur, in fraudem constitutionum videri adiectum, quod usuram legitimam excedit: diversamque causam commissoriae esse ait, cum ea specie, inquit, non faenus illicitum contrahatur, sed lex contractui non improbata dicatur. Si quis colludente procura- 27 tore meo ab eo emerit, an possit agere ex empto? et puto 61 hactenus, ut aut stetur emptioni aut discedatur. Sed et si quis 28 minorem viginti quinque annis circumvenerit, et huic hactenus dabimus actionem ex empto, ut diximus in superiore casu. Si 29 quis a pupillo sine tutoris auctoritate emerit, ex uno latere 12 constat contractus: nam qui emit, obligatus est pupillo, pupillum sibi non obligat. Si venditor habitationem exceperit, ut 30 inquilino liceat habitare, vel colono ut perfrui liceat ad certum tempus, magis esse Servius putabat ex vendito esse actionem: 99 denique Tubero ait, si iste colonus damnum dederit, emptorem ex empto agentem cogere posse venditorem, ut ex locato cum colono experiatur, ut quidquid fuerit consecutus, emptori reddat. Aedibus distractis vel legatis ea esse aedium solemus 31 dicere, quae quasi pars aedium vel propter aedes habentur, ut puta putealia,

14. *POMPONIUS libro trigesimo primo ad Quintum Mucium* 99 (id est quo puteum operitur),

15. *ULPIANUS libro trigesimo secundo ad edictum* lines et labra, salientes. fistulae quoque, quae salientibus iunguntur, quamvis 99 longe excurrant extra aedificium, aedium sunt: item canales: pisces autem qui sunt in piscina non sunt aedium nec fundi,

16. *POMPONIUS libro trigesimo primo ad Quintum Mucium* 99 non magis quam pulli aut cetera animalia, quae in fundo sunt.

17. *ULPIANUS libro trigesimo secundo ad edictum* Fundi nihil est, nisi quod terra se tenet: aedium autem multa esse, quae 98, 99 aedibus adfixa non sunt, ignorari non oportet, ut puta seras claves claustra: multa etiam defossa esse neque tamen fundi aut villae haberi, ut puta vasa vinaria torcularia, quoniam haec instrumenti magis sunt etiamsi aedificio cohaerent. Sed et 1 99 vinum et fructus perceptos villae non esse constat. Fundo 2 99 vendito vel legato sterculinum et stramenta emptoris et legatarii sunt, ligna autem venditoris vel heredis, quia non sunt fundi, tametsi ad eam rem comparata sunt. in sterculino autem distinctio Trebatii probanda est, ut, si quidem stercorandi agri causa comparatum sit, emptorem sequatur, si vendendi, venditorem, nisi si aliud actum est: nec interest, in

3 stabulo iaceat an acervus sit. Quae tabulae pictae pro tectorio
4 includuntur itemque crustae marmoreae aedium sunt. Reticuli
circa columnas, plutei circa parietes, item cilicia vela aedium
5 non sunt. Item quod insulae causa paratum est, si nondum
perfectum est, quamvis positum in aedificio sit, non tamen
6 videtur aedium esse. Si ruta et caesa excipiantur in venditione,
ea placuit esse ruta, quae eruta sunt, ut harena creta et similia:
caesa ea esse, ut arbores caesas et carbones et his similia.
Gallus autem Aquilius, cuius Mela refert opinionem, recte ait
frustra in lege venditionis de rutis et caesis contineri, quia, si
non specialiter venierunt, ad exhibendum de his agi potest
neque enim magis de materia caesa aut de caementis aut de
harena cavendum est venditori quam de ceteris quae sunt pre-
7 tiosiora. Labeo generaliter scribit ea, quae perpetui usus causa
in aedificiis sunt, aedificii esse, quae vero ad praesens, non esse
aedificii: ut puta fistulae temporis quidem causa positae non
sunt aedium, verum tamen si perpetuo fuerint positae, aedium
8 sunt. Castella plumbea, putea, opercula puteorum, epitonia
fistulis adplumbata (aut quae terra continentur quamvis non
9 sint adfixa) aedium esse constat. Item constat sigilla, columnas
quoque et personas, ex quorum rostris aqua salire solet, villae
10 esse. Ea, quae ex aedificio detracta sunt ut reponantur, aedificii
11 sunt: at quae parata sunt ut imponantur, non sunt aedificii. Pali,
qui vineae causa parati sunt, antequam collocentur, fundi non
sunt, sed qui exempti sunt hac mente ut collocentur, fundi sunt.

18. *IAVOLENUS libro septimo ex Cassio* Granaria, quae ex
tabulis fieri solent, ita aedium sunt, si stipites eorum in terra de-
1 fossi sunt: quod si supra terram sunt, rutis et caesis cedunt. Te-
gulae, quae nondum aedificiis impositae sunt, quamvis tegendi
gratia allatae sunt, in rutis et caesis habentur: aliud iuris est
in his, quae detractae sunt ut reponerentur: aedibus enim
accedunt.

19. *GAIUS ad edictum praetoris titulo de publicanis* Veteres
in emptione venditioneque appellationibus promiscue utebantur.

20. *IDEM libro vicesimo primo ad edictum provinciale* Idem
est et in locatione et conductione.

21. *PAULUS libro trigesimo tertio ad edictum* Si sterilis ancilla
sit, cuius partus venit, vel maior annis quinquaginta, cum id
1 emptor ignoraverit, ex empto tenetur venditor. Si praedii

venditor non dicat de tributo sciens, tenetur ex empto: quod 60, 106 si ignorans non praedixerit, quod forte hereditarium praedium erat, non tenetur. Quamvis supra diximus, cum in corpore 2 consentiamus, de qualitate autem dissentiamus, emptionem esse, tamen venditor teneri debet, quanti interest non esse 56, 190 deceptum, etsi venditor quoque nesciet: veluti si mensas quasi citreas emat, quae non sunt. Cum per venditorem steterit, quo 3 minus rem tradat, omnis utilitas emptoris in aestimationem venit, quae modo circa ipsam rem consistit: neque enim si potuit ex vino puta negotiari et lucrum facere, id aestimandum 92, 109 est, non magis quam si triticum emerit et ob eam rem, quod non sit traditum, familia eius fame laboraverit: nam pretium tritici, non servorum fame necatorum consequitur. nec maior fit obligatio, quod tardius agitur, quamvis crescat, si vinum hodie pluris sit, merito, quia sive datum esset, haberem emptor, sive non, quoniam saltem hodie dandum est quod iam olim dari oportuit. Si tibi fundum vendidero, ut eum conductum 4 certa summa haberem, ex vendito eo nomine mihi actio est, 67, 68 quasi in partem pretii ea res sit. Sed et si ita fundum tibi 5 vendidero, ut nulli alii · eum quam mihi venderes, actio eo 26, 176 nomine ex vendito est, si alii vendideris. Qui domum vendebat, 6 excepit sibi habitationem, donec viveret, aut in singulos annos decem: emptor primo anno maluit decem praestare, secundo anno habitationem praestare. Trebatius ait mutandae voluntatis 99 potestatem eum habere singulisque annis alterutrum praestare posse et quamdiu paratus sit alterutrum praestare, petitionem non esse.

22. *IULIANUS libro septimo digestorum* Si in qualitate fundi venditor mentitus sit, non in modo eius, tamen tenetur emptori: pone enim dixisse eum quinquaginta iugera esse vineae et quin- 59 quaginta prati et in prato plus inveniri, esse tamen omnia centum iugera.

23. *IDEM libro tertio decimo digestorum* Si quis servum, quem cum peculio vendiderat, manumiserit, non solum peculii nomine, quod servus habuit tempore quo manumittebatur, sed et eorum, 110 quae postea adquirit, tenetur et praeterea cavere debet, quidquid ex hereditate liberti ad eum pervenerit, restitutu iri. *MARCEL-LUS notat*: illa praestare venditor ex empto debet, quae haberet emptor, si homo manumissus non esset: non continebuntur igitur, quae, si manumissus non fuit, adquisiturus non esset.

24. *IULIANUS libro quinto decimo digestorum* Si servus, in quo usus fructus tuus erat, fundum emerit et antequam pecunia numeraretur, capite minutus fueris, quamvis pretium solveris, actionem ex empto non habebis propter talem capitis deminutionem, sed indebiti actionem adversus venditorem habebis. ante capitis autem minutionem nihil interest, tu solvas an servus ex eo peculio quod ad te pertinet: nam utroque casu 1 actionem ex empto habebis. Servum tuum imprudens a fure bona fide emi: is ex peculio quod ad te pertinebat hominem paravit, qui mihi traditus est. posse te eum hominem mihi condicere Sabinus dixit, sed si quid mihi abesset ex negotio quod is gessisset, invicem me tecum acturum de peculio. Cassius veram opinionem Sabini rettulit, in qua ego quoque 2 sum. Servo vendente hominem fideiussor venditionis omnia praestare debet, in quae obligaretur, si pro libero fideiussisset: nam et in dominum actio sic datur, ut emptor eadem consequatur, quae libero vendente consequi debuisset, sed ultra peculii taxationem dominus non condemnatur.

25. *IDEM libro quinquagesimo quarto digestorum* Qui pendentem vindemiam emit si uvam legere prohibeatur a venditore, adversus eum petentem pretium exceptione uti poterit 'si ea pecunia, qua de agitur, non pro ea re petitur, quae venit neque tradita est.' ceterum post traditionem sive lectam uvam calcare sive mustum evehere prohibeatur, ad exhibendum vel iniuriarum agere poterit, quemadmodum si aliam quamlibet rem suam tollere prohibeatur.

26. *ALFENUS VARUS libro secundo digestorum* Si quis, cum fundum venderet, dolia centum, quae in fundo esse adfirmabat, accessura dixisset, quamvis ibi nullum dolium fuisset, tamen dolia emptori debebit.

27. *PAULUS libro tertio epitomarum Alfeni* Quidquid venditor accessurum dixerit, id integrum ac sanum tradi oportet: veluti si fundo dolia accessura dixisset, non quassa, sed integra dare debet.

28. *IULIANUS libro tertio ad Urseium Ferocem* Praedia mihi vendidisti et convenit, ut aliquid facerem: quod si non fecissem, poenam promisi. respondit: venditor antequam poenam ex stipulatu petat, ex vendito agere potest: si consecutus fuerit, quantum poenae nomine stipulatus esset, agentem ex stipulatu

doli mali exceptio summovebit: si ex stipulatu poenam consecutus fueris, ipso iure ex vendito agere non poteris nisi in id, quod pluris eius interfuerit id fieri.

29. IDEM *libro quarto ex Minicio* Cui res sub condicione 23 legata erat, is eam imprudens ab herede emit: actione ex empto poterit consequi emptor pretium, quia non ex causa legati rem habet.

30. AFRICANUS *libro octavo quaestionum* Servus, quem de me cum peculio emisti, priusquam tibi traderetur, furtum mihi fecit. quamvis ea res quam subripuit interierit, nihilo minus retentionem eo nomine ex peculio me habiturum ait, id est ipso iure ob id factum minutum esse peculium, eo scilicet, quod debitor meus ex causa condictionis sit factus. nam licet, si iam traditus furtum mihi fecisset, aut omnino condictionem eo nomine de peculio non haberem aut eatenus haberem, quatenus ex re furtiva auctum peculium fuisset, tamen in proposito et retentionem me habiturum et, si omne peculium penes te sit, vel quasi plus debito solverim posse me condicere. secundum quae dicendum: si nummos, quos servus iste mihi subripuerat, tu ignorans furtivos esse quasi peculiares ademeris et consumpseris, condictio eo nomine mihi adversus te competet, quasi res mea ad te sine causa pervenerit. Si sciens alienam rem igno- 1 ranti mihi vendideris, etiam priusquam evincatur utiliter me 19, 59, 89, ex empto acturum putavit in id, quanti mea intersit meam esse 90, 102, factam: quamvis enim alioquin verum sit venditorem hactenus 121, 134 teneri, ut rem emptori habere liceat, non etiam ut eius faciat, quia tamen dolum malum abesse praestare debeat, teneri eum, qui sciens alienam, non suam ignoranti vendidit: id est maxime, si manumissuro vel pignori daturo vendiderit.

31. NERATIUS *libro tertio membranarum* Si ea res, quam ex empto praestare debebam, vi mihi adempta fuerit: quamvis 38, 89, 102, eam custodire debuerim, tamen propius est, ut nihil amplius 107, 108 quam actiones persequendae eius praestari a me emptori oporteat, quia custodia adversus vim parum proficit. actiones autem eas non solum arbitrio, sed etiam periculo tuo tibi praestare debebo, ut omne lucrum ac dispendium te sequatur. Et 1 non solum quod ipse per eum adquisii praestare debeo, sed et id, quod emptor iam tunc sibi tradito servo adquisiturus fuisset. Uterque nostrum eandem rem emit a non domino, cum emptio 2

venditioque sine dolo malo fieret, traditaque est: sive ab eodem emimus sive ab alio atque alio, is ex nobis tuendus est, qui prior ius eius adprehendit, hoc est, cui primum tradita est. si alter ex nobis a domino emisset, is omnimodo tuendus est.

32. *ULPIANUS libro undecimo ad edictum* Si quis a me oleum quod emisset adhibitis iniquis ponderibus accepisset, ut in modo me falleret, vel emptor circumscriptus sit a venditore ponderibus minoribus, Pomponius ait posse dici venditorem sibi dare oportere quod plus est petere: quod habet rationem: ergo et emptor ex empto habebit actionem, qua contentus esse possit.

33. *IDEM libro vicesimo tertio ad edictum* Et si uno pretio plures res emptae sint, de singulis ex empto et vendito agi potest.

34. *IDEM libro decimo octavo ad edictum* Si fundo vendito in qualitate iugerum captio est, ex empto erit actio.

35. *IDEM libro septuagesimo ad edictum* Si quis fundum emerit, quasi per eum fundum eundi agendi ius non esset, et interdicto de itinere actuque victus sit, ex empto habebit actionem: licet enim stipulatio de evictione non committatur, quia non est de iure servitutis in rem actione pronuntiatum, tamen dicendum est ex empto actionem competere.

36. *PAULUS libro septimo ad Plautium* Venditor domus antequam eam tradat, damni infecti stipulationem interponere debet, quia, antequam vacuam possessionem tradat, custodiam et diligentiam praestare debet et pars est custodiae diligentiaeque hanc interponere stipulationem: et ideo si id neglexerit, tenebitur emptori.

37. *IDEM libro quarto decimo ad Plautium* Sicut aequum est bonae fidei emptori alterius dolum non nocere, ita non est aequum eidem personae venditoris sui dolum prodesse.

38. *CELSUS libro octavo digestorum* Si venditor hominis dixit peculium cum habere decem nec quemquam adempturum, et si plus habet, totum praestet, nisi hoc actum est, ut dumtaxat decem praestaret, si minus est, praestet esse decem et talem 1 servum esse, ut tantum peculii habeat. Si per emptorem steterit, quo minus ei mancipium traderetur, pro cibariis per arbitrium indemnitatem posse servari Sextus Aelius, Drusus dixerunt, quorum et mihi iustissima videtur esse sententia. 2 Firmus a Proculo quaesiit, si de plumbeo castello fistulae sub

terram missae aquam ducerent in aenum lateribus circum-
structum, an hae aedium essent an ut ruta caesa vincta fixaque
quae aedium non essent. ille rescripsit referre, quid acti esset.
quid ergo si nihil de ea re neque emptor neque venditor
cogitaverunt, ut plerumque in eiusmodi rebus evenisse solet,
nonne propius est, ut inserta et inclusa aedificio partem eius
esse existimemus?

39. *MODESTINUS libro quinto responsorum* Quaero, si quis
ita fundum vendiderit, ut id venum datum esse videatur, quod
intra terminos ipse possedit, sciens tamen aliquam partem
certam se non possidere non certioraverit emptorem, an ex
empto iudicio teneatur, cum haec generalis adiectio ad ea, quae
specialiter novit qui vendidit nec excepit, pertinere non debeat,
ne alioquin emptor capiatur, qui fortasse, si hoc cognovisset, vel
empturus non esset vel minoris empturus esset, si certioratus
de loco certo fuisset: cum hoc et apud veteres sit relatum in eius
persona, qui sic exceperat: 'servitutes si quae debentur, debe-
buntur:' etenim iuris auctores responderunt, si certus venditor
quibusdam personis certas servitutes debere non admonuisset
emptorem, ex empto eum teneri debere, quando haec generalis
exceptio non ad ea pertinere debeat, quae venditor novit quaeque
specialiter excipere et potuit et debuit, sed ad ea, quae ignoravit
et de quibus emptorem certiorare nequivit. Herennius Modestinus respondit, si quid circumveniendi emptoris causa venditor
in specie de qua quaeritur fecit, ex empto actione conveniri
posse.

40. *POMPONIUS libro trigesimo primo ad Quintum Mucium*
super Quintus Mucius scribit: dominus fundi de praedio arbores
stantes vendiderat et pro his rebus pecuniam accepit et tradere
nolebat: emptor quaerebat, quid se facere oporteret, et verebatur,
ne hae arbores eius non viderentur factae. *POMPONIUS*: arborum, quae in fundo continentur, non est separatum corpus a
fundo et ideo ut dominus suas specialiter arbores vindicare
emptor non poterit: sed ex empto habet actionem.

41. *PAPINIANUS libro tertio responsorum* In venditione
super annua pensitatione pro aquae ductu infra domum Romae
constitutum nihil commemoratum est. deceptus ob eam rem
ex empto actionem habebit: itaque, si conveniatur ob pretium
ex vendito, ratio inprovisi oneris habetur.

42. *PAULUS libro secundo quaestionum* Si duorum fundorum venditor separatim de modo cuiusque pronuntiaverit et ita utrumque uno pretio tradiderit, et alteri aliquid desit, quamvis in altero exsuperet, forte si dixit unum centum iugera, alterum ducenta habere, non proderit ei, quod in altero ducenta decem inveniuntur, si in altero decem desint. et de his ita apud Labeonem relatum est. sed an exceptio doli mali venditori profutura sit, potest dubitari, utique si exiguus modus silvae desit et plus in vineis habeat, quam repromissum est. an non facit dolo, qui iure perpetuo utitur? nec enim hic quod amplius in modo invenitur, quam alioquin dictum est, ad compendium venditoris, sed ad emptoris pertinet: et tunc tenetur venditor, cum minor modus invenitur. videamus tamen, ne nulla querella sit emptoris in eodem fundo, si plus inveniat in vinea quam in prato, cum universus modus constat. similis quaestio esse potest ei, quae in duobus fundis agitata est, et si quis duos statuliberos uno pretio vendat et dicat unum decem dare iussum, qui quindecim dare debebat: nam et hic tenebitur ex empto actione, quamvis emptor a duobus viginti accepturus sit. sed rectius est in omnibus supra scriptis casibus lucrum cum damno compensari et si quid deest emptori sive pro modo sive pro qualitate loci, hoc ei resarciri.

100, 124, 126
43. *IDEM libro quinto quaestionum* Titius cum decederet, Sciae Stichum Pamphilum Arescusam per fideicommissum reliquit eiusque fidei commisit, ut omnes ad libertatem post annum perduceret. cum legataria fideicommissum ad se pertinere noluisset nec tamen heredem a sua petitione liberasset, heres eadem mancipia Sempronio vendidit nulla commemoratione fideicommissae libertatis facta: emptor cum pluribus annis mancipia supra scripta sibi servissent, Arescusam manumisit, et cum ceteri quoque servi cognita voluntate defuncti fideicommissam libertatem petissent et heredem ad praetorem perduxissent, iussu praetoris ab herede sunt manumissi. Arescusa quoque nolle se emptorem patronum habere responderat. cum emptor pretium a venditore empti iudicio Arescusae quoque nomine repeteret, lectum est responsum Domitii Ulpiani, quo continebatur Arescusam pertinere ad rescriptum sacrarum constitutionum, si nollet emptorem patronum habere: emptorem tamen nihil posse post manumissionem a venditore consequi. ego cum meminissem et Iulianum in ea sententia

esse, ut existimaret post manumissionem quoque empti actionem durare, quaero, quae sententia vera est. illud etiam in eadem cognitione nomine emptoris desiderabatur, ut sumptus, quos in unum ex his quem erudierat fecerat, ei restituerentur. idem quaero, Arescusa, quae recusavit emptorem patronum habere, cuius sit liberta constituta? an possit vel legatariam quae non liberavit vel heredem patronum habere? nam ceteri duo ab herede manumissi sunt. respondi: semper probavi Iuliani sententiam putantis manumissione non amittitur eo modo. de sumptibus vero, quos in erudiendum hominem emptor fecit, videndum est: nam empti iudicium ad eam quoque speciem sufficere existimo: non enim pretium continet tantum, sed omne quod interest emptoris servum non evinci. plane si in tantum pretium excedisse proponas, ut non sit cogitatum a venditore de tanta summa (veluti si ponas agitatorem postea factum vel pantomimum evictum esse eum, qui minimo veniit pretio), iniquum videtur in magnam quantitatem obligari venditorem,

44. *AFRICANUS libro octavo quaestionum* (cum et forte 126 idem mediocrium facultatium sit: et non ultra duplum periculum subire eum oportet)

45. *PAULUS libro quinto quaestionum* idque et Iulianum agitasse Africanus refert: quod iustum est: sicut minuitur 125 praestatio, si servus deterior apud emptorem effectus sit, cum evincitur. Illud expeditius videbatur, si mihi alienam aream 1 vendideris et in eam ego aedificavero atque ita eam dominus evincit: nam quia possim petentem dominum, nisi impensam aedificiorum solvat, doli mali exceptione summovere, magis est, 127 ut ea res ad periculum venditoris non pertineat. quod et in servo dicendum est, si in servitutem, non in libertatem evinceretur, ut dominus mercedes et impensas praestare debeat. quod si emptor non possideat aedificium vel servum, ex empto habebit actionem. in omnibus tamen his casibus, si sciens quis alienum vendiderit, omnimodo teneri debet. Superest tertia 2 deliberatio, cuius debet esse liberta Arescusa, quae recusat emptorem. et non sine ratione dicetur eius debere effici 100 libertam, a quo vendita est, id est heredis, quia et ipse ex empto actione tenetur: sed hoc ita, si non Arescusa elegerit emptoris patronatum: tunc etenim et illius remanet liberta et

ille ex empto actionem non habet, quia nihil eius interest, cum eam libertam habet.

46. *IDEM libro vicensimo quarto quaestionum* Si quis alienam rem vendiderit et medio tempore heres domino rei exstiterit, cogetur implere venditionem.

47. *IDEM libro sexto responsorum* Lucius Titius accepta pecunia ad materias vendendas sub poena certa, ita ut, si non integras repraestaverit intra statuta tempora, poena conveniatur. partim datis materiis decessit: cum igitur testator in poenam commiserit neque heres eius reliquam materiam exhibuerit, an et in poenam et in usuras conveniri possit, praesertim cum emptor mutuatus pecuniam usuras gravissimas expendit? Paulus respondit ex contractu, de quo quaeritur, etiam heredem venditoris in poenam conveniri posse. in actione quoque ex empto officio iudicis post moram intercedentem usurarum pretii rationem haberi oportere.

48. *SCAEVOLA libro secundo responsorum* Titius heres Sempronii fundum Septicio vendidit ita: 'fundus Sempronianus, quidquid Sempronii iuris fuit, erit tibi emptus tot nummis' vacuamque possessionem tradidit neque fines eius demonstravit: quaeritur, an empti iudicio cogendus sit ostendere ex instrumentis hereditariis, quid iuris defunctus habuerit et fines ostendere. respondi id ex ea scriptura praestandum, quod sensisse intelleguntur: quod si non appareat, debere venditorem et instrumenta fundi et fines ostendere: hoc etenim contractui bonae fidei consonat.

49. *HERMOGENIANUS libro secundo iuris epitomarum* Qui per collusionem imaginarium colonum circumveniendi emptoris causa subposuit, ex empto tenetur nec defenditur, si, quo facilius excogitata fraus occultetur, colonum et quinquennii pensiones in fidem suam recipiat. Pretii, sorte licet post moram soluta, usurae peti non possunt, cum hae non sint in obligatione, sed officio iudicis praestentur.

50. *LABEO libro quarto posteriorum a Iavoleno epitomatorum* Bona fides non patitur, ut, cum emptor alicuius legis beneficio pecuniam rei venditae debere desisset antequam res ei tradatur, venditor tradere compelletur et re sua careret. possessione autem tradita futurum est, ut rem venditor aeque amitteret, utpote cum petenti eam rem petitor ei neque vendidisset neque tradidisset.

51. *IDEM libro quinto posteriorum a Iavoleno epitomatorum* Si et per emptorem et venditorem mora fuisset, quo minus vinum praeberetur et traderetur, perinde esse ait, quasi si per emptorem solum stetisset: non enim potest videri mora per venditorem emptori facta esse ipso moram faciente emptore. Quod si 1 fundum emisti ea lege, uti des pecuniam kalendis Iuliis, et si ipsis calendis per venditorem esset factum, quo minus pecunia ei solveretur, deinde per te staret quo minus solveres, uti posse adversus te lege sua venditorem dixi, quia in vendendo hoc ageretur, ut, quandoque per emptorem factum sit, quo minus pecuniam solvat, legis poenam patiatur. hoc ita verum puto, nisi si quid in ea re venditor dolo fecit.

52. *SCAEVOLA libro septimo digestorum* Creditor fundum sibi obligatum, cuius chirographa tributorum a debitore retro solutorum apud se deposita habebat, vendidit Maevio ea lege, ut, si quid tributorum nomine debitum esset, emptor solveret: idem fundus ob causam eorum tributorum, quae iam soluta erant, a conductore saltus, in quo idem fundus est, venit eumque idem Maevius emit et pretium solvit: quaesitum est, an empti iudicio vel aliqua actione emptor a venditore consequi possit, ut solutionum supra scriptarum chirographa ei dentur. respondit posse emptorem empti iudicio consequi, ut instrumenta de quibus quaereretur exhibeantur. Praedium aestimatum in 1 dotem a patre filiae suae nomine datum obligatum creditori deprehenditur: quaesitum est, an filius, qui hereditatem patris retinet, cum ab ea se filia abstinuisset dote contenta, actione ex empto teneatur, ut a creditore lueret et marito liberum praestaret. respondit teneri. Inter venditorem et emptorem militiae ita 2 convenit, ut salarium, quod debeatur ab illa persona, emptori cederet: quaesitum est, emptor militiae quam quantitatem a quo exigere debet et quid ex eiusmodi pacto venditor emptori praestare debeat. respondit venditorem actiones extraordinarias eo nomine quas haberet praestare debere. Ante domum mari 3 iunctam molibus iactis ripam constituit et uti ab eo possessa domus fuit, Gaio Seio vendidit: quaero, an ripa, quae ab auctore domui coniuncta erat, ad emptorem quoque iure emptionis pertineat. respondit eodem iure fore venditam domum, quo fuisset priusquam veniret.

53. *LABEO libro primo pithanon* Si mercedem insulae accessuram esse emptori dictum est, quanti insula locata est, tantum

emptori praestetur. *PAULUS*: immo si insulam totam uno nomine locaveris et amplioris conductor locaverit et in vendenda insula mercedem emptori cessuram esse dixeris, id accedet, quod tibi totius insulae conductor debebit. Si cum fundum vendidisti, in quo sepulcrum habuisti, nec nominatim tibi sepulcrum excepisti, parum habes eo nomine cautum. *PAULUS*: minime, si modo in sepulcrum iter publicum transit. Si habitatoribus habitatio lege venditionis recepta est, omnibus in ea habitantibus praeter dominum recte recepta habitatio est. *PAULUS*: immo si cui in ea insula, quam vendideris, gratis habitationem dederis et sic receperis: 'habitatoribus aut quam quisque diem conductum habet,' parum caveris (nominatim enim de his recipi oportuit) itaque eos habitatores emptor insulae habitatione impune prohibebit.

54. *IDEM libro secundo pithanon* Si servus quem vendideras iussu tuo aliquid fecit et ex eo crus fregit, ita demum ea res tuo periculo non est, si id imperasti, quod solebat ante venditionem facere, et si id imperasti, quod etiam non vendito servo imperaturus eras. *PAULUS*: minime: nam si periculosam rem ante venditionem facere solitus est, culpa tua id factum esse videbitur: puta enim eum fuisse servum, qui per catadromum descendere aut in cloacam demitti solitus esset. idem iuris erit, si eam rem imperare solitus fueris, quam prudens et diligens pater familias imperaturus ei servo non fuerit. quid si hoc exceptum fuerit? tamen potest ei servo novam rem imperare, quam imperaturus non fuisset, si non venisset: veluti si ei imperasti, ut ad emptorem iret, qui peregre esset: nam certe ea res tuo periculo esse non debet. itaque tota ea res ad dolum malum dumtaxat et culpam venditoris dirigenda est. Si dolia octoginta accedere fundo, quae infossa essent, dictum erit, et plura erunt quam ad eum numerum, dabit emptori ex omnibus quae vult, dum integra det: si sola octoginta sunt, qualiacumque emptorem sequentur nec pro non integris quicquam ei venditor praestabit.

55. *POMPONIUS libro decimo epistularum* Si servus, qui emeretur vel promitteretur, in hostium potestate sit, Octavenus magis putabat valere emptionem et stipulationem, quia inter ementem et vendentem esset commercium: potius enim difficultatem in praestando eo inesse, quam in natura, etiamsi officio iudicis sustinenda esset eius praestatio, donec praestari possit.

REFERENCES TO OTHER TITLES IN THE DIGEST AND CODE.

[*The references are to the preceding pages.*]

DIG. XVIII. 2.
DE IN DIEM ADDICTIONE.

1. 160.	6. pr. 163–165.	13. 1. 162.
2. pr. 157, 160, 170.	— 1. 164.	14. pr. 162, 163.
— 1. 164.	7. 163.	— 1. 162, 165.
3. 165.	8. 163.	— 3. 14, 162.
4. pr. 162.	9. 165, 166.	— 5. 161.
— 2. 165.	10. 166.	15. 1. 161, 162.
— 3. 160, 165.	11. pr. 167.	16. 164, 165.
— 4. 164, 165.	— 1. 166.	17. 166.
— 6. 161.	12. 166.	18. 162.
5. 14, 161.	13. pr. 166.	19. 161.

DIG. XVIII. 3.
DE LEGE COMMISSORIA.

1. 170.	4. 2. 173.	6. pr. 172.
2. 170–172.	— 3. 170.	— 2. 171.
3. 172.	— 4. 170, 171.	7. 171.
4. pr. 170, 172.	5. 170, 171.	8. 170, 171.
— 1. 172.		

DIG. XVIII. 4.
DE HEREDITATE VEL ACTIONE VENDITA.

1. 22.	4. 37.	14. 1. 33.
2. 1. 34, 35.	5. 37.	15. 33.
— 4. 34.	6. 37.	16. 33.
— 10. 35.	7. 22, 33.	17. 37.
— 11. 35.	8. 33, 38.	20. pr. 35.
— 15. 35.	9. 33.	21. 34.
— 16. 35.	10. 33, 131.	23. pr. 37.
— 18. 35.	11. 33, 131.	24. 35.
3. 34.	13. 33.	25. 34.

DIG. XVIII. 5.

DE RESCINDENDA VENDITIONE ET QUANDO LICET AB EMPTIONE DISCEDERE.

2. 180.	5. 1. 179.	7. pr. 79, 158, 180.
3. 180.	— 2. 76.	— 1. 12.
4. 180.	6. 80, 174, 179.	10. 1. 171.

DIG. XVIII. 6.

DE PERICULO ET COMMODO REI VENDITAE.

1. pr. 76, 77, 81–83, 90.	4. 1. 72, 76, 77, 82, 83.	12. 77, 90.
— 1. 77, 87.	— 2. 81.	14. 89, 99.
— 2. 81, 99.	5. 86.	15. pr. 108, 148.
— 3. 88, 148.	6. 190.	— 1. 30, 77, 82, 83.
— 4. 88.	7. pr. 94.	16. 77.
2. pr. 88.	8. pr. 40, 76, 77–79, 163.	17. 154.
— 1. 87, 107, 108.	— 1. 79.	18. 87, 148.
3. 107.	— 2. 17.	19. 1. 19, 128, 133.
4. pr. 77, 81, 83, 107.		20. 147.

DIG. XXI. 1.

DE AEDILICIO EDICTO ET REDHIBITIONE ET QUANTI MINORIS.

1. pr. 194.	4. 4. 196, 212.	14. 7. 215.
— 1. 193, 202, 212.	6. pr. 196.	— 9. 215.
— 2. 201.	— 2. 215.	— 10. 198.
— 6. 198.	7. 215.	15. 210.
— 7. 195.	10. 2. 195.	16. 197.
— 8. 195, 196.	— 5. 215.	17. pr. 196.
— 9. 196, 212.	11. 215.	— 14. 196.
— 10. 196, 212.	12. 1. 195, 215.	— 17. 197.
— 11. 196.	— 2. 215.	18. pr.–1. 212.
4 pr. 196, 212.	— 4. 215.	19. pr.–1. 191.
— 1–3. 196.	14. 3. 215.	— 2. 191, 212.

TO OTHER TITLES.

19. 3. 191.	31. 5. 209.	39. 200.
— 4. 201.	— 6. 206, 209.	40. pr. 200.
— 5. 5, 195.	— 7. 209.	43. pr. 196, 197.
— 6. 209.	— 9. 203, 209.	— 1–3. 196.
21. pr. 201, 202.	— 10. 208, 209.	— 5. 202.
— 1. 203.	— 11–15. 203, 206.	— 8. 203, 206.
— 2–3. 207.	— 16. 211.	— 9. 214.
22. 207.	— 17. 202.	44. 1. 192, 209.
23. pr. 203.	— 18. 201.	— 2. 206.
— 1. 202.	— 19. 202.	45. 208.
— 2–3. 196.	— 20. 192, 193.	46. 203.
— 4. 207.	— 22. 83, 174.	47. pr.–1. 206.
— 7. 202.	— 23. 83.	48. pr. 206.
— 8. 205.	— 24. 176.	— 1. 210.
— 9. 202.	32. 199.	— 2. 211.
25. pr.–2. 203.	33. pr. 199, 200.	— 3–4. 197.
— 3. 202, 203.	— 1. 199.	— 8. 214.
— 4–8. 203.	34. pr.–1. 133, 200.	49. 194.
— 10. 207.	35. 200.	51. 1. 198, 199.
26. 207.	36. 204.	54. 197.
27. 204.	38. pr. 194, 199, 209.	55. 209.
28. 193.		57. pr. 208.
29. pr. 208.	— 3. 206.	— 1. 207.
— 1. 205.	— 5. 194.	58. pr.–1. 205.
— 2. 161, 204.	— 8. 197.	59. pr.–1. 201.
— 3. 204.	— 9. 195, 197.	60. 22.
30. pr. 207.	— 11. 199.	61. 210, 211.
— 1. 204.	— 12. 200.	63. 194.
31. pr. 204, 205.	— 13. 211.	64. pr. 200, 204.
— 2–4. 202.	— 14. 200.	— 1. 200.

DIG. XXI. 2.

DE EVICTIONIBUS ET DUPLAE STIPULATIONE

2. 112.	9. 114, 129.	15. 1. 131.
4. pr. 118.	11. pr. 115.	16. pr. 127.
5. 132.	12. 44.	— 1, 114, 133.
6. 122.	13. 130.	21. pr. 89, 90, 115.
8. 111, 124, 131.	14. 130.	131.

21. 1. 89, 115.	45. 55.	62. 1. 120.
— 2. 121.	47. 128.	— 2. 117.
22. 1. 113.	48. 105.	63. pr. 121.
24. 100, 114.	49. 117.	— 1. 116–118, 131.
27. 116.	51. pr. 115, 118, 131.	— 2. 116, 131.
28. 116, 118.	— 3. 128.	64. pr. 129.
29. pr. 115, 128.	53. pr. 130.	— 1. 130.
— 1. 116.	— 1. 118, 121.	— 2. 118, 130.
— 2. 120.	54. 1. 132.	— 3. 130.
31. 193.	55. pr. 112, 116, 122, 131.	66. pr. 116, 131.
32. pr. 193.		— 1. 117.
— 1. 211.	— 1. 116, 121.	— 2. 122.
34. 1–2. 117.	56. 1. 116.	67. 128.
35. 117.	— 4. 116, 119.	69. 3. 132.
37. pr. 111, 112, 122.	— 5–6. 121.	— 5. 105.
— 1. 112, 123, 193.	— 7. 119.	— 6. 55.
39. pr. 117.	57. pr. 114.	70. 124, 125.
— 1. 119.	— 1. 129.	72. 128.
— 2. 113.	59. 120.	74. 3. 38.
— 3. 54.	60. 112, 124.	75. 105, 191.
41. 1. 114, 129.	61. 113.	76. 116.
— 2. 129.		

COD. IV. 38.

DE CONTRAHENDA EMPTIONE.

3. 74.	8. 173.	12. pr. 173.
4. 22.	9. 74, 173.	13. 69.
5. 10.	10. 22.	15. pr. 70.

COD. IV. 39.

DE HEREDITATE VEL ACTIONE VENDITA

1. 36.	5. 36.	9. 36.
2. 36.	6. 34.	

COD. IV. 44.
DE RESCINDENDA VENDITIONE.

1. 64.	8. 64, 181, 183.	12. 128.
2. 75, 181, 182.	9. 67.	14. 173.
5. pr. 61.	10. 61.	

COD. IV. 48.
DE PERICULO ET COMMODO REI VENDITAE.

1. 92.	2. 1. 76.	5. 76, 78.
2. pr. 84, 86.	4. 90, 107.	6. 90.

COD. IV. 49.
DE ACTIONIBUS EMPTI ET VENDITI.

2. 2. 92.	7. 143.	13. 92, 146, 147.
3. 42.	9. 106.	14. 193.
4. 109.	10. 109.	16. 92, 148.
5. 146.	12. 109.	17. 115.

COD. IV. 58.
DE AEDILICIIS ACTIONIBUS.

1. 205.	3. pr. 197.	5. 207.
2. 210, 211.	4. pr. 194.	

COD. VIII. 44.
DE EVICTIONIBUS.

1. 132.	8. 97, 118.	21. 1. 118.
3. 89, 102, 112, 133, 134.	9. 127.	23. 124.
	14. 118.	24. pr. 128, 133.
4. 195.	15. 131.	25. 112.
5. 101, 128, 134.	16. 127.	26. 89, 115.
6. 112.	17. 128.	27. 123, 132.
7. 118, 119.	20. pr. 121.	30. 132.